MEDIA, FEMINISM, CULTURAL STUDIES

The Cinema of Hayao Miyazaki
by Jeremy Mark Robinson

Spirited Away: Pocket Guide
by Jeremy Mark Robinson

Princess Mononoke: Pocket Guide
by Jeremy Mark Robinson

The Sacred Cinema of Andrei Tarkovsky
by Jeremy Mark Robinson

Liv Tyler
by Thomas A. Christie

Stepping Forward: Essays, Lectures and Interviews
by Wolfgang Iser

Wild Zones: Pornography, Art and Feminism
by Kelly Ives

The Cinema of Richard Linklater
by Thomas A. Christie

Walerian Borowczyk
by Jeremy Mark Robinson

Andrea Dworkin
by Jeremy Mark Robinson

Cixous, Irigaray, Kristeva: The Jouissance of French Feminism
by Kelly Ives

Julia Kristeva: Art, Love, Melancholy, Philosophy, Semiotics
by Kelly Ives

Luce Irigaray: Lips, Kissing, and the Politics of Sexual Difference
by Kelly Ives

Helene Cixous I Love You: The Jouissance *of Writing*
by Kelly Ives

FORTHCOMING BOOKS

Legend of the Overfiend
The Twilight Saga
Harry Potter
Bleach
Naruto

THE CINEMA OF JASON FRIEDBERG AND AARON SELTZER

THE CINEMA OF JASON FRIEDBERG AND AARON SELTZER

Jeremy Mark Robinson

CRESCENT MOON

Crescent Moon Publishing
P.O. Box 1312
Maidstone, Kent
ME14 5XU, Great Britain
www.crmoon.com

First published 2024.
© Jeremy Mark Robinson 2024.

Set in Times New Roman 10 on 14pt.
Designed by Radiance Graphics.

The right of Jeremy Mark Robinson to be identified as the author of this book has been asserted generally in accordance with sections 77 and 78 of the Copyright, Designs and Patents Act 1988.

All rights reserved. No part of this book may be reprinted or reproduced, stored in a retrieval system, or transmitted, in any form or by any means, electronic, mechanical, photocopying, recording or otherwise, without permission from the publisher.

British Library Cataloguing in Publication data available for this title.

ISBN-13 9781861719164 (Pbk)

CONTENTS

Acknowledgements ✳ 1
Picture Credits ✳ 1

PART ONE: BIOGRAPHY AND COMEDY

1 Jason Friedberg and Aaron Seltzer: Introduction ✳ 17
2 Spoof Movies ✳ 60
3 Comedy and Criticism ✳ 69

PART TWO: THE MOVIES

1 *Maximum Risk* ✳ 79
2 *Spy Hard* ✳ 83
3 The *Scary Movie* Series ✳ 90
4 *Date Movie* ✳ 112
5 *Epic Movie* ✳ 128
6 *Meet the Spartans* ✳ 146
7 *Disaster Movie* ✳ 165
8 *Vampires Suck* ✳ 182
9 *The Starving Games* ✳ 203
10 *Best Night Ever* ✳ 220
11 *Superfast!* ✳ 232

Appendices
Some Movies Linked To the Work of Friedberg and Seltzer ✳ 246

Viewers On the Movies of Friedberg and Seltzer ✻ 257

Bibliography ✻ 259

ACKNOWLEDGEMENTS

To the authors and publishers quoted.
To the copyright holders of the illustrations.

PICTURE CREDITS

Regency. New Regency. Fox. Miramax. Safran Company. 3 In the Box. Lionsgate. Momentum. Ketchup Entertainment. Blumhouse.

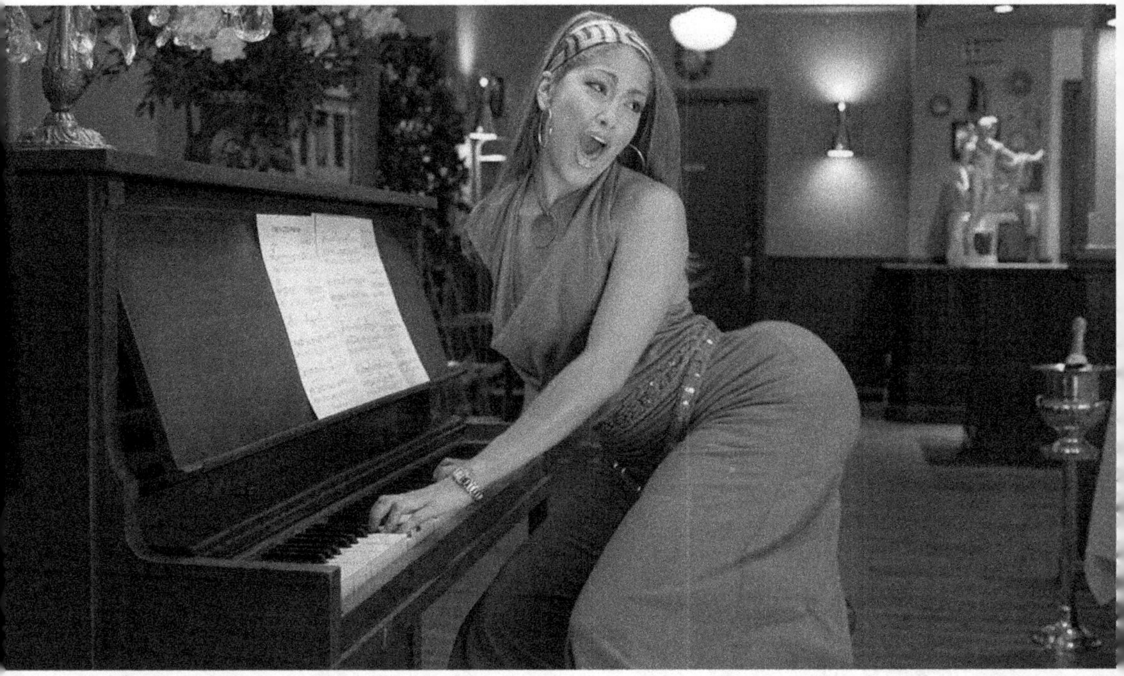

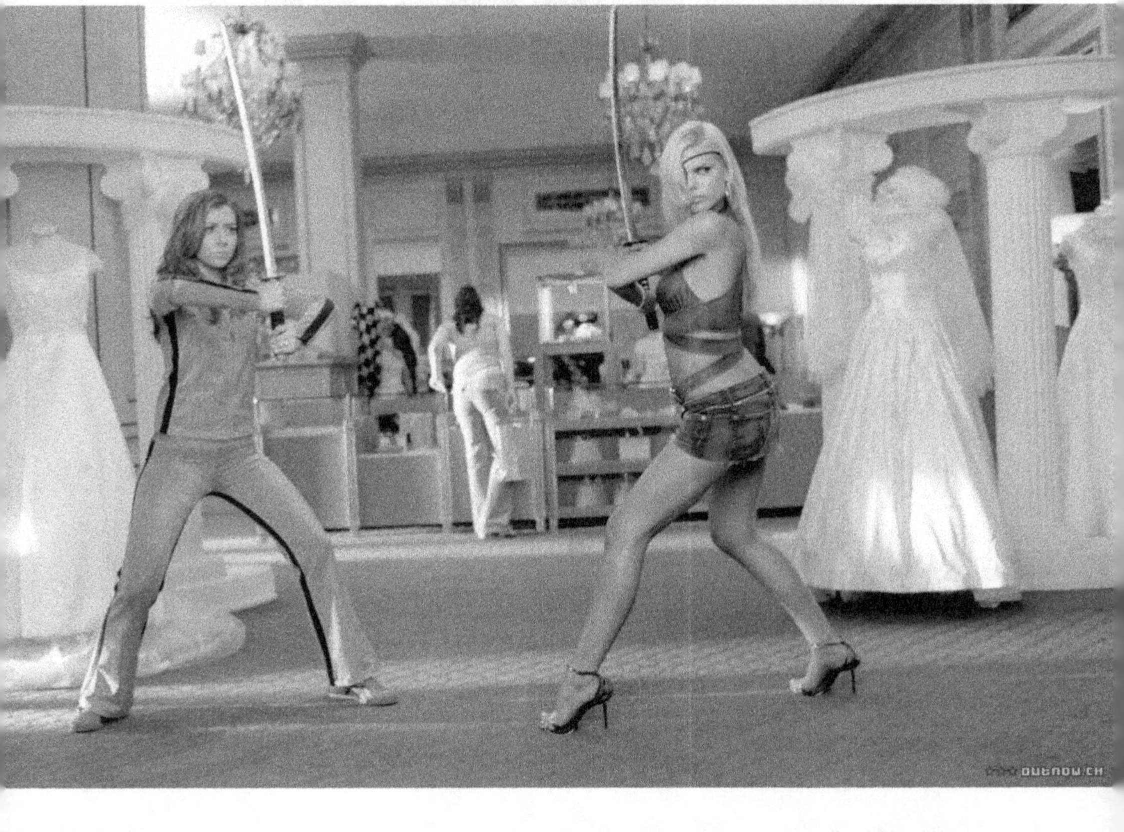
outnow.ch

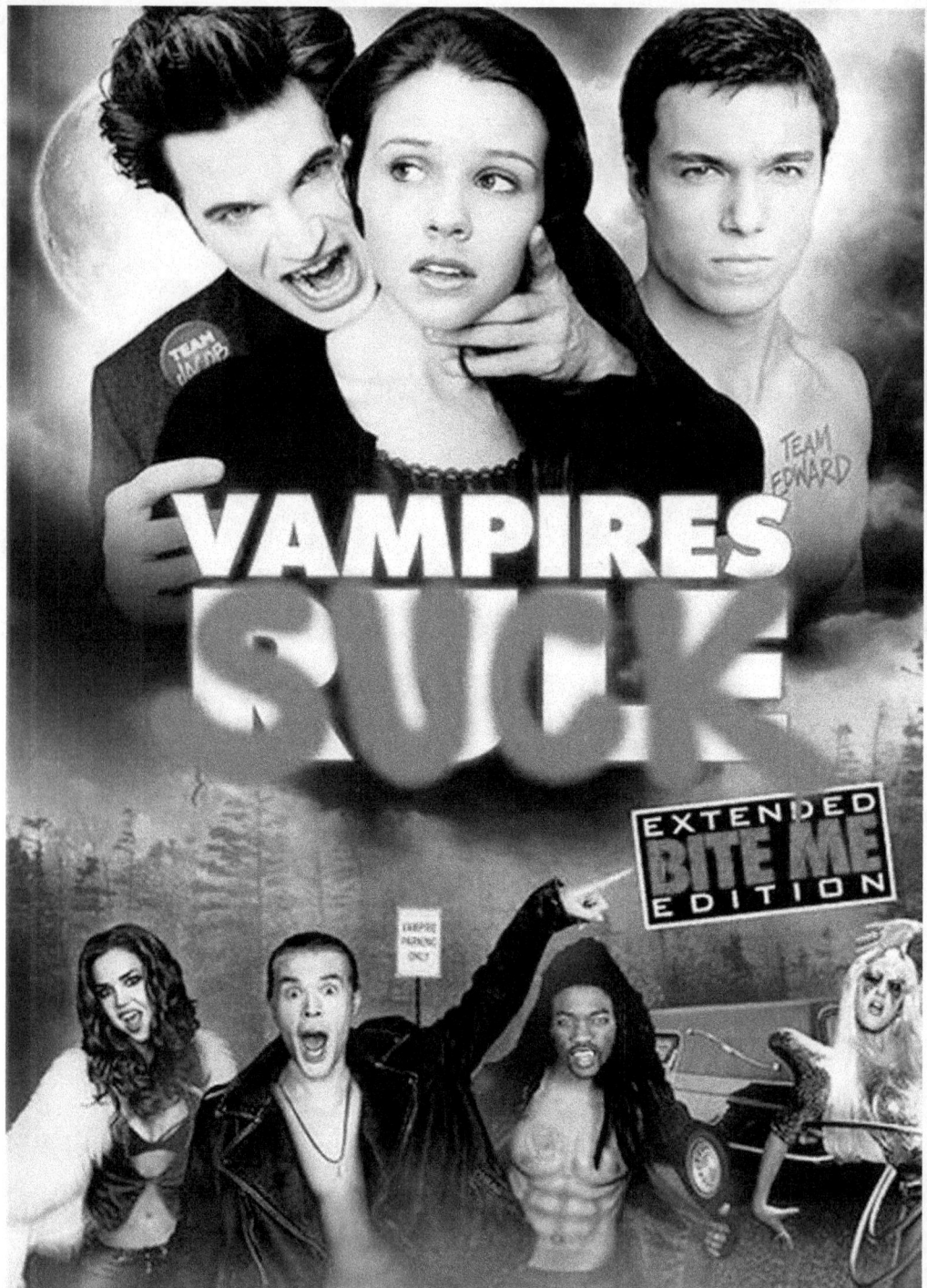

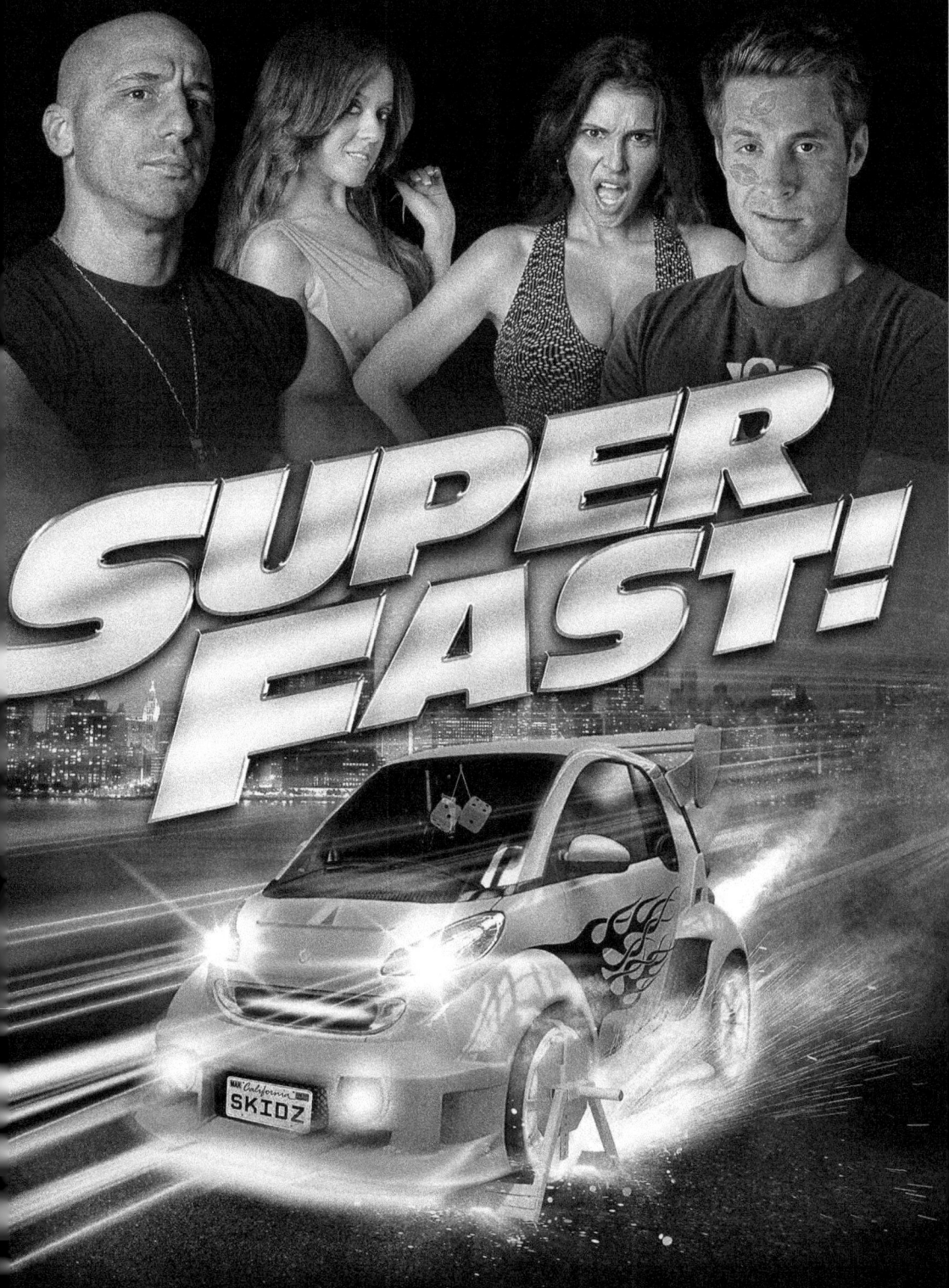

PART ONE

BIOGRAPHY AND COMEDY

1

JASON FRIEDBERG AND AARON SELTZER: INTRODUCTION

What is a rebel? A man who says no.
(Albert Camus, *The Rebel*)

BIOGRAPHY

The co-directors and co-writers Jason Friedberg and Aaron Seltzer were certainly on a roll in the 2000s and 2010s: they co-wrote the first *Scary Movie*, then set to work on a series of parody movies, beginning with *Date Movie* in 2006, followed by *Epic Movie* (2007), *Disaster Movie* (2008), *Meet the Spartans* (2008), *Vampires Suck* (2010), *The Starving Games* (2013) and *Superfast* (2015). Some of these movies were released with only a year between them (very few mainstream, commercial filmmakers achieve that kind of productivity). The factory system of Hollywood loves a series, so it churns out the same product repeatedly: the parodies of Friedberg and Seltzer are not a series, but they do come across as a series, with the word *Movie* in the titles of the first three spoofs (they feature some of the same cast and crew – and some of the same jokes!). The finest of the spoof movies of Friedberg and Seltzer are *Date Movie*, *Vampires Suck* and *Meet the Spartans*; *Vampires Suck* is probably the best-known, because of its association with the *Twilight Saga* (and *Vampires Suck* is certainly the premier send-up of *Twilight*).

Jason Friedberg (b. October 13, 1970, Newark, NJ),[1] grew up in Paterson, New Jersey (cue Noo Joisey jokes!),[2] and Aaron Seltzer (b. January 12, 1974), hailed from Mississauga, Ontario, Canada (cue Canadian jokes!). Seltzer's family were in the shoe business. They met at the University of Cali, in Santa Barbara, where they were studying history (Friedberg) and art history (Seltzer).[3] Jason's sister Alix Friedberg is a costume designer (she works mostly in television, and also designed the clothes for *Date Movie*).

Up to 2018, the films of Jason Friedberg and Aaron Seltzer had grossed around $400 million ($800+ million more if you include the *Scary Movie* franchise). After the first *Scary Movie* movie, Friedberg and Seltzer were not directly involved with the series – however, each *Scary Movie* is credited as 'based on characters by' Friedberg and Seltzer (they were known as 'two of the six writers of *Scary Movie*' – which they put on their movie posters).

The movies of Jason Friedberg and Aaron Seltzer as directors include:

Date Movie (2006)
Epic Movie (2007)
Meet the Spartans (2008)
Disaster Movie (2008)
Vampires Suck (2010)
The Starving Games (2013)
Best Night Ever (2013)
Superfast! (2015)

Eight movies in nine years, and two movies a year in 2008 and 2013. As writers, their produced credits include:

Spy Hard (1996)
Maximum Risk (1996)

---
1 Some sources say 1971.
2 Yes, jokes about New Jersey pop up in their films.
3 Seltzer had ambitions to be an artist.

There are 100s of parodies in all forms of media of the big, popular film franchises, such as *Star Wars, Star Trek, Lord of the Rings,* the *Twilight Saga, Harry Potter*, etc. Jason Friedberg and Aaron Seltzer have taken on many of the most well-known movie franchises, and based films around franchises such as *Twilight, The Hunger Games,* and *The Fast and the Furious.*

The comedies helmed by Jason Friedberg and Aaron Seltzer are budgeted at around $20 million. For some Hollywood observers, that would count as 'low budget'. Maybe. But the filmmakers make those 20 million dollar bills go a long way. They squeeze every cent out of the low budgets of their ambitious recreations of movies costing up to ten times more. There are many expensive elements: large crowd scenes, numerous costumes, big stunts, location shooting and tons of visual effects. Indeed, the spoof movies of recent times look as impressive and as effective as movies costing $100m, $150m or $200m. (Between 2014-2018, the average budget for an adventure film was $75 million, $20 million for a comedy, and $12 million for a drama.)

Actually, $20 million is regarded as 'low budget' *only* within the American film industry, and only compared to high budget or ultra-high budget productions. In *any* other film industry, in any other part of the world, $20 million is a substantial budget, or it's a high budget.

Also, within the American film business, $20 million (at 2006 prices) was a decent budget for a comedy movie. Budgets are spent by producers and companies in relation to how much movies are expected to generate (similarly with Prints and Advertizing).

We could get into film budgets and production costs in detail here, but it doesn't add much to the analysis of the cinema of Friedberg and Seltzer, except to point out that using the notion of the 'low budget' to attack their films, by fans and critics, is beside the point. (Critics, who should know better, actually understand very little about the costs of movie-making).

At their height, the movies of Friedberg and Seltzer had very wide releases, comparable with any ultra-high budget blockbuster movie: 3,233 screens for *Vampires Suck,* and 2,643 for *Meet the Spartans,* for example. In the U.S.A., *Vampires Suck* grossed $36,661,504, and *Meet the*

Spartans $38,233,676.

Friedberg and Seltzer join a small sub-group of directors who co-direct (many of the co-directing teams are brothers): the Wachowskis,[4] the Coens, the Farrellys, the Russos, the Hugheses, the Quays, the Tavianis, Jeunet & Caro, and Parker & Stone. Co-directing is common in Hong Kong cinema, often with one director overseeing the action, and the other doing the actorly, dramatic bits. In Japanese *anime*, it's common for the chief director to oversee the whole production (often working on the pre-production), while the second director runs the day-to-day production of the animation. (There are film directors you can't imagine sharing the directoral reins: Cecil B DeMille, D.W. Griffith, Woody Allen, Akira Kurosawa, Stanley Kubrick and Alfred Hitchcock).

There have been rumours of writers pitching jokes to Jason Friedberg and Aaron Seltzer, but their producer Peter Safran denies that, claiming that Friedberg and Seltzer write their own movies. In some areas of television, of course, comedies are created by whole teams (a tradition which goes back to the origins of TV in the U.S.A.). And in the movie industry, scripts are regularly rewritten numerous times (sometimes a *lot* of writers work on a single movie if it's been in development over years or even decades). A series of movies from the same team having only one or two screenwriters is very rare.

•

Aaron Seltzer and Jason Friedberg were entrepreneurs before they got into film production (to pay for college): they sold shoes[5] (Seltzer's father was a shoe salesman), they had a food delivery service, and hawked homemade Tee shirts (M. Patches, 2014). They were fans of movie comedies such as *Caddyshack, Airplane!, The Simpsons* and *The Naked Gun*. (Some of the crew of the Zucker-Abrahams-Zucker comedies worked on Friedberg and Seltzer's films, such as their production designer, William Elliott, and Leslie Nielsen starred in their first comedy script to be produced – *Spy Hard*). You can also spot the influence of Mel Brooks and *Saturday Night Live*,[6] among many others, in the films of Friedberg and Seltzer.

---
4 Should that now be the Wachowski 'sisters'?
5 They had two stores in Los Angeles (on Melrose Avenue).
6 Some of the skits that appear in Friedberg and Seltzer's movies resemble *Saturday Night Live* sketches.

The first big success for Jason Friedberg and Aaron Seltzer was *Spy Hard*:[7] the co-written script was shown to Friedberg's father Rick, a TV and film director (working mainly in television). Friedberg senior handed it to Leslie Nielsen, with whom he was making some comic golf training videos. Nielsen enjoyed it – and it became *Spy Hard* (1996), helmed by Friedberg senior (and also co-written and co-produced by him).

Friedberg and Seltzer thus created and developed two important and very good comedy movies – *Spy Hard* and *Scary Movie*. True, their scripts were rewritten and rejigged by other writers, but they originated the ideas for *Spy Hard* and (some of) *Scary Movie,* two comedy movies which have been enjoyed by millions, which have been well-received by some critics, and which have generated lots of $$$$.

Following *Scary Movie,* Jason Friedberg and Aaron Seltzer wrote and sold upwards of forty scripts. Writers can exist on selling scripts, even it they're not produced (that is, if they get a decent amount of money for each sale). I would imagine that material from some of the unproduced screenplays was used in the run of Friedberg-Seltzer's films beginning with *Date Movie*.

Many scripts were sold, but only one was green-lit (*Maximum Risk,* 1996), their rewrite[8] of a Jean-Claude van Damme actioner directed by Hong Kong legend Ringo Lam Ling-tung. They had sold a Jackie Chan action movie to Columbia called *The Bridge*, which wasn't made, but it led to them being hired to rewrite *Maximum Risk*. (The producer, Moshe Diamant, was at the time developing projects with Western stars and Hong Kong directors/ teams, including superstar directors such as John Woo and Tsui Hark. Diamant has extensive credits in TV and cinema).

Friedberg and Seltzer adapted Christopher Buckley's *Little Green Men* (and did other book adaptations), wrote a parody of a talking animals[9] movie in the manner of *Babe,* sold a script to Disney,[10] and did other work-for-hire gigs.

Liberace[11] was a script[12] that Jason Friedberg and Aaron Seltzer were

---
[7] The first movie to be produced from one of their scripts – *Spy Hard* – grossed $84 million, very good going for a comedy.
[8] Larry Ferguson has screen credit.
[9] Animals – usually puppets – pop up regularly in their movies.
[10] Which apparently became *Cars*.
[11] There's a reference to Liberace in *Epic Movie*.
[12] The *Liberace* script impressed producer Peter Safran, who worked with Friedberg and Seltzer on the *Scary Movie* project and later became their regular producer.

keen to see made. They had screenwriters Larry Karaszewski and Scott Alexander (*Ed Wood, The People vs. Larry Flynt*) on their side in 2000, with Philip Kaufman as director,[13] and Independent Pictures as the producer (actors such as Nicolas Cage, Robin Williams and Johnny Depp were interested).

But *Liberace* proved to be a pricey project (requiring period recreations of the razzle-dazzle of Las Vegas in its heyday, for example). It ended up as a different production, on Home Box Office (many movies are reworked as mini-series for cable networks).

Following the mega-success of the first *Scary Movie,* more work came their way: Jason Friedberg and Aaron Seltzer developed a mock documentary called *The Batchelor Party* (presumably this surfaced as *Best Night Ever* in 2013); for director Ivan Reitman (*Ghostbusters, Evolution*), they wrote a *Looney Tunes* script; an adaptation of *H.R. Pufnstuf* by Sid and Marty Krofft (this script was also backed by Larry Karaszewski and Scott Alexander); and a story in the manner of *Groundhog Day* (1993), where a guy discovers he's in a mental living hell.

If a movie is successful, as *Date Movie* was in 2006, the first thing a studio will ask for is a sequel or for More Of The Same, or for something very similar. Thus, altho' Jason Friedberg and Aaron Seltzer had many unproduced scripts, it was another parody movie that New Regency wanted, as Aaron Seltzer explained in the 2014 interview:

> We like to work. And know how difficult it is to get a movie made. So if you have a movie that worked financially, then the studios are much more apt to do that again than something more original.

After *Date Movie* and *Epic Movie,* *A Christmas Carol*-style holiday movie was pitched to New Regency, to star Rainn Wilson (*The Office*). But the studio cancelled the production days before principal photography (citing budgetary concerns). Friedberg and Seltzer sold them the idea of a *300* parody instead, called *Meet the Spartans*, which New Regency were more confident about.

Backing the Jason Friedberg and Aaron Seltzer parody movies was Regency Enterprises, founded by Arnold Milchan (b. 1944) in 1991. A

---

[13] A celebrated name director – *The Right Stuff, The Unbearable Lightness of Being, The Moderns*, etc.

major Hollywood mogul, billionaire Milchan (he was worth $3.5 billion in 2018)[14] was the producer of 130 movies (including *J.F.K., Heat, King of Comedy, Once Upon a Time In America, Brazil, Under Siege, Free Willy, Falling Down, Pretty Woman, Fight Club, City of Angels, Entrapment, L.A. Confidential, Alvin and the Chipmunks, Fantastic Mr Fox, Assassin's Creed, Birdman, Noah, 12 Years a Slave, Jumper, Daredevil* and *The Devil's Advocate*). Regency's *Big Momma* films were forerunners of the Friedberg and Seltzer movies.

Regency had distribution deals with Warners and subsequently Fox. It had a television dept (*Malcolm In the Middle, Roswell, The Bernie Mac Show,* etc).

By the time of *The Starving Games* in 2013, Jason Friedberg and Aaron Seltzer changed the way they worked with film studios. *The Hunger Games* spoof was pre-sold to distributors and overseas markets by Peter Safran's company. (The budget was considerably smaller, at $4.5 million, compared to the usual budgets of $15-20 million of other Friedberg and Seltzer movies).

The business model of *The Starving Games* also had the movie being released in theatres and as video-on-demand, by the new company, Ketchup Entertainment. The scheme was also employed for *Best Night Ever* the same year.

Several of Friedberg and Seltzer's movies have been based in Louisiana: since 2002, tax incentives have encouraged productions to film there (the tax deals favour hiring local residents, for example. Productions such as *Twilight, Jurassic World, Fantastic Four* and *Captain Marvel* have filmed in Lousiana).

•

One aspect that film critics haven't been able to explain is that the films of Jason Friedberg and Aaron Seltzer have been commercially successful. These are the critics who, like 10 year-old nerds, rate movies with stars or marks out of five or out of ten. It's unbelievably idiotic.

Think about it: *Citizen Kane*, if released today, would get three stars out of five and a 'could try harder' warning from film critics. And *Gone With the Wind* and *The Wizard of Oz* – from Hollywood's miracle year of

---

14 $5.6 billion in 2015, according to Forbes.

1939 – would be absolutely trashed as cheesy, melodramatic, indulgent, etc etc etc.

But the film critics who rely so heavily on stars and ratings systems can't square their beloved numbers with the financial revenue generated by the movies directed by Jason Friedberg and Aaron Seltzer.

•

Jason Friedberg and Aaron Seltzer don't do much press, interviews, TV chat shows, etc (many people in show business would rather be doing *anything* than sitting in hotels with journos or attending press conferences). So some observers wonder if they even exist. One of the very few interviews with Friedberg and Seltzer can be found in *Grantland*, published in January, 2014. It's a telephone interview. Even this, tho', might be a wind-up – after all, Friedberg and Seltzer spent an entire audio commentary making up non-existent technical guff (for *Epic Movie*). However, their commentaries for *Date Movie* and *Meet the Spartans* are in a regular format.

Like many artists, Friedberg and Seltzer prefer to work, and to live their lives. They might choose privacy, but they're not 'recluses': you can't be a recluse when you're a filmmaker! You're surrounded by 50 people on a set – and if you're the director, people are asking you stuff all the time. (And don't forget the countless meetings during pre-production, when movies are *really* made. In the pre-production cycle of making movies, you are meeting all sorts of people all the time).

Jason Friedberg and Aaron Seltzer like to work: they not only write and direct (demanding enough – try it), they also co-produce their movies. But because they're not messing about on Twitter or Facebook or other 'social media', or appearing on inane TV chat shows, people think they're either recluses, or they are really Steven Soderbergh, or some other director working under a pseudonym.

•

Jason Friedberg and Aaron Seltzer don't take on just any movie for their spoofs: they have to be high profile movies, with a satisfying narrative structure. It's no good sending up movies that nobody has seen (similarly, Friedberg and Seltzer nix jokes which only play to a section of the audience). That also means that spoof movies are dependent on the movie market, and are *reacting* to the movies that're out there.

But as each year passes, you can probably guess the movies that will be parodied by Jason Friedberg and Aaron Seltzer. Some movies are just asking for it: *50 Shades of Grey*, the dreadful films directed by M. Night Shyamalan, *Bridget Jones' Diary*, the cretinous *Hunger Games*, and the *Twilight Saga*.

However, because the budgets are in the $20 million range, that automatically limits what can be put on screen – movies with digitally animated creatures, exotic locations, 100s of extras and costumes, vehicles, and 100s of sets are going to be expensive. Dinosaurs from *Jurassic Park*, aliens from *Star Wars* or *Star Trek*, giant robots from *Transformers* or *Pacific Rim*, monsters from *Harry Potter* or *Avengers* – these are extremely costly visual effects. (But comedy movies can get away with cheapo and cheesy visual effects, because they're not being earnest and serious).

One wonders if some of the movies parodied by Jason Friedberg and Aaron Seltzer are not really high profile enough to sustain a whole movie: *300* was a big movie, but maybe not iconic enough for a whole spoof movie. The *Fast and the Furious* franchise was a bigger earner at the box office, as a series, but again perhaps not well-known enough to sustain a whole parody movie. (This may account for the low box office returns of *Superfast!*).

On the other hand, movies such as *Vampires Suck, Meet the Spartans* and *Superfast!* benefit from following the plot of a single source movie (in the main), rather than combining the plots from several unrelated movies, as with *Epic Movie*, *Date Movie* and others. But those movies that draw on multiple films are sometimes funnier because they have more targets to send up.

The home entertainment releases of Jason Friedberg and Aaron Seltzer's films include deleted scenes or unrated scenes which were cut from the theatrical versions (partly, presumably, to obtain the all-important 'PG-13' rating). Unfortunately, the wonderful music is mixed too low, as with almost every home entertainment release of Western movies. A pity, because the composers of Friedberg and Seltzer's movies deliver amusing send-ups of the pompous scores found in so many

Hollywood flicks.

Rather than being the heartless cynics as portrayed in the meeja, Jason Friedberg and Aaron Seltzer are actually total softies: consider the predominance of romance in their comedies, the lovers who are united at the end, etc.

•

Jason Friedberg and Aaron Seltzer work in the 'PG-13' rating arena – which means many trips to the M.P.A.A. to reduce the 'R' rated gags (they didn't enter the world of 'Rs' until *Best Night Ever* in 2013). The natural zone for Friedberg and Seltzer is probably 'R' rated, but in the world of commercial cinema, 'PG-13' is more lucrative (particularly as much of the target audience for Friedberg and Seltzer's comedies is teenage). (Home releases added more material, which became 'R' rated – thus, for videos, DVDs, Blu-rays and the like, the movies of Friedberg and Seltzer are 'Rs', tho' soft 'Rs', compared to 'Rs' which're close to 'NC-17').

The ratings system in North America since the Nineties has been set by the Motion Picture Association of America (the M.P.A.A.).[15] The classifications are 'G' (general audience); 'PG' (parental guidance suggested); 'PG-13' (parental guidance suggested, some material not suitable for under 13 year-olds); 'R' (anyone under 17 must be accompanied by an adult), and 'NC-17' (no children under 17 admitted).

Earlier, the C.A.R.A. (Code and Ratings Administration) had divided films into 4 categories: 'G' (general admission), 'M' (parental guidance), 'R' (children under 16 must be accompanied by an adult) and 'X' (16 and over). The 'M' category was changed to 'GP' in 1970, and the age restriction was raised to 17 (in response to parents regarding the 'M' category as too stern, said Jack Valenti). 'GP' became 'PG' in 1972. C.A.R.A. became the Classification and Ratings Administration in 1977. The 'PG-13' rating was added in 1984, due largely to the second *Indiana Jones* film, directed by Steven Spielberg. (According to Valenti, any reference to drugs, for example, would require a 'PG-13'; 'sexual nudity' or repetitive violence would take a film into 'R' rating.)

There is a feeling about the films of Jason Friedberg and Aaron

---

[15] The M.P.A.A. ratings board is made up of 8 to 13 members, who serve for varying lengths of time.

Seltzer of middle-age guys pretending to act like crude teenagers – but then, that applies to much of the output of the North American film industry. (It also appears that if they could, Friedberg and Seltzer would sail happily beyond 'R' rated material *and* beyond 'NC-17' material, into the zones of being totally 'offensive'. Many comedians would, if they could get away with it, be *much* cruder. It depends partly on the context: in the arena of stand-up comedy, for ex, more extreme material is commonplace. Ditto in novels. In comics. But television and cinema are different cultural territories, more carefully policed than printed fiction or stand-up comedy or comicbooks).

The movies of Jason Friedberg and Aaron Seltzer are overtly political all over the place, but they don't stem from the right-on, pseudo-left-wing political activism of U.S. filmmakers such as Michael Moore and Spike Lee. Instead, Friedberg and Seltzer tend to use directly political jokes sparely, and only when a big laugh is possible. U.S. Presidents are thus fair game, but not raising complex political issues (which are harder to turn into laffs).

Altho' critics and fans have complained repeatedly that the scripts of Jason Friedberg and Aaron Seltzer's films are feebly structured, the team insists that they are carefully crafted. Which they are – it's obvious, anyone can see that these are structured, planned plots and scripts. For a start, each spoof movie takes up the narrative of the target movie, and arranges it into a suitable form. This is actually the part where a lot of thought is taken – which movies to parody, and how to fit them into a compelling plot (target movies for parody will be discarded if a suitable narrative structure doesn't present itself). Some of Friedberg and Seltzer's spoof movies use a single plot from a single movie – *Meet the Spartans* – some use the plots of two movies – *Vampires Suck* – and some are amalgams of several movies – *Date Movie*, *Epic Movie* and *Disaster Movie*. Notice that the later movies use a single plot as the main spine of the movie: *The Starving Games* and *Superfast!*.

It's obvious that the scripts of Friedberg and Seltzer perform all of the usual functions of a regular film script: they have clear plots that develop to a resolution, with sometimes a subplot (the romantic subplot in *Disaster Movie*, for instance); other elements include foreshadowing, call-backs, sometimes flashbacks, running gags, and all the usual ingredients of a film script.

For example, Friedberg and Seltzer introduce characters in the standard manner, with basic characteristics, names, what they do for a living (if it's important), what their relationship is with other characters, their goals, desires, motives, etc. And if the characters are the protagonists, their story will develop and include some sort of resolution. Where Friedberg and Seltzer depart from the norms of scriptwriting, however, is how they go about delivering the dramatic functions. For example, the most extreme version of ending a character's narrative trajectory is simply to kill them off (and very rapidly, too – with a bus slamming into them *à la Final Destination*).[16]

There's a tradition of the 'worst' films being enjoyable, the 'so bad they're good' syndrome: *Plan 9 From Outer Space*, *Battlefield Earth* and *Jaws: The Revenge*. Films like *Showgirls* are panned across the board by crrritics, but're fabulous. Of course, some movies are so bad they stink, and nothing redeems them: *The Avengers* (1998), *Snow White and the Huntsman*, *Where the Wild Things Are*, *Batman Begins*, *King Arthur*, *The Hulk*, the *Narnia* series, the *Bridget Jones* movies, *Kill Bill*, *50 Shades of Grey*, etc.

Many of the movies parodied by Jason Friedberg and Aaron Seltzer cried out for parodies – *300*, *The Hunger Games*, *Twilight*, *The Fast and the Furious*, *Narnia*, etc. As soon as dreck like *Narnia* or *The Hunger Games* is released, you beg for someone – anyone! – to lampoon it.

The movies of Jason Friedberg and Aaron Seltzer, the *Scary Movie* series, the *Naked Gun* films – even if they are among the 'worst' films of recent times, people still enjoy them. Movies can't gross $80 million at the box office or $18 million in DVD sales unless *someone* wants to see them. Or put it like this:

• It's great to see movies you hate get a kicking (*The Hunger Games*, *Narnia*, ditzy rom-coms);

• It's great to see movies you love get a kicking (*Twilight*, *Harry Potter*);

• And it's great to see movies you find creepy and disturbing get a

---

[16] A rubbish horror franchise, but *Final Destination* did give Friedberg and Seltzer a way of simply wasting characters when their function's over.

kicking (*300*, superhero flicks).

Jason Friedberg and Aaron Seltzer preview their movies (as do the Zucker, Abrahams and Zucker team) – and the whole point of the preview process is simple, as it often is with comedies: *are people laughing*? All art hopes for some kind of response, but comedies are one of the very few genres where a physical reaction is the number one goal. If there aren't laughs, out go the jokes. As Aaron Seltzer says: 'People have to laugh, they have to like it'.

And a parody movie is not a regular comedy; it has *lots* of jokes, some of which have to be big laughs. 'You have to have big belly laughs; you have to have people screech at some things. We just go for it.' (The Marx Brothers road-tested some of their movies before they filmed them: they undertook short tours of vaudeville theatres before making films such as *A Night At the Opera* and *A Day At the Races*, to see which material worked. The films were not only filmed in response to the knowledge of the live shows, they were also edited that way, too. Thus, some of the pauses in the movies were built in because the Marxes knew there would be laughs there).

Who do studios preview and market test movies to? Not audiences of critics, or industry professionals, but audiences of regular folk – the Zucker-Abrahams-Zucker movies used college audiences, for example (the Mall at Sherman Oaks was a regular previewing theatre for them).[17] Of course, an audience of critics might be useful, if they really did their work, and offered ways of improving the movie. But they don't, or they can't: that's why they're critics! Not filmmakers! There are famous examples of critics who wrote movies that weren't that good (Pauline Kael and Roger Ebert come to mind). However, one group of critics *did* go on to become world-class filmmakers: the *Cahier du Cinéma* crowd (Jean-Luc Godard, François Truffaut, Claude Chabrol *et al*).

Today, tho', what major film critic in Europe or the U.S.A. is also a world-class filmmaker, or screenwriter? Indeed, *are* there any major film critics anymore?

British producer and artists' manager Peter Safran, who has produced

---

[17] As the Zuckers joked, there was a rail by the cinema, up on the third floor – it was the director's rail, to jump from when their movie tanked.

Jason Friedberg and Aaron Seltzer since *Date Movie*, says they don't even bother to test movies for over-25s: teens are their target audience (African American and Latino audiences also partial to their movies, as they are to the spoofs of the Wayans family, and Z.A.Z.). One reason offered by critics is that spoof movies are a potent way of analyzing American society and culture from the viewpoint of marginalized groups. As Linda Hutcheon put it in *A Poetics of Postmodernism*:

> parody has certainly become a most popular and effective strategy of the other ex-centrics – of black, ethnic, gay, and feminist artists – trying to come to terms with and to respond, critically and creatively, to the still predominantly white, heterosexual, male culture in which they find themselves. (35)

Indeed, it's worth noting that these two white, Jewish[18] filmmakers include more non-white actors than most of their contemporaries (there are many Latino performers in their films, for instance) – and beyond the usual token roles for non-white actors (as sidekicks, for instance, or the victim who gets eaten by the monster early on). In *Epic Movie*, for example, two of the four heroes are non-white.

And Friedberg and Seltzer must be the blackest of white film directors in the U.S.A. – they include heaps of African American pop culture in their movies – in music, fashion, interactions, characters, and dialogue. Their go-to music is hiphop or rap, and they happily give black characters (or Latino characters) the best jokes.

FRIEDBERG AND SELTZER ARE *AUTEURS*.

Fans – and critics, who should know better – also forget that North American commercial cinema is a market-driven industry. If a movie is a big hit, there will be official sequels, cash-ins, and downright rip-offs, as with any commercial film business around the globe. In other words, if film studios and producers see that parody comedies can be made for under $20 mil and can gross four times that, well, they will order up some more.

It's not a case of Jason Friedberg and Aaron Seltzer acting as Great

---

[18] Friedberg and Seltzer don't make a big deal of their Jewish background in their movies like, say, Mel Brooks or Woody Allen or Neil Simon.

Artists, who step down from their ivory tower to announce that they would like a film studio to back their latest artistic masterpiece (which they have spent the past three decades perfecting). It's the other way around: studios and producers want to make money, and they will consider projects that can do that. They buy properties, then they hire people to develop them. Studios have *lots* of scripts and projects in development at any one time (100 might be in official development). The movie parodies of Friedberg and Seltzer are just one part of a much bigger industrial practice.

Also, Jason Friedberg and Aaron Seltzer would be the first to admit that they are not *auteurs*, not arty directors with 'important' things to say, who're worshipped by critics as significant filmmakers – the Scorseses, the Kurosawas, the Bergmans and the Dreyers of the movie world. (And Friedberg and Seltzer don't own their movies – no commercial film director does – it's the *studios* who own the movies, and the copyrights, and the right to exploit the material).

But wait – Friedberg and Seltzer are actually genuine *auteurs*, as defined in contemporary film criticism: they *write* as well as *direct* their movies. Most film directors *don't* write their own scripts, and they *don't* originate their projects – they are hired, like everybody else. The American film business is a factory-type system run by studios and producers; it's not a collective of artists expressing themselves on a film-by-film, individual-project basis.

Friedberg and Seltzer are also *auteurs* as defined by contemporary film criticism in other ways: they have recurring themes, motifs and even images in their work. Now, we know that film critics will froth at the mouth at the very idea that Friedberg and Seltzer could be regarded as *auteurs* as revered as Akira Kurosawa and Orson Welles. But they are.

THE CASTS.

Actors who've worked for Jason Friedberg and Aaron Seltzer have remarked how they have been encouraged to go all-out, to try all sorts of things. And actors just love directors who provide the space and the time and the freedom to do that. The context, the script, the story, the setting, the characters, the themes and everything else are already set, but there's still plenty that a decent performer can bring to a scene.

But few (i.e., none) of the critics have appraised the performances in the Friedberg-Seltzer spoof movies – they seem to see everything in their films as gormless goofing around. It's not: have a look at amateur videos of weddings or parties or one of those TV shows that trades on viewers sending in their 'funny' or 'accidental' camcorder pieces, to see how bad some 'acting' can be. No – the performances in recent spoof movies are more skilful than that.

For instance, compare the range of performance styles in the recent spoof movies to your typical Hollywood/ American/ European movie, and you'll see right away how strait-laced, how buttoned-up, and how restrained actors usually are (in any movie, in any genre). Because most movies and TV shows either emulate what they perceive as 'realism'/ 'naturalism', or they try to evoke it (even in stories with a fantastical or unreal premise). In the recent spoof movies, you'll find the regular performance styles of Western TV and cinema (the spoofs still aim at creating some semblance of 'reality' – usually in order to work against it), but they also allow room for some *really* out-there performances.

Also worth noting is how much screen time is generously given to actresses in the Friedberg-Seltzer spoofs – in thousands of mainstream and Hollywood comedies, it's the main star, the comedian, who is given the all-important jokes and punchlines. And the girls are not only given punchlines, they are encouraged to goof around as energetically as the guys. Again, unusual. In the movies of Friedberg and Seltzer, actresses such as Nicole Parker, Crista Flanagan, Carmen Electra and Jennifer Coolidge shine.

The actors in a Jason Friedberg and Aaron Seltzer movie love to make the people they're working for laugh, and the people they're acting with. They'll look over at the directors during a take and see them laughing, which encourages them further. Many actors have said the same – Johnny Depp with Tim Burton, and Jack Nicholson with anybody. Dorothy Tutin, appearing in *Savage Messiah* (1972), said that the actors felt like they were performing not for the camera, but for the director, Ken Russell: 'He knows *exactly* what the film will be like, and we weren't doing it for the camera – we were doing it for *him*'.[19]

They may be hated by *some* audiences and *some* critics, and dubbed the 'worst' film directors by *some* critics and *some* audiences, but not *all* critics and *all* audiences. And Jason Friedberg and Aaron Seltzer are loved by their actors and crew, by many accounts. Crew and cast keeping coming back to work with them. Friedberg and Seltzer are not among the well-known jerk film directors in the industry – the ones who intimidate, yell at, and coerce crew members and actors. (Directors known for their harsh behaviour on set include James Cameron, Michael Bay, David O. Russell and Roman Polanski).

Actors like to work for Jason Friedberg and Aaron Seltzer for obvious reasons: (1) most actors are out of work, so any work is great. (2) Their work will be seen by thousands of people in movies that're released around the world in theatres and then on home releases. (3) They get to do things they never usually do: sing, and dance, and go for it in many other ways. (4) They can appear in many kinds of scenes within one production (in the spoofs in different genres). (5) The shooting schedules are short, so they don't tie up too much time.[20] (6) They get to work with some great actors. (7) They have a laugh making the films (the social angle is a key part of any job).

Ditto with the crew. The costume, props, art, set dressing, camera, vfx, practical fx and design departments get to create Ancient Greece, the Louvre Museum, Hogwarts, Narnia, Pandora, Forks, a Caribbean pirate ship, TV game shows, and Willy Wonka's Chocolate Factory.

An ensemble of sorts have appeared in several Friedberg and Seltzer movies, including Carmen Electra, Crista Flanagan, Nicole Parker, Jennifer Coolidge, Ike Barinholtz, Diedrich Bader, Tony Cox, Nick Steele, etc.

Several of the regular actors in the Jason Friedberg and Aaron Seltzer comedies were cast members of *Mad TV* (1995-2009),[21] including Christa Flanagan, Nicole Parker, Ike Barinholtz and Josh Meyers.

Enhancing the feeling of all of this being a pantomime, of putting on a theatrical show, the films of Friedberg and Seltzer have actors playing

---
19 J. Baxter, 196.
20 Shooting in towns like L.A. is a bonus.
21 Broadcast on Fox, the distributors of some of Friedberg and Seltzer's films.

multiple roles. So the wonderful Nicole Parker will turn up in *Meet the Spartans* playing Paris Hilton, Britney Spears, Paula Abdul and Ellen DeGeneres. In a theatre company, that's a common practice, to cut down on the size of the ensemble, on logistics, on travel, and of course on salaries.

And then there's Carmen Electra (Tara Patrick, b. 1972), the singer/ actress/ TV celebrity/ *Playboy* model, who's appeared in many parody flicks (she first worked for Jason Friedberg and Aaron Seltzer in *Date Movie* – and had already been in the *Scary Movie* series; her other films include *Starksy and Hutch, Christmas Vacation, Perfume, Get Over It, Dirty Love, Cheaper By the Dozen 2, I Want Candy,* and *Book of Fire.* On TV, Electra's appeared in *Baywatch, Hyperion Bay, The Simpsons, Off Centre, Dance Fever, Summerland, Manhunt, 90210, Stacked* and *Jane the Virgin,* and her own TV show on M.T.V.) She was the face of Max Factor. Electra dated Prince and was one of the many acts he nurtured: he created and produced her first album, and oversaw her stage show and dancers (and she supported his band on tour, too).

When Carmen Electra worked for them, Jason Friedberg said, she was paid scale, and she liked to be part of the team and work hard.

Carmen Electra remarked in 2008:

I'm always attracted to doing parodies, and especially to Jason and Aaron's specific brand of humor. Their films are a lot of fun to make. I love to go to work every day and laugh, get to do all this silly stuff, and even make fun of myself. You do have to walk into a movie like this with an open mind and be willing to poke fun at yourself a little bit and put yourself out there.

Friedberg on Electra: 'Carmen really gets our comedic spin. She's obviously beautiful and very sexy, but she also has great comic skills'.

THE CREW.

Composer Christopher Lennertz studied at Thornton School of Music (U.S.C.). His film credits include: *Frailty, Saint Sinner, The Deal, Soul Plane, Alvin and the Chipmunks, The Perfect Christmas, The Comebacks, Free Willy 2, Dr Doolittle 3, The Jungle Book,* and *101 Dalmatians,* and TV shows such as *Supernatural, Brimstone,* and *The*

Strip. Lennertz has also scored video games such as *Medal of Honor* and *James Bond*. (There's more on Lennertz in the *Meet the Spartans* chapter).

One of the unsung heroes of the cinema of Jason Friedberg and Aaron Seltzer is the music producer and composer Ali Dee Theodore (b. 1970, New York City). Theodore (who sometimes uses the moniker Ali Dee, has worked with many hiphop and rap artists, and provided the soundtracks for flicks such as *Night At the Museum, Daredevil, Iron Man, Ghost Rider, Transformers,* and *Sex and the City*. Whenever Friedberg and Seltzer need a hiphop song or two (or ten), they often turn to Theodore (as well as using the originals). Many of the rap/ hiphop tunes you hear in a Friedberg and Seltzer are thus composed by Theodore.

The production designer of Friedberg and Seltzer's films, William Elliott, is a veteran of numerous movies, including some spoof movies: the two *Hots Shots!* movies, *Scary Movie 3* and *Undercover Brother*. Elliott's credits include: *Roll Bounce, Malibu's Most Wanted, Ghosts of Mars, The Nutty Professor 1* and *2, Doctor Doolittle, Metro, For Better or Worse, Andre, Ace Ventura: Pet Detective, Honeymoon In Vegas* and *Impulse*. Elliott designed *Jane Austen's Mafia!,* a forerunner of the Friedberg and Seltzer comedies, doing a great job of recreating the historical era of *The Godfather II* (including the Ellis Island sequence), and many swipes at the classic 1970s movies.

Editor Peck Prior has credits that include: *Planes, Trains and Automobiles, The Benchwarmers, Deuce Bigalow: European Gigolo, Joe Dirt, Without a Paddle, Dating Games People Play, I Still Know What You Did Last Summer, Terminal Velocity, The Hot Chick, Ray, The Master of Disguise* and *The Animal*.

THE SELTZER-FREIDBERG FORMULA.

In a typical Jason Friedberg and Aaron Seltzer movie, there's more music and dancing and dressing up and other elements regarded as 'feminine'/ 'female'/ 'girlie' than in many comparable movies (their first movie as co-directors was a romantic comedy about a young woman. *Date Movie,* like the *Scary Movie* series, has a young woman as the central character, automatically shifting it away from your typical Hollywood movie. And a young woman in a comedy – again unusual.)

• There's usually a song or two,[22] and a dance number (typically hiphop/ rap, with break-dancing).

• Figures of fun will pop up regularly – like Michael Jackson with a young boy, or Captain Jack Sparrow, or James Bond. Friedberg and Seltzer exploit lookalike actors to the max.

• Babes in bikinis (or at least in tight dresses revealing curves and cleavages) are recurring characters. (Someone in the Friedberg-Seltzer team is very fond of beautiful, young women – tits and ass are plentiful in their movies).

• Someone will fart/ piss/ defecate.

• Characters are killed off rapidly and violently.[23]

• Dummies are thrown about with gleeful abandon, as charas are dispatched (squashing is a favourite device from a body dropping from above).

• Puppets are everywhere.

• Gags are repeated serially beyond the usual comedic requirements.

• TV commercials and joke products are typical gags.

• TV shows (game shows especially) are aped.

• Friedberg and Seltzer are fond of printed gags – joke signs, parody book covers, humorous magazine articles and newspaper headlines.

• Going out-of-date is a concern: hence, topical gags are often included near the completion of the movie, or the subjects tackled are strong enough to last (hence only well-known movies are satirized).

ASPECTS OF THE COMEDY OF FRIEDBERG AND SELTZER.

Among the topics that recur in the comic vision of Jason Friedberg and Aaron Seltzer are: irregular body types (fat people, midgets, hairy people – anyone is fair game), simple (often violent) slapstick, gross/ toilet humour, pomposity/ pretension, pointless cleverness, disguises, irritating pop culture icons, terrible pop stars/ music, homosexuality/ lesbianism, and of course movies.

Jason Friedberg and Aaron Seltzer deliberately flout the 'rules' of comedy – their most stubborn 'fuck you' to thousands of years of humour is to flog a joke to death via repetition. In *Epic Movie*, for example, Lucy

---

[22] Actually, *lots of songs and* pieces of music.
[23] This drives critics nuts!

repeats what Susan's just said. A couple of times it's funny, but the joke is retained throughout the movie. In another scene in *Epic Movie*, Susan vomits after chugging beer – the scene goes beyond the 'rule of three' in comedy into endless repetition.

Instead of abiding by some of the 'rules' of comedy, Jason Friedberg and Aaron Seltzer simply go for the laugh, every time. Well, there aren't any comedy 'rules', but there are certainly ways of constructing scenes, introducing characters, setting up the joke, which many comedy writers follow.

A typical joke features a set-up and a pay-off, as we know – but critics complain that Jason Friedberg and Aaron Seltzer think it's funny just to wheel on a celebrity lookalike. For critics, Friedberg and Seltzer are simply lazy and obvious.

Slapstick is an ingredient in the comedy of Friedberg and Seltzer; though slapstick comedy and pratfalls are seen as crude and cheap by critics, even verbal, sophisticated comic writers such as Woody Allen and Steve Martin use them. And silent comedy cinema took slapstick to sublime heights in the films of Charlie Chaplin and Buster Keaton.

Perhaps one could see the sudden deaths from speeding vehicles in the films of Friedberg and Seltzer as a kind of black humour version of traditional slapstick. In *American Film Comedy*, the Siegels define slapstick thus:

> Slapstick is usually considered a lowbrow form of physical humor that depends upon pain and humiliation for its laughter: the archetypal slapstick gags have their victim falling on a banana peel or being hit in the face with a pie. In general, slapstick depends heavily upon chases, pratfalls, seemingly dangerous comic collisions, practical jokes, and otherwise turbulent, 'roughhouse' antics. (263)

The films of Friedberg and Seltzer vary between spoofs of a single movie (or a single movie franchise): *Meet the Spartans, The Starving Games, Vampires Suck* and *Superfast!*, and films which lampoon a genre: *Date Movie, Epic Movie, Spy Hard* and *Disaster Movie*.

The films of Friedberg and Seltzer employ satire in its Ancient Roman sense of ridiculing or lampooning the vices or follies of the era. No film critic has acknowledged that the parody movies of Friedberg and

Seltzer use satire in this way; but, yes, they do contain scenes which ridicule authority figures, cultural trends, and social institutions such as television, the media, the family and the Great American Dream.

One of their targets is easy to ridicule: the contemporary obsession with celebrities, with cel phones, the internet, Facebook, social media, fashion, etc.

Friedberg and Seltzer are very fond of joke props:[24] crew in the prop department have created all sorts of weird props for their films, including the Model Turned Actress's survival kit in *Superfast!* (fake breasts, a barf bag), numerous joke signs, and J. Lo's over-size butt.

For some critics, what Jason Friedberg and Aaron Seltzer do is not parody, it's quotation: 'we're just supposed to laugh because they mention another movie, and know that we've heard of it too, and that's funny, I guess?' (Jason Bailey, *Flavorwire*). Partly true – in films like *Epic Movie*, but not true of films like *Vampires Suck*, which do construct a whole movie with a single dramatic structure, and where the comedy comes very definitely from parodying the original movie/s and from the situations.

Audience stand-ins are a recurring dramatic device in Jason Friedberg and Aaron Seltzer's comedies: if someone's kicked in the crotch (which's regularly), there'll be someone else to look on and wince. Witnesses are everywhere in parody movies, to enhance the joke with their own reactions. Indeed, if you want to show that something is scary/ silly/ painful/ boring/ funny, have some characters reacting in that way (to guide the viewer).

Attacks on gay culture are scarily commonplace in the Jason Friedberg and Aaron Seltzer comical formula. (And the hypocrisy of people covering up the fact that they're gay is just as harshly judged). Easy jokes? Probably.

Every Jason Friedberg and Aaron Seltzer movie has someone being kicked or punched in the balls (these guys have a real thing for ball jokes!).

Violence is everywhere in the comic shtick of Friedberg and Seltzer – victims are mown down by buses and cars regularly; or they're pushed

---

[24] Is this inspired by the Zucker, Abrahams and Zucker movies?

into pits, or blown away by shotguns; and the weapon of choice is a baseball bat (preferrably metal).

This kind of rough treatment of characters really irks film critics, who forget that you cannot simply apply the same critical criteria you use with a serious drama to a ridiculous comedy which features puppets. The multiple deaths in a William Shakespeare tragic play like *Macbeth* or *Hamlet,* or the vast body count of a 'serious' war movie like *Saving Private Ryan* or *We Were Soldiers,* is a very different artistic/ dramatic enterprise from a crude comedy movie.

Seltzer-Friedberg seem to be fans of rap and hiphop music – it crops up in most of their parody movies. So it's not the usual white rock music, the go-to music for parodists when they're trying to be cool, or the dance music when they're trying to be contemporary. (And that's why they selected break-dancing as their go-to form of choreography, instead of many types of dancing. Break-dancing is urban, and cool, aggressive and very flashy. It's incredible to see first-hand on the street – especially when it's combined with acrobatics. Friedberg and Seltzer are also fond of dance battles, with two duellists trying to out-dance each other).

These days, quite a few Hollywood directors have helmed a movie with dancing in it; occasionally a director will be known for featuring dance in more than one movie. Not Friedberg and Seltzer: they have dancing in all of their films.

When the Seltzer-Friedberg films send up U.S. television (which's often), it's usually hiphop that's played, emphasizing the slick, urban culture that advertizing in television evokes as it aims for an upwardly mobile, middle-class audience. (Friedberg and Seltzer are two white, middle-class, university-educated guys, but their movies are sprinkled with mock urban, street-wise dialogue: 'get your punk ass up', 'you messed shit up with Amy', etc.)

A significant proportion of the parodies in the films of Jason Friedberg and Aaron Seltzer are not of other films, but of TV shows. Some movies, such as *Meet the Spartans*, are full of send-ups of the inane quiz shows and talent shows that TV broadcasters use to fill up the schedules. Sometimes you get the impression that Friedberg and Seltzer spend much of their down-time watching TV.

Most of the references in Friedberg and Seltzer's movies are to North American pop culture – television, movies, sport, celebrities, magazines, politics, etc. If a movie or fad originated somewhere else – such as *Harry Potter* – it will only be included if it's made a big impact in North America. Similarly, all of the movies and movie franchises that Friedberg and Seltzer take up as the basis for a story are North American. *Meet the Spartans* might be set in Ancient Greece – but it's a parody of a North American movie, *300*.

Many of the gags in spoof movies centre around celebrity lookalikes[25] – tying into the celebrity culture of the 1990s and after, where every live venue in every city on Earth includes tribute bands, where whole TV shows're based on people wanting to be stars impersonating the famous, and where karaoke rules in bars. And lookalikes're wandering around theme parks, hanging about on Hollywood Boulevard, and attending every Hallowe'en party.

Friedberg and Seltzer are fond of drawing attention to the mechanics of making movies – by pointing out visual effects, for instance. This has been a staple of parody movies, which're always aware of their movieness.

Is product placement part of the deals made for the parodies of Jason Friedberg and Aaron Seltzer? Apple computers, Subway sandwiches, Coca Cola and others crop up regularly. (Bearing in the mind the target audience for these movies is teens, it makes sense).

THEY'RE SOFTIES.

No one can miss the fact that Friedberg and Seltzer have taken on many genres and cinematic forms regarded as 'feminine' or 'for women' or 'women's movies': rom-coms, musicals, dance, and romantic dramas; or that their first movie as directors had a female lead (*Date Movie*); or that they have directed subsequent movies with women in the main roles: *The Starving Games, Best Night Ever* and *Vampires Suck* (4 out of 8 movies, up to 2015). And two of their 8 movies are romances: *Date Movie* and *Vampires Suck*.

In *Meet the Spartans*, for ex, Queen Margo (Carmen Electra) has her

---

[25] Such as the lookalikes outside Grauman's/ Mann's Chinese Theater on Hollywood Boulevard.

own plotline: she's back home in Sparta, trying to persuade the Council and the Elders to send more troops to the Hot Gates. In the event, she dances before the Council members (a bunch of grey-haired extras culled from around New Orleans), and has to deal with Traitoro (played by Diedrich Bader).

Jason Friedberg and Aaron Seltzer are not iconoclasts or radicals – cinematically or politically, at least. Critics and audiences loathe their work, apparently, but they are not setting out to debase or destroy the parody genre, or cinema itself (as if filmmakers could do that).

Indeed, for their first film as directors, Jason Friedberg and Aaron Seltzer selected the most traditional, the most conventional and the most conservative form of narrative – the romance.

If you want to bring down Western civilization, or challenge the global media (or a part of it – cinema) – you wouldn't choose a romantic comedy! (In movies, super-villains do not announce that in order to rule the world, or to destroy the world, they will start with a shopping trip to Rodeo Drive, or by directing a romantic comedy movie!).

STYLE, DESIGN, LOOK.

Cinematically, comedy movies tend to be clear and clean in their staging, camerawork, angles and shots – in order to allow the humour to come through. It's regular master shots, singles, two-shots and over-the-shoulder shots. Arty and gimmicky camerawork is avoided, because it draws unnecessary attention to itself, which takes away power from the gag. If you want your audience to be focussing on getting laughs, you don't want them admiring a fancy boom or drone shot.

Thus, the lighting in the films of Jason Friedberg and Aaron Seltzer tends to be over-lit, as DP Shawn Maurer and others fill the set with light. Why? Because these are comedies, and we need to see the gags. However, the cinematographers, like the production designers, the set dressers and everyone else doing a spoof movie, get to try out all sorts of looks, as they emulate the appearance of supernatural dramas, or rom-coms, or sci-fi extravaganzas.

The sound, too, is bright and clear – it's sound design for knockabout cartoons, where sound effects are mixed high, rather than the subtle, 100-channels of sound of a prestige movie.

In the editing, there are shots to help set up the jokes (like the sign gags). Even this has irritated some critics as being too 'obvious', as with characters announcing the name of another character. But movies do that all the time: a character enters a scene, and someone else says, 'Gandalf! Whazzup?' Just so we know.

The shooting schedules of the films of Friedberg and Seltzer seem very short: 32 days for *Date Movie*, for ex. In the audio commentaries, some of the actors mention filming at one in the morning – but in the studio, not a night shoot outdoors. So it seems as if the movies were sometimes shot outside of regular union hours.

The movies of Jason Friedberg and Aaron Seltzer are wholly North American – the popular cultural allusions are all to North American items. Which means that, for overseas audiences, some of the cultural references aren't picked up (the U.S.A. exports massive amounts of TV, music, radio and cinema, but not everything).

And, needless to say, Jason Friedberg and Aaron Seltzer have only filmed in the U.S.A. thus far. No exotic overseas shooting for them! (Actually, you could make the same movies in China or Hong Kong or India for a fraction of the price).

Most of the movies written/ directed Jason Friedberg and Aaron Seltzer have been filmed in the studio or the backlot. Budget is an issue here, but there are other issues: for example, it can be easier to control a production æsthetically as well as logistically in a studio. The spoofs that Friedberg and Seltzer are creating are drawing on blockbuster movies that're also filmed chiefly in the studio – for the same reasons. If you want to conjure up a world that doesn't exist, like Hogwarts, or Narnia, or Ancient Greece, or a spaceship, a studio and a set can be the way to go. We're talking about highly stylized spoof movies of highly stylized movies. And for extreme stylization, filmmakers often prefer to work in the studio, where everything can be built from scratch.

MUSIC.

The cinema of Friedberg and Seltzer is full of dance, and singing, and thus it's also full of music. Jason Friedberg: 'We use music in our movies whenever possible.' No film critic, as they jump up and down in anger, flailing away at the movies of Friedberg and Seltzer with their faces turning red, mentions the music (but critics hardly ever draw attention to the soundtracks in movies). But Friedberg and Seltzer have some great music in their movies – hiphop is obviously a big deal for them, as is disco. Their movies are full of pop songs (if they can afford the rights), or references to pop songs (if they can't) – or they commission a composer to come up with joke songs.

Hats off to the music supervisors, then – Dave Jordan and Jojo Villanueva – and to composers such as Christopher Lennertz and Ali Dee Theodore – for creating those wild soundtracks to the films of Jason Friedberg and Aaron Seltzer.

How wonderful, for ex, is the latent homosexual, war-mongering song from *Meet the Spartans*. Crude, yes, 'offensive' even, sure, but it nails the even more 'offensive 'ideology in the movie *300* (and in many other Hollywood movies and war movies where, yes, the links between masculinity, violence, aggression and war-mongering are evoked straight, and taken straight. Sometimes, watching a North American movie, you wonder if they are secretly being paid for by the U.S. military machine and orchestrated by the C.I.A. – they come across as extended commercials for (1) the Great American Way of Life, and (2) the domination of the U.S.A. over all other countries).

Composers such as Christopher Lennertz produced marvellous scores of the movies of Friedberg and Seltzer – they *hommage* the original scores as well as satirize them. Lennertz's score for *Meet the Spartans* 'competes favorably with 2008's most dramatic action scores', noted Christian Clemmensen (see below).

The scores of the films of Friedberg and Seltzer give them a heroic scale (in *Meet the Spartans* or *Epic Movie*), or an action movie energy (in *Disaster Movie*), which helps the humour along, and expands the scope of the movies which are modestly budgeted (typically $20 million). Low budget filmmakers know that one sure way of adding production value to a movie is with music. (For instance, if you can't afford lavish sets and costumes, a piece of music can help to create the scene).

But the scores of Friedberg and Seltzer's movies are more than one or two source songs: they are full, orchestral scores for some of the parody movies, so that the parodic scenes play like the ones in the original films.

MUSICALS AND MORE ON MUSIC.

Musicals are – alas! – a much-maligned (yet also much-loved) genre, and, in recent times, an under-used genre. I think musical movies are the Hollywood Dream Factory at its very finest (from a social, political, ideological and philosophical point-of-view, but also a technical and cinematic point-of-view). Musical movies are, at their best, all about pure performance, pure visual filmmaking, and pure storytelling. Musical movies foreground the whole technical arsenal of the modern film studio, and they also tend to feature stars in all their glory, and physical prowess, the body in motion.

So it's a delight to see so many musical numbers, involving music, song and dance, in the recent spate of spoof movies. A comedy movie is a way of shoe-horning a musical number into an otherwise dramatic format. (At times, Jason Friedberg and Aaron Seltzer are really delivering Broadway musical skits, or MTV pop promos, in the midst of spoof movies. Indeed, several of their spoof movies would make great musical shows. Eric Idle and John Du Prez did it with *Spamalot* in 2005, and Mel Brooks with *Young Frankenstein* in 2007).

Spoof movies also act like the vaudeville or variety shows of old, where, on stage, a variety of acts would be presented in an evening: a stand-up comedian, a magician, a showgirls number (or burlesque), comedy sketches, a puppet act, an animal act, musical soloists or bands, and so on. Spoof movies allow all sorts of forms of performance to be included, which's a key reason why actors like to perform in them, because they get to do what they normally never get to do.

DANCE.

No critic mentions an element of the movies of Friedberg and Seltzer that pops out all over and is such a fundamental ingredient of their cinema: dance. Critics will complain about the crudity, the stupidity, the insipidity, and the waste of talent/ money/ time, etc, but not a single critic mentions that these movies are jammed with dancing.

Dancing is there in every Friedberg and Seltzer movie – these guys might be fonder of dance than even humour or parodies. They are the Bob Fosses of the spoof genre – if there's a chance to put in a dance number, Friedberg and Seltzer will take it, and run with it. When the ancient Greeks clash with the Persians in *Meet the Spartans*, they dance; when Julia Jones is first introduced in *Date Movie*, she dances (and she dances throughout the film); in *Disaster Movie*, there's a lavish send-up of *High School Musical* (a movie Friedberg and Seltzer perhaps wish that Disney had given *them* to direct!); in the bid to work for the crime lord in *Superfast!* the characters stage a dance competition.

And, as anybody knows, a dance routine in a movie isn't a throwaway bit of business that can be filmed on the wing – it requires rehearsal-rehearsal-rehearsal, plus casting actors or dancers who can actually do it, plus of course pre-recorded music (or clearance for rights). Music rights plus rehearsal plus choreography plus dancers are other elements of the Friedberg and Seltzer circus that will drive up the budget. (A producer wishing to cut the costs of a Friedberg and Seltzer production would automatically slash the dance routines. But that is also where some of the biggest laughs occur. It's funny watching characters in historical costumes launching into contemporary dances).

MOVIE-MOVIES.

Spoof/ parody movies are completely movie-movies – movies about other movies, and about popular culture (and television in particular). In this respect, spoof/ parody films can be viewed as supremely postmodernist – all about surfaces (with no depth), and completely self-reflexive.

Spoof/ parody movies can be seen as another instance of the media exploring itself: the media likes nothing better than talking about other media (there are television shows about other television shows. Even what people say on television is sometimes reported on news shows). Spoof/ parody movies are thus part of celebrity culture, media gossip, reducing complex issues to soundbites.

As movies about other movies, spoof/ parody films are bound to endear themselves to filmmakers and the *cognoscenti* (but not to film critics! who persist in denigrating them with scary loathing).

Is there a bad movie about movies? I don't think so; they are all enjoyable (even the less compelling ones): the great ones include: *8 1/2, Contempt, Sunset Boulevard, F For Fake, The Bad and the Beautiful, Singin' In the Rain, Millennium Actress, Stardust Memories, Day For Night, A Star Is Born, Peeping Tom* and *The Player*. And there are many more, all entertaining: *Ed Wood, Living In Oblivion, Chaplin, The Last Tycoon, Passion, High Risk, Boogie Nights, Valentino* and *Shadow of the Vampire*.

Spoof/ parody movies are movie-movies, but they are not about the making of spoof/ parody movies (spoof/ parody movies don't spoof other spoof/ parody movies). So you don't have *Scary Movie* (2000) spoofing *The Naked Gun* (1988) spoofing *Blazing Saddles* (1974) spoofing *Casino Royale* (1967), and so on.

FRIEDBERG AND SELTZER AND *STAR WARS*.

Some movie-goers have complained that Jason Friedberg and Aaron Seltzer have 'ruined' parody movies. *Eh? What?* You can't 'ruin' other movies because one movie in that genre or form sucks, or because all of the spoof movies of Friedberg and Seltzer suck! And you can't 'destroy' an abstract, cultural entity like a movie genre.

It's like those scarily toxic *Star Wars* fans who loathed *The Phantom Menace* (1999) and claimed that it 'ruined' the *Star Wars* franchise. Hell, *no!* You can't 'ruin' (or 'corrupt' or 'kill') other movies in a franchise because one of them stank!

The comparison with *Star Wars: The Phantom Menace* is useful: the reaction to that 1999 movie over the years has reached frightening levels of venom, totally out of proportion to the movie itself (which, let's not forget, not only rocked, but was the top movie financially at the global box office in 1999. A film that's supposedly that dreadful simply *cannot* attract millions of people paying money to see it. Also, have a look at the contemporary reviews of *Episode One*: they are not all negative, as is assumed nowadays).

But this hatred... *Hmmm...* Is it irrational? Easy to do? Lets off steam? Done because everyone else is doing it? Is it because people now have access to the internet and instant communication and can write reviews which can be seen the world over? (And they can hide behind pseudonyms and avatars).

Maybe it's because the movies of Friedberg and Seltzer expose the mechanics of humour. But not in the usual flattering, modernist manner. Instead, it's done in a way that makes viewers feel uncomfortable: there's a cynical, even cruel attitude on display (which leads critics to complain that Friedberg and Seltzer dislike movies, don't know comedy, and disdain their audiences).

The *intention* of the parody is important, according to Linda Hutcheon in *A Theory of Parody*:

> when we speak of parody, we do not just mean two texts that interrelate in a certain way. We also imply an intention to parody another work (or set of conventions) and both a recognition of that intent and an ability to find and interpret the backgrounded text in its relation to the parody. (22)

Just why the parody movies of Jason Friedberg and Aaron Seltzer have been the target of so much loathing is a mystery, as with *Star Wars: The Phantom Menace*. Even if a movie sucked, why would anyone spend so much energy and time saying so?

Certainly, *expectation* is part of the reason: people go to a comedy hoping to enjoy it and laugh, right? (And the diehard *Star Wars* fans went to *The Phantom Menace* hoping for a wild ride). When a movie disappoints (no movie could've lived up to the expectations of *Star Wars* fans at that particular time), or isn't what an audience expected, that's when the dissatisfactions can become fiery. (Hence, the Disney-era *Star Wars* movies (from 2015 onwards) have gone for the safe option, reworking the elements they reckon the market and the fans want to see).

But it's also a certain sector of the audience, let's admit, that is very loud and vocal in making its opinions known. Some fans of some franchises are well-known for it (*Twilight, Star Wars, Star Trek, Barry Trotter*, etc). Which unbalances the media image of some franchises and movies. But there hasn't been a backlash or campaign like those in the realm of *Star Wars* fandom (by comparison with that, the bile aimed at

Friedberg and Seltzer by movie-goers is nothing!).

Star Wars fans are, though, a very special case – no other movie franchise in film history has had people camping out a theatre for *forty-two days* before the movie opens!

WHAT ABOUT SINCE 2015?

Two movie franchises are high profile enough and rich enough for parodies from Jason Friedberg and Aaron Seltzer: *Star Wars* and *Harry Potter*. Friedberg and Seltzer have already taken on parts of both series, but not for a whole film. A *Star Wars* spoof was announced by them in the film trades on Feb 8, 2017:[26] *Star Worlds Episode XXXIVE=MC2: The Force Awakens the Last Jedi Who Went Rogue* (I can't wait to see this one!).[27] *Star Worlds* would be produced by Covert Media/ Broken Road, with a shoot in Autumn, 2017.

Of course, the Disney-era *Star Wars* movies – beginning with *Star Wars: The Force Awakens* in 2015 – were already parodies of the *Star Wars* franchise. They were like $200 million fan fiction movies, in which all of the famous motifs and characters from the *Star Wars* universe were re-jigged into a 'new' movie that was actually a shameless re-run of the first *Star Wars* movie of 1977 (plus generous selections from all six of the George Lucas-era *Star Warses*).

A parody of the *Taken* thrillers, which starred Liam Neeson, *Who the F#@K Took My Daughter?*, has also been announced by Friedberg and Seltzer. (There are low budget parodies of *Taken* around). And *Avatar* was rumoured in 2011 (to be filmed in 3-D).

THE CRITICS ON FRIEDBERG AND SELTZER'S FILMS.

Jason Friedberg and Aaron Seltzer and their movies have been described as 'abominations', 'horrifying' (*Flavorwire*) • 'a plague' (*Austin Chronicle*) • 'evildoers' (*Slate*) • 'cultural blight' (A.V. Club) • 'comic terrorists' (A.V. Club) • 'the worst filmmakers in Hollywood' (*New York Post*).

And on the Rotten Tomatoes website, the films of Jason Friedberg

---
[26] There was a press release, with plans to film in late 2017.
[27] Yet the too-long, multiple-movie title was a clue that perhaps this *wasn't* a Friedberg and Seltzer project.

and Aaron Seltzer regularly attain 'scores' of less than 10 (7 for *Date Movie*, and 0 for *The Starving Games*!).

Mad! How you can give 'stars' or 'scores' or 'numbers' to a movie? The 'ratings' system, applied to everything these days, is loathsome. What would you give the Sistine Chapel of Michelangelo Buonarrotti? Three 'stars' out of four? – and a snidey remark: 'could try harder, Mickey'. What about Leonardo da Vinci's *The Last Supper*? One 'star' out of four? – 'good try, dude, but why'd'ya use that crappy paint which doesn't last?'

Linked to that are the Golden Raspberry Awards – again, this is another category error, where a 'bad' performance in a comedy or parody is directly compared, using the same criteria, to a performance in a straight or dramatic movie.[28]

Nominations for the Golden Raspberry For Worst Director have included Friedberg and Seltzer, of course. But wait – directors who've also been nominated for the Worst Director Award include Stanley Kubrick, George Lucass and Oliver Stone (I'd be happy to be included in the same list as Kubrick, Lucas and Stone).

However, some heavyweight cultural philosophers have praised the films of Friedberg and Seltzer very highly:

• French cultural theorist Jean Baudrillard thought that *Date Movie* was 'a sublime exploration of the anxiety of heterosexual relationships in an uncertain, postmodern world';

• Slavoj Zizek admired *Vampires Suck* for its 'delirious evocation of contemporary vampires' as the return of the repressed;

• and in-your-face feminist Camille Paglia celebrated *Epic Movie*, *Date Movie* and others: 'these movies offer a devilish, ironic and very welcome Dionysian attack on the empty values of modern America'.

Just kidding![29]

Kenny Byerly, one of the comedians who wrote a YouTube spoof of Jason Friedberg and Aaron Seltzer, wonders:

---

[28] Carmen Electra received a Golden Raspberry nomination for her role as King Kong's victim in *Date Movie*. Eh?! She's only on screen for 15 seconds!
[29] Actually, Camille Paglia, bless her, has come out with some surprising statements on contemporary cinema – like her view of the *Star Wars* prequel movies as great, operatic spectacles.

> The big question to me, dramatized in the sketch, is whether they are really that unfunny, or whether they are really that cynical. Are they lucky idiots? Or trapped in a career that's beneath them? I don't know.

Critics have complained that Friedberg and Seltzer are either very cynical or very stupid, and that they regard their audiences as idiots. In interviews, Friedberg and Seltzer do exhibit plenty of cynicism (name me a professional writer in comedy or a successful comedian who *isn't* cynical!), but I reckon the real cynics in the entertainment industry are the film producers, TV broadcasters and movie studios that really do blatantly exploit the audience and the market by churning out pap and dreck.

Josh Levin (in *Slate*) timed a screening of *Meet the Spartans* in 2008 and complained that it was criminal charging $10.50 for a cinema ticket to see a flick that hardly went beyond 60 minutes. Well, *duh*, plenty of the greatest movies ever made run for 60-70 minutes (many Disney features in the 'Golden Age' of the Mouse House, for instance, and the Marx Brothers' comedies). And is it more 'value' if a movie runs over two hours, as so many movies do today? Not if it's a bad movie! You're just getting an extra 30-50 minutes of ≠$‡¡. (Yes – because watching a really bad movie can be unbearable even for two minutes!).[30]

Meanwhile, Owen Gleiberman in *Entertainment Weekly* is one of the very few professional film critics who've enjoyed the comedies of Jason Friedberg and Aaron Seltzer (Gleiberman liked *Epic Movie* and *Disaster Movie*). Occasionally critics will gingerly pop their heads out of the trenches: Jim Schembri (in *The Age*) said that *Disaster Movie* was 'dumb but undeniably funny', and A.O. Scott (in the *New York Times*) remarked of *Epic Movie* that 'the humour is coarse and occasionally funny'.

Some critics have complained that Friedberg-Seltzer don't understand comedy. Rubbish. Critics carp that Friedberg-Seltzer don't know how comedy works. Horse-dung.

Critics often complain that the scripts of Jason Friedberg and Aaron Seltzer's movies are badly written. In terms of humour, maybe, but not structurally: if you write forty screenplays, as Friedberg and Seltzer did, you soon learn how to construct a story for the screen. And comedy

---

[30] Yet a masterpiece can be just one minute long – *Mothlight*, for example (Stan Brakhage, 1962).

scripts are much tougher, because of the over-riding pressure to make audiences laff.

However, if you are constructing a parody/ spoof/ send-up script, a good deal of your work is done for you in terms of creating characters and developing characterizations, in setting up scenarios, and in forging stories. If you quote a *Narnia* or *Harry Potter* fantasy, or a rom-com, or a goofy vampire romance, the audience is already there with you: they know the charas, the relationships, the motives, the goals, and the scenarios.

Let's remember that even comic geniuses deliver turkeys: Woody Allen, for one. Among recent movies from the Woodman, *To Rome, With Love* (2012) and *Magic In the Moonlight* (2014) fail utterly as comedies (no matter how strong the talent is in front of or behind the camera). *To Rome With Love* was the umpteenth feature film written and directed by Woody Allen, with a great cast, but it didn't work.

Yes, it was written and directed by Woody Allen, without question one of the most remarkable filmmakers of any era. Yes, it was produced by Allen's regular team of highly skilled, professional filmmakers. Yes, it contained a high profile cast – which included Penelope Cruz, Roberto Benigni, Judy Davis, Alec Baldwin and Ornella Mutti. Yes, it looked like a million dollars, and yes it was mainly filmed in one of the great cities of the Western world – Rome, Italy. But it didn't work.

To Rome With Love was a romantic comedy. But it wasn't romantic, and it wasn't a comedy. *To Rome With Love* didn't fly largely due to the script, the ideas, the construction of the scenes, and the overwhelming feeling of *déja vu*.

Why do many critics and many viewers claim that they really dislike (or downright hate) silly comedies and spoof movies? I've put forward a few possible reasons – about what audiences expect, about the contract between a movie and the viewer, about humour being *very* culture specific (and humour not travelling national borders),[31] about some comedies not being funny, etc.

Or is it because critics react badly when the movies they have to

---

[31] Comedy not traversing national borders and cultures means that actors such as Stephen Chow Sing-chi and Michael Hui can be giants in China, but hardly known at all in the West. The comedies of Chow and Hui are very funny, but they aren't part of the celebrated films in the Western world.

review for a living – many of which are really dumb and politically and ideologically offensive – are attacked? Is it because the concept of art is being debased? Or the value of art in the contemporary world? Or the notion of storytelling? The task of film critics, after all, is to watch and write about movies. Thus, critics enjoy movies-about-movies which *celebrate* movies, which *flatter* them with witty commentaries, or which *gently* poke fun at movies. But they don't respond well when movies are given a good kicking by movies themselves (critics might complain that it's the *critics'* job to kick movies, *not* filmmakers!). But I don't understand it: why don't film critics relish movies which remind us how stupid movies are?

Viewers and critics expect (nay, *demand*) that certain genres of movies deliver what is advertized: a horror film must be scary, an action-adventure film must be exciting, and a comedy film must be funny. When they don't deliver, the pact between the viewer and the film is broken.

But more loathing is hurled at comedy films that don't deliver than any other film genre. And yet we could point to many movies that are released which do *not* deliver what they seem to promise:

From 2004: *Collateral, Ocean's Twelve, The Bourne Supremacy, King Arthur, A Series of Unfortunate Events, Aliens vs. Predator, Finding Neverland, Kill Bill, Home On the Range*, etc. From 2006: *The Da Vinci Code, Casino Royale, Superman Returns, Eragon, Poseidon, The Host*, etc. From 2008: *Iron Man, Prince Caspian, Quantum of Solace, The Incredible Hulk*, etc. From 2014: *Dawn of the Planet of the Apes, The Hobbit, The Hunger Games*, etc.

Ultimately, it probably boils down to a simple fact: some people don't like some things.

Some people don't like the Beatles.
Some people don't like *Star Wars*.
Some people don't like the films of Akira Kurosawa.
Some people don't like chocolate.
Some people don't like spoof movies.

It's that simple. Personally, I think it's physically, biologically, humanly impossible to dislike the Beatles or Akira Kurosawa.

We all have blind spots in entertainment. In comedy, the following don't seem funny at all: Adam Sandler, Ben Stiller, Ricky Gervais, Kevin Smith and Sacha Cohen. Oh, there's no doubt that Stiller, Gervais and Sandler have clever collaborators, and you can admire the smart writing in the scripts written for them. But they aren't funny (for me).

•

Jason Friedberg and Aaron Seltzer are sometimes dubbed 'the worst filmmakers' in Hollywood/ the world. Oh hell, *no*, they are so not! There are far, *far* more untalented hacks out there.

But Jason Friedberg and Aaron Seltzer have become punchbags for critics and audiences to hit from time to time. Other hated directors include Michael Bay, Michael Winner, Joel Schumacher,[32] Paul W.S. Anderson, M. Night Shyamalan, Kevin Smith, Danny Boyle, McG, Lars 'von' Trier, Mike Leigh, Michael Cimino, Ken Loach, Roland Emmerich, Ken Russell and Uwe Boll.

Uwe Boll (b. 1965) was certainly a character: his movies were routinely trashed by film critics, to the point where Boll offered to have boxing matches with his fiercest critics (which he did!). Filmmakers often joke about summat like that, but hardly any have actually done it! Boll is also a despised director, like Friedberg and Seltzer, a director that people love to hate. So there have been petitions to stop Boll making more films.

My recommendations for film directors I would pay to take up knitting socks or stamp collecting instead of making films include: Guy Ritchie, Shawn Meadows, Catherine Breillat, Sam Mendes, Quentin Tarantino, Danny Boyle, Ken Loach, Kevin Smith, Mike Leigh, Paul W.S. Anderson, Lars 'von' Trier, McG, and M. Night Shyamalan.

•

Much of the humour in the films of Jason Friedberg and Aaron Seltzer is pitched at a mid-teens mind-set. It's often crude, or violent, or dumb, or cheesy. But there are some gags aimed at an older audience, and an intellectual audience. But not enough, it seems, to appease film critics.

---

[32] Joel Schumacher was blamed by fans for 'ruining' the *Batman* franchise with the two entries, of 1995 and 1997. But those are both wonderful, very entertaining movies!

Shows like *The Simpsons* are much admired by the media because they are clearly incredibly witty and smart, and brilliantly written (and rewritten and rewritten) – they flatter the eggheads, the *literari*, the PhDs in the audience who can appreciate the cultural refs to Susan Sontag and John Updike. The movies of Friedberg and Seltzer don't often go that route – their intellectual material is blink and you miss it. They'd much rather stage a skit of TV quiz shows or have someone being kicked in the crotch (well, yeah, but *The Simpsons* does that, too!).

Causing offence seems inevitable in any spoof comedy, or in comedy as a whole. Someone somewhere will be offended by the jokes: the films of Friedberg and Seltzer are self-consciously crude, sometimes racist, homophobic, and sexist. Everyone is fair game – fat people, small people, ugly people, black people, white people, media people, celebrities, television shows, Hollywood, women's magazines, TV commercials, U.S. politics and Presidents, pop stars, and so on.

Another aspect of the films of Friedberg and Seltzer seems to irritate critics: much of the comedy is *not* carried in witty dialogue, in lines or quips that can be quoted in film reviews (like the humour of Woody Allen or Groucho Marx). If you look at the film scripts written by Friedberg and Seltzer, it's the *visual* gags, the imagery of pop culture, the slapstick and the *situations* that carry much of the humour, *not* the dialogue.

And film critics and journalists continually emphasize dialogue in films: they seem to think that the structure of a movie, the story of a movie, and what a movie 'means', or what a movie 'says', or what 'messages' a movie has, is contained in the dialogue. If you buy into the version of filmmaking found in film criticism and film reviews in the mainstream media, you'd think that films are created by a single author coming up with witty lines of dialogue, like a Robert Benchley or a Dorothy Parker or an S.J. Perelman. As director Akira Kurosawa remarked, if he wanted to produce a 'message', he'd hold up a placard.

Filmmakers, on the other hand, emphasize issues such as structure, action, situations, introductions, pay-offs, tone, pace, timing, rhythm, and technical elements such as editing, music, sound effects, and of course the camera. Filmmakers will make a movie just to get to one particular, amazing scene, which might have nothing to do with what the characters say.

Some critics (like Josh Levin) reckoned that when audiences got to know who Jason Friedberg and Aaron Seltzer were, they would avoid their movies in the future. No. Audiences don't *care* who's behind the camera, who the DP was, or where the costume designers bought her tweed (was it from that amazing boutique on Melrose? Was it hand-sewn by actual, real elves from Middle-earth? *No one cares*!). They just want entertainment. (Do you know anybody who'll go see a movie mainly because superstar cinematographers Vittorio Storaro, say, or Gordon Willis, was the DP? I mean, apart from movie fans like us! Do you know anyone who's heard of Storaro or Willis?).

Another thing that's odd about the negative response to the films of Friedberg and Seltzer is that some viewers returned to their movies and were disappointed a second time. When I've seen one abysmal film directed by Guy Ritchie (*Lock, Stock and Two Smoking Critics*), or got halfway thru a Lars 'von' Trier film (*Scandinavian Ordure, Volume 15*), I never go back and see another.

Altho' critics have asserted many times that Aaron Seltzer and Jason Friedberg hate movies or aim to denigrate movies, and audiences, and pop culture, they are clearly massive fans of it all. They seem to have seen every big movie from the past 30 years several times, and know North American television and pop music inside-out.

The films of Friedberg and Seltzer clearly do *not* disdain the audience or cinema in general (tho' it's certainly skeptical and scathing about the entertainment business, and television in particular). If you *really* had a cynical and disdainful attitude towards your audience, you would *not* include seven dance and musical numbers in a single movie. You would *not* include jokes and scenes which are absolutely, definitely designed to make people laugh. You would *not* include several schmaltzy, sentimental scenes. And you would *not* exalt romantic love and lovers. (But you wouldn't direct movies, either).

For the detractors, Friedberg and Seltzer produce anti-movies and anti-comedies: movies which try to subvert their very existence, and comedies are designed *not* to be funny. Thus, Friedberg and Seltzer are viewed as anti-filmmakers, or anti-writers. They make movies not to celebrates cinema, but to disparage it, along with television, and pop music, and celebrities, and anything else that they fancy.

Critics often complain that movie comedies aren't funny. Jean-Luc Godard had a simple way of looking at movies: Godard was asked at a press conference in Venice in 1965 whether his new movie *Pierrot le Fou* was a comedy: his response was classic Godard: 'if you laughed, yes, if not, no.'[33] You can use the same approach to contemporary spoofs and comedies: did you laugh? Then it was a comedy!

Producer Peter Safran insists that the films of Jason Friedberg and Aaron Seltzer work very well with their target audience of teens:

> Their movies are *obviously* not made for a very broad audience. It's mostly that teen demographic, but that teen demographic seems to really enjoy it. When you sit in the theater and watch *Meet the Spartans* or *Vampires Suck* with a group of teens, they are absolutely loving it.

Critics and viewers who attack the films of Jason Friedberg and Aaron Seltzer forget that the movie industry is an *industry*, not a realm of exquisite, æsthetic beauty, where 'artistes' 'create' 'films' like painters create paintings on their own in an isolated studio. And it's a market-driven industry: the market dictates the products (to a degree that no artist or filmmaker wants to acknowledge). Companies and studios churn out movies, release them, and hope that something sticks and makes money. If there's a hit movie about mud-wrestling grannies, you will find that in a few months (even shorter if it's Hong Kong), cash-in movies will appear.

So the movie market wants the spoof movies of Friedberg and Seltzer and many other filmmakers, because they generate $$$$. Yes, the market loves the giant blockbuster movies best of all, which employ thousands of people, and have all sorts of side benefits and spin-offs. But modestly-priced movies have a place, too – especially ones that'll do well on DVD, Blu-ray and TV channels.

Indeed, back in 1978, David Denby complained that the spoof movie came out of a conservative, timid film industry:

---

33 R. Brody, 2008, 249.

Why all the spoofing? I think the main reason is simple fear of putting new experiences on the screen. Along with remakes and sequels, parodies have become endemic in a panicky industry intent on endless replication of past successes as a safeguard again risk.

•

The vitriol that Jason Friedberg and Aaron Seltzer have attracted is startling: one hopes that they don't take any of it to heart, and keep making movies. I mean, this is loathing worse than that endured by film directors such as Ken Russell, Michael Winner, James Cameron, Joel Schumacher, Russ Meyer or George Lucas (well, maybe not Lucas! We know how intense and bitter *Star Wars* fans can be!).

But why? Why have Aaron Seltzer and Jason Friedberg angered so many viewers and critics?

If filmmakers really took criticism seriously, they would be lying on the floor weeping, swearing they'll never make another movie. Ken Russell said that bad press was personally hurtful (Russell received plenty during his career), but it never changed what he created. Hayao Miyazaki and Woody Allen claim they don't read the critics – they're not interested. And pop star Prince pointed out that no matter what critics wrote, he never learned anything from them.

Dwelling on the reactions of audiences or critics isn't that useful in the long run. You can't hang on to everything that everyone says. Aaron Seltzer remarked:

> I think the first movie, you're always surprised, like, 'Oh, wow, we're not getting a 100 Rotten Tomatoes score?' And then you go, 'It's not a critic's cup of tea,' and some people don't like it and then you move on. Otherwise, you go crazy.

Aaron Seltzer and Jason Friedberg say they have lives, they get on with their work; yes, they're aware of the negative reactions, but they don't respond to them. (There *are* filmmakers who reply to critics or fans, but that doesn't go anywhere, doesn't help anybody, and takes away valuable time and energy from creative work).

In the 2014 *Grantland* interview, Aaron Seltzer says that they just get on with their work and lead regular lives, and don't take too much notice of the negative criticism:

We love writing, we love directing, we love the actors we work with. We have our own families that we raised. Jason has kids, I have kids, we have wives,[34] so we don't sit around [reading reactions]. Honestly, we don't have a lot of ego that needs to be stroked. We don't want to be condemned, but we don't pay that much attention. We just kind of do our work.

The response of Jason Friedberg and Aaron Seltzer to film critics – when they're being polite or on the record – is to ignore them, or claim they don't take much notice of them (if you're busy working, you haven't got time to go through all of the reviews). However, at the end of *Date Movie*'s audio commentary, their response is blunter:

'Go fuck yourself!'

---

[34] Their spouses have appeared in bit parts in their movies.

Friedberg and Seltzer on set.

2

SPOOF MOVIES

THE SPOOF MOVIE AND THE PARODY MOVIE.
The spoof movie and the parody movie – no film critic seems to agree on exactly what they are (the terms, spoof and parody, are used interchangeably in film criticism, along with satire, send up, take off, put-on, lampoon, comedy-satire, etc). Similarly, the definitions of satire, parody and comedy in literary criticism are subject to dispute. Anyhow, most film critics agree that the parody movie and the spoof movie are sub-sets of the comedy genre,[1] and that the modern era of spoof movies began with *Airplane!* in 1980 (some go back to the great Mel Brooks comedies of the 1970s).

> Doctor: We've got to get him to a hospital.
> Air stewardess: What is it?
> Doctor: A large white building with doctors and nurses inside, but that's not important now. (*Airplane!*)

According to the Siegels in their excellent book *American Film Comedy,* Mel Brooks launched the modern trend in film parodies, with films such as *Blazing Saddles* and *Young Frankenstein* in 1974: 'It was also Brooks who established the unwritten rule of such parodies: anything for a laugh!' (220)

---

[1] However, some see spoof and parody as a mode of fiction, not a genre in itself, because 'parody has no subject matter other than what is parodied, since furthermore it is a relation and not the specific form that the relation takes', as Terry Ceasar put it in "Violating the Shrine", 1979.

One thing's for sure: when you start researching spoof/ parody movies, it's a tiny, teeny, itsy-bitsy group of films that is put forward as the classic examples. Look at any list of spoofs or parodies, by critics or fans, from 1960s to the present day, and the same movies will crop up:

• Mel Brooks' movies: *Blazing Saddles, Young Frankenstein, Silent Movie, Spaceballs, High Anxiety,* etc).

• Woody Allen (*Love and Death, Sleeper, Bananas*).

• Monty Python (*Life of Brian, Monty Python and the Holy Grail*).

• The *Carry On* series.

• *The Kentucky Fried Movie* and *National Lampoon* series.

• *Airplane!*[2]

• The Zucker, Abrahams and Zucker films (*The Naked Gun* series, the *Hot Shots!* films, *Top Secret!*).

• *The Rocky Horror Picture Show.*

• Steve Martin (*Dead Men Don't Wear Plaid, The Jerk, The Man With Two Brains*).

• *This Is Spinal Tap.*

• The *Scary Movie* series.

• The *Austin Powers* series.

Early spoof/ parody movies before the Mel Brooks era include: *The Great Dictator, Helzzapoppin', What Price Hollywood?, Sons of the Desert,* and the *Abbott and Costello* movies. Add to that *Mad* magazine, the improv comedy groups and *Saturday Night Live.*

The same movies in the tiny sub-genre of the spoof/ parody movie are held up as the great, shining, super-radiant examples: *Airplane!, Blazing Saddles, Young Frankenstein,* the *Naked Gun* series, the *Hot Shots!* films, *This Is Spinal Tap,* the better Monty Python flicks *(Life of Brian, Monty Python and the Holy Grail)*, the better early Woody Allen films *(Bananas, Love and Death, Sleeper), Mars Attacks!, Kentucky Fried Movie,* the better *National Lampoon* films, *Caddyshack,* the finer Steve Martin films, etc.

Below that front rank group, there's a larger pool of movies sometimes grudgingly accepted as decent parodies/ spoofs: *Not Another Teen Movie, Borat, Superhero Movie, Spy Hard, Loaded Weapon, Don't*

---

2 *Airplane 2* is generally disregarded, being from a different production team.

Be a Menace To South Central While Drinking Your Juice In the Hood, Johnny English, Galaxy Quest, Kung Fu Hustle, the *Our Man Flint* films, and the better *Carry On* films, among others.

Even in the above selection of the shining examples of the spoof/ parody movie, there's disagreement over placing many of those movies in the parody movie or spoof movie category. Some critics maintain that many spoof/ parody movies are comedies, featuring some spoofing or parodying in parts.

There are many more spoof/ parody movies produced than the ones that are recognized as the finest of the sub-genre. Every year, more spoof/ parody movies are made. Typically, they are low budget (or *very* low budget) productions, and many (most?) don't have a theatrical release.

Most spoofing and parodying occurs in other media, not in theatrically-released movies. Television (and related media) is the chief area of production in the filmed/ video arts. It's a standard procedure in any long-running comedy series to include some parodies of well-known properties, franchises, items, or issues of the day.

Thus, when we consider full-length movies that have a theatrical release, and not television, radio, comics, novels, magazines, newspaper strips, online/ streaming, etcetera, the field is automatically narrowed down considerably.

And when you add that the spoofing or parodying must run for the whole length of the film, and not in one or two scenes, or as throwaway lines, it whittles down the group of examples even further.

Today, the spoof/ parody movie is taken to mean a movie with an instantly recognizable story and characters, a very fast pace, 100s of jokes (most referring to popular culture), gross humour, lookalikes, and celebrity cameos.

The recent spoof spate is a gag-a-beat comedy, jokes upon jokes, 200 jokes in 70 minutes. The running time of modern comedies is typically 70-80 minutes. By that time, the audience is laughed out, they've had enough. And this is one of the *very* appealing aspects of comedy films: they don't out-last their welcome, they don't bloat out, like far too many movies today do, to beyond the two-hour mark. (A three-hour comedy movie does not exist for very obvious reasons).[3]

Forerunners of the spoof/ parody movie include the Marx Brothers films and screwball comedies – both from the 1930s: the fast pace, the rapid delivery of gags and – in the Marx Brothers' case – surreal, abstract humour. (Certainly, the *speed* of the jokes (and the dialogue) in the Marx Brothers' films has helped them to endure).

Silent movies are the golden age of comedy in cinema – and spoof/ parody films continue to use the same gags, the same knockabout, physical humour, even the same plots. (Keaton, Lloyd, Chaplin *et al* got there first with literally thousands of gags that are still used everywhere in the comedy genre).

Why aren't Zucker-Abrahams-Zucker or the Wayans Brothers and their comedy movie teams running the whole of Hollywood?! Why can't we have their fabulously entertaining movies in the place of distended, gloomy, 200 million dollar blockbusters which over-do everything except generating laughter? Just one of those gargantuan special effects extravaganzas could pay for 200 new scripts (at $1m each! Or, hell, if writers'll work for $100,000 a script (and I know they will!), we could have *two thousand new scripts*! *From one movie's budget!*).

ASPECTS OF SPOOF MOVIES.

Here are some observations on parody/ spoof movies:

• If you look at a really big dic (such as *The Oxford English Dictionary*), you'll discover that:

> 'spoof' means swindle, hoax or parody;

> 'parody' means a work which humorously imitates an author;

> and 'satire' is an Ancient Roman term for ridiculing/ lampooning contemporary vices or follies or individuals.

• Some movies and events are so ridiculous there's no need to spoof them: *Star Wars, The Lord of the Rings,* superhero movies, many television shows, any sports event, etc. So, the best spoof of *Star Wars* would simply be… to show *Star Wars.*

• Spoof movies don't spoof other spoof movies. Thus, you don't

---

[3] True, *It's a Mad, Mad, Mad, Mad World* (1963) initially ran for 192 minutes, but it was subsequently cut down to 154 minutes for general release. And *It's a Mad, Mad, Mad, Mad World* is a very rare case, an all-star 'ultimate comedy'.

find send-ups of the *Airplane!* films or the *Naked Gun* films in a parody movie. (But you will of course see many outright steals of jokes). So an intriguing new form of spoof movie would be one that only spoofs other spoof movies. (Would it work?).

• A good parody movie works if you *love* the original, but also if you *hate* the original. And also, if you don't know the original at all.

• Titles are all-important. Some spoof/ parody movies tried to include a bunch of the targets of their comedy in the title: *The 41-Year-Old Virgin Who Knocked Up Sarah Marshall and Felt Superbad About It, 30 Nights of Paranormal Activity With the Devil Inside the Girl With the Dragon Tattoo, Shriek If You Know What I Did Last Friday the Thirteenth*, etc. (Friedberg and Seltzer had a go at the multiple title – *Star Worlds Episode XXXIVE=MC2: The Force Awakens the Last Jedi Who Went Rogue*).

THE PLOTS OF SPOOF MOVIES.

Many critics attack spoof movies and comedies as possessing terrible scripts with rubbish stories. For the detractors (and they are seemingly everywhere), recent spoofs feature 'simple' plots which are used as an excuse or a pretext for a bunch of skits and gags.

Maybe – actually, the plots of most comedies and spoofs, when you consider them closely, conform to the same narrative structures of any other kind of movie, in any genre. Critics seem to be dazzled (or irritated) by the froth, the colour, the noise, the dialogue, the performances and the pop culture references in comedies and parodies, so they don't really see the narrative forms.

A common criticism of recent spoof movies and comedy movies is that they're badly written. Actually, comedies, as any screenwriter knows, are much more carefully constructed and written than many straight dramas. Why? Because they're trying to make audiences laugh! And that isn't easy – so comedies have to try harder. Typically, at least six months is taken for a comedy script.

These are the same film critics who complain that contemporary blockbuster movies are nothing but special effects and flashy visuals and one set-piece after another, and they don't really have stories like Ye Olde

Movies used to have.

Rubbish.

Take any mega-picture or blockbuster movie, and you will find a carefully worked-out narrative structure. True, the politics is often offensive and the ideology of those blockbusters can be repulsive in its pro-militarism and promotion of what I call 'Amerika Über Alles'. But the scripts conform to classical models of narrative and structure.

OK – another way of looking at contemporary spoofs, parodies and comedies is to think of them as sharing the same narrative form as musical movies. A musical film will have a story, yes (most often it's a love story), but it will use the narrative as the basis for a series of set-pieces, dances and musical numbers.

That's expected from a musical movie (and it's a form that can also apply to many blockbuster movies, too). But it is also a narrative form that *isn't* the same as a drama, a thriller, or a historical picture. In Bollywood cinema, they arer called 'masala' movies – a bit of everything.

A musical movie is a narrative form where it's expected that the story will stop and the characters will sing or dance. Comedies do the same – there'll be a moment when the story is simply halted in favour of a set-piece. (Hong Kong action movies can also be considered as using a musical movie form, with the musical numbers consisting of *kung fu* and martial arts sequences).

SOME THEORIES OF JOKES AND COMEDY.

Jokes and gags typically involve two elements, like a narrative: a preparation and resolution, a build-up and a punchline. In the typical joke, for Sigmund Freud, there are three components: the teller, the addressee, and the target or butt of the joke. The comic, meanwhile, is about observation, involving two elements: the observer and the observed or butt. Though ambiguous, jokes nearly always have a set of limits, are never completely illogical, so that their absurdities have meaning. Though humour seems to be 'subversive', disrupting norms and conventions, it is also conservative and reactionary, endorsing stereotypes, tradition and conventional views (S. Neale, 1990, 82). Aside from scapegoats, humour also involves incongruity, a mismatch of ideas and meanings; lastly, humour allows the harmless release of repressed feelings (O. Double, 89).

For Evanthius (14th century), comedies consist of 3 elements: exposition (*protasis*), complication (*epitasis*) and resolution (*catastrophe*). A further complication (*catastasis*), to occur after the complication stage, was later added by Joseph Scaliger. The reversal of fortune (*peripeteia*) was part of Neoclassical theory. The *anagnorisis* was another part of the reversal, indicating a movement from ignorance to knowledge. Surprise and suspense was crucial to comedy (and narrative), with knowledge being distributed between the characters and spectators. Keeping certain information secret, or pretences and disguises, combined with schemes and plans, are common narrative forms.

Much humour relies on repetition: the audience knows that particular events are going to happen and expect them; the humour plays with delivering the expected, or slight variations on a theme, or by altering the emphasis, or additional complications, or extending the motif, or reversing expectations. Another common rule in comedy is the rule of three: the first thing is expected, the second is expected, the third is unexpected, and thus funny.

Parodies are in constant dialogue with their targets, and seem to exist only in relation to them. Thus, Peter Wollen noted that parody 'constantly veers towards the hybrid, towards the graft, both compatible and incompatible with its apparent model'.[4] For some film fans this is where a spoof movie can produce an uneasy response: is it parasytic, feeding off the original, but offering nothing of its own? Is it textual cannibalism? Does it cheapen or corrupt the original? (As in, spoof movies 'ruin' the movies they parody).[5]

For Dan Harries, no, that doesn't happen: he dubs the parody movie 'conservative transgression':

> parody does have *some* effect through its unsettling of established normative system, yet ends up losing most of its radical verse by becoming a normative system itself. (120)

---

[4] P. Wollen, "Komar & Melamid Exhibition Catalogue", Fruitmarket Gallery, Edinburgh, 1985, 39.
[5] Dan Harries suggests that parody movies 'signal the end of a particular phase of a canon', not the demise of a whole tradition. Harries reckons that parodies in fact rejuvenate movies: 'film parody can be seen as a source of renewal by breathing new life into worn-out canons with specifically burying that tradition' (123).

And parody might even by the leading edge of culture, according to Terry Caesar: 'if we see parody not as living off popular culture but hosting it, then may not we also see parody as a route to the leading edge?' (1979)

The viewer is an active participant in contemplating a parody for Linda Hutcheon – parodies require the viewer to be familiar with the original text. Parodies, in short, need audiences. They are necessary to make the parodic process work: 'the parodic function can only be completed by a viewer', as Dan Harries put it (107).

There is an enormous amount of critical theory and analysis of parody and satire – in literature as well as cinema and television. Many studies are available which explore typical issues concerning parody and satire such as intertextuality, how a parody or satire relates to the original work or target, how viewers/ readers respond to parody and satire, how parody and satire relate to straight comedy, and so on.

RECENT SPOOF MOVIES.

Parody movies of the 2000s include:

2001: A Space Travesty, Shriek If You Know What I Did Last Friday the Thirteenth, The Bogus Witch Project, Not Another Teen Movie, Shrek, Wet Hot American Summer, Kung Pow!, Reality Kills, Austin Powers 3, Johnny English, Down With Love, G-Sale, A Mighty Wind, Shaun of the Dead, Kung Fu Hustle, Team America: World Police, My Big Fat Independent Movie, Hoodwinked!, Another Gay Movie, Borat, Bikini Bloodbath, Man of the Year, Hot Fuzz, The Comebacks, Walk Hard, Enchanted, Superhero Movie, The Onion Movie, Another Gay Sequel: Gays Gone Wild, An American Carol, Extreme Movie, Tropic Thunder, The World Is Hot Enough, Dance Flick, Not Another Not Another Movie, Transylmania, Stan Helsing, Land of the Lost, Cloudy With a Chance of Meatballs, Spanish Movie, Dark and Stormy Night and *Alien Trespass*.

Parodies of the 2010s include:

MacGruber, The 41-Year-Old Virgin Who Knocked Up Sarah Marshall and Felt Superbad About It, I Am Virgin, Johnny English Reborn, Hoodwinked Too! Hood vs. Evil, Hotel Transylvania, Movie 43, iSteve, A Haunted House, 30 Nights of Paranormal Activity with the Devil Inside the Girl with the Dragon Tattoo, Inappropriate Comedy, This Is The End, The World's End, Not Another Celebrity Movie, A Haunted House 2, The Hungover Games, They Came Together, A Million Ways to Die in the West, The Walking Deceased, Tooken, Ridiculous 6, Imaginary Movie, Fifty Shades of Black, Donald Trump's The Art of the Deal: The Movie, Meet the Blacks, Popstar: Never Stop Never Stopping, Sausage Party and *The Lego Batman Movie.*

3

COMEDY AND CRITICISM

- Surely you can land this plane?
- Yes I can, and stop calling me Shirley!
(*Airplane!*)

COMEDY AND THE CRITICS.
The *Scary Movie* movies, the *Naked Gun* movies, the Zucker, Abrahams and Zucker flicks and the Seltzer-Friedberg movies, like most comedies, and certainly most recent parody movies, are for mass audiences at a multiplex cinema on a Friday night, and *not* for critics. Film critics don't like them. They sit in screening rooms, surrounded by other stony-faced critics, on cold mornings in New York or London or L.A. or Paris or Rome. They don't laugh, they sit there seething or bored (according to their reviews). And they give the movies bad write-ups.

In fact, critics virulently despise spoof movies; the level of animosity that spoof movies (and the filmmakers) attract is striking (but not perhaps surprising). The filmmakers are called idiots, scourges, lazy, and inept.

But go to a comedy movie on the weekend, to a packed house, and then see how it plays! You can't beat seeing an audience reacting positively to a movie – whether it's thrills and chills (*Jaws, Alien, The Exorcist*), or laughs (*Airplane!, Tootsie, Aladdin*). We've all seen those movies (and 1,000s more) at the cinema, and audiences love them. They *love* to laugh, they *love* to be entertained. These movies are *designed* for huge audiences, chomping popcorn and slurping soda, yelling to their mates, chatting on their cel phone – not sitting there in stony silence.

Film critics, meanwhile, prefer parodies or spoofs that flatter their intellect. They like the send-ups of Michelangelo Antonioni's po-faced, Italian modernism that Woody Allen delivers in *Everything You Wanted To Know About Sex*. They like clever comedy writing (the early Marx Brothers, 1930s wise-cracking screwball comedies, Jacques Tati sight gags, Buster Keaton's deadpan, balletic routines, and early Woody Allen ('the early, funny ones').) They like comedy that makes them smile knowingly (with an occasional 'hrrumph' or snort of repressed but mild amusement – critics never belly laugh); they like comedy that flatters them, that reminds them that they're smart enough to get the joke. They don't like gross-out comedy, teenage comedy, or dumb comedy.

You will notice that no film critic has ever suggested ways in which a movie could be made funnier in their film reviews, no film critic has ever offered to rewrite jokes or situations, or has ever demonstrated in clear, precise prose how to improve the comical movies they attack.

That's what Jean-Luc Godard said: when he hears people complaining about the dialogue in a movie, he asks: *what did you do to improve it?*

Comedy movies are under-valued everywhere in critical circles. They seldom win major awards (if there's a dead-serious movie about World War One or yet another adaptation of a classic, 19th century novel (with a Great Performance from a Great Actor) nominated in the same category, a comedy picture hasn't got a chance).

Altho' comedy movies make money, and often offer an attractive cost-to-profit ratio to producers and financial backers, they are seldom listed in a year's top ten movies, critically. They are not often placed in film critics' top ten lists. The comedies that do feature in the top ten lists are the usual suspects: the Marx Brothers, *Dr Strangelove,* Billy Wilder (*The Apartment* or *Some Like It Hot*), 1930s screwball comedy (*His Girl Friday, Bringing Up Baby, The Philadelphia Story*), Charlie Chaplin and Buster Keaton, Laurel & Hardy, and the odd Jerry Lewis comedy.

So if you are making comedy movies, you have to accept that the critics are going to kick you repeatedly (and sometimes astonishingly violently, as if you'd just murdered their Moms in front of their eyes). And in recent years, the film critics give out their garlands for comedies even rarer, as if the times are getting more'n more cynical, to the point where no darn critic wants to laugh, or is even physically capable of laughing.

Look at Woody Allen, a towering genius and one of the most remarkable talents ever produced by the American film business. Leave aside Allen's 'early, funny ones' (*Sleeper, Annie Hall, Love and Death, Bananas*), which film critics still celebrate (*some* critics, that is, but not *all* critics). Let's look at the recent comedies of the 2000s and 2010s. For me, movies such as *Small Time Crooks, Anything Else, Hollywood Ending, The Curse of the Jade Scorpion* and *Whatever Works* are classy, fun, intelligent comedies, and *Midnight In Paris* is a simply gorgeous romantic comedy. Consult the film critics, tho', and just look at the kicking that Allen and his movies receive![6]

•

Twelve comedies appeared in the American Film Institute's 100 Greatest American Films of 1998: *Some Like It Hot, Dr Strangelove, Annie Hall, It Happened One Night, The Philadelphia Story, M.A.S.H., Tootsie, The Gold Rush, City Lights, Modern Times, Duck Soup* and *Bringing Up Baby* (in addition, films such as *Singin' In the Rain, American Graffiti, The Graduate*, and *The Apartment* could be seen as comedies, and indeed were included in the American Film Institute's list of top comedy movies, the 100 Laughs list, published in 2000).

In the American Film Institute's list of top comedy movies ('100 Laughs', from 2000), spoof/ parody movies include: *Blazing Saddles* (at no. 6), *Airplane!* (10), *Young Frankenstein* (13), and *This Is Spinal Tap* (29). The top ten comedies, according to the A.F.I., were: *Some Like It Hot, Tootsie, Dr Strangelove, Annie Hall, Duck Soup, Blazing Saddles, M.A.S.H., It Happened One Night, The Graduate* and *Airplane!*.

The British Film Institute's Top 100 movie lists, published in 2012, featured only 7 comedy films in the directors' list and only 6 in the critics' list. The 1970s and 1980s are the cut-off point: very few comedy films made after that seem to make the Top 100 film lists. Also, silent

---

[6] Woody Allen has produced some clunkers in the 2000s and 2010s, however: *From Rome With Love* and *Magic In the Moonlight*, for instance.

comedy classics continue to be revered (the output of Charlie Chaplin and Buster Keaton in particular).

The greatest movies ever, which feature in every list of Top 100 Movies, are mostly dramas, historical films, the odd thriller, and some genre outings (like horror, adventure, sci-fi or fantasy): *Citizen Kane, Casablanca, The Godfather, Gone With the Wind, Lawrence of Arabia, The Wizard of Oz, On the Waterfront, Schindler's List, It's a Wonderful Life, Sunset Boulevard, The Bridge On the River Kwai* and *Star Wars*.

•

It's partly a *category error*, perhaps: spoofs of other movies are incorrectly categorized. They are a particular form of comedy that secretly enjoys the object of parody (sometimes, the original movie is regarded as 'trashy', like *Fifty Shades of Grey* or *Twilight*).

But critics – *and* audiences – incorrectly assess the movies. Read any review of any recent spoof or comedy movie, and you'll discover a disappointment, an irritation, which stems from a movie delivering something that isn't what the critic expected, or that the critic rejects (almost with an automatic reaction).

This is actually a crucial point: recent comedy/ spoof movies do something that critics weren't expecting, or didn't want, or that went against the critics' sensibilities. So critics (and audiences) never buy into the movie in the first place, but set themselves in constant conflict with it. From the first shot, they are fighting the movie. Which is a waste of their time, of everyone's time.

Look at a film critically, consciously, carefully, but don't reject it outright for the wrong reasons – then there's no point sitting through the next ninety minutes.

That categorization error and flat rejection creates a stumbling block that no comedy movie – or *any* movie – can overcome. The issue of whether a comedy movie is funny, or whether it's well-written, is not even important anymore if the movie is rebuffed from the outset.

Meanwhile, movie-goers often react very negatively to recent spoof films. Why? The movies of Friedberg-Seltzer and the Wayans Brothers, among others, come in for incredible gouts of venom (that is, if the user reviews, the buyers' reviews, on sites such as Internet Movie Database and Amazon are to be believed).

Are the scary levels of loathing justified? Not by a mere movie, no. Is it because, then, spoof movies reveal that what viewers are buying into and consuming by the ton (movies) are actually dumb, superficial entertainment? Same with critics: do critics really come down hard on recent spoof films because they demonstrate clearly that what critics are spending so much of their time contemplating is puerile junk.

Because many North American and Western movies are just dumb – banal, self-righteous, patronizing and smug. Oh, *and* they're politically offensive with their pro-militaristic stance, and their promotion of racist, white supremacist, nationalistic ideology (what I call 'Amerika Über Alles').

Parody/ spoof/ send-up movies vividly reveal the idiotic premises and stories of the North American movies that're eaten up by audiences around the world and earn billions. In *Epic Movie*, the White Bitch admits that her nefarious plan is the same as that in *Superman Returns*. Yes – and in the immensely lucrative Disney *Star Wars* sequels of 2015 onwards, movies that critics and audiences have gone nuts over, it's the same dreadful super-villain scheme of taking over the universe.

I wonder if some film critics loathe the recent spate of spoof and parody comedies because they aggressively attack and rip to pieces not only the movies that critics write about every week, but also every film convention, every motif, every issue and every trick and gimmick that movies use (a movie is nothing but tricks and gimmicks – cinema is all fakery, smoke and mirrors).

The spoof movies also reveal, loud and clear, that most North American movies, and certainly all mainstream, Hollywood movies, are telling pathetically simplistic stories, with one-dimensional characters, with a trite, childish morality of good vs. evil, in a tired, stereotypical and worn-out fashion, and promulgating pro-war, pro-military Western ideology.

Go and look at any of the film critics writing in Western newspapers, or online, or in magazines, or on TV, and you'll see so-serious, so-respectful reviews of movies that are, let's face it, often dumb. Spoof movies expose the idiocy of the movies themselves, and of the people who write about them so solemnly and reverentially.

SPOOFS AND TURKEYS.

Compared to so many crappy movies, bloated movies, incredibly expensive movies, creepily politically pro-American and pro-military movies, and often repulsively violent movies of recent times, the comedies of Zucker-Abrahams-Zucker, the Wayans family, Friedberg and Seltzer *et al* are wonderful! All those Summer blockbuster movies that last way too long (2h 30m! Or more!), that feature cretinously stupid plots, and that hammer home a horrible, pro-aggression, pro-capitalist ideology: they stink!

Here are some turkeys, far worse than any of the comedies of Zucker-Abrahams-Zucker, the Wayans family, Friedberg and Seltzer *et al*:

The Hobbit, King Kong, The Lion, the Witch and The Wardrobe (cost: $180m), *Prince Caspian* ($200m), *Voyage of the Dawn Treader* (cost: $140-155m), *Kill Bill, Black Hawk Down, Hannibal* (cost: $87 million!), *50 Shades of Grey, Quantum of Solace, Casino Royale, The Beach, Billy Elliot,* the *Charlie's Angels* movies, *Unbreakable, Jungle Book 2, Lemony Snicket, Snow White and the Huntsman* (cost: $170 million!),[7] *Sin City, Lara Croft, Chocolat, Vanilla Sky, Amélie, Kingdom of Heaven, Oceans 11, Alien vs. Predator, About a Boy, Batman Begins, King Arthur, The Village,* the *Bourne* series, *Spider-man 3* (cost: $270-350 million), *X-Men Origins: Wolverine, 8MM, The Hulk,* the *Bridget Jones* movies, *Where the Wild Things Are, Home On the Range* (cost $110 million), etc.

Here's one of the mysteries and ironies of mega-budget movies that flop or stink: they were produced by very talented people, many of whom were highly paid, and veterans of the business. They are technically superlative, with $$$$ spent on sets, costumes, props, stunts, visual effects and all the rest.

When you spend *more money* on an item, it is usually *better quality*, right? You spend a *lot* of money on clothes, and you get *nicer* clothes,

---

[7] A complete flop, *Snow White* and the Huntsman (Universal, 2012), was... a series of empty shots, a fairy tale eviscerated of all magic. There's literally *nothing here*, nothing going on. I wait and wait for *something* to happen. But it doesn't.
  What a waste of money! *Snow White* isn't 'bloated' or over-done or OTT (some of the usual accusations against current blockbuster flicks), it's not 'done' at all (uncooked). It's just empty. There really is nothing there at all.

right? You can even have clothes tailor-made to your exact specifications, if you spend enough.

So the elements in ultra-high budget movies are top of the range – the production values, the cast, the effects, the technical aspects, etc. But there's one area which lets everything down: the concept and the script.

This is the irony of massively expensive movie productions: the *more* you spend does not automatically equal *better* movies!

(It's worth reminding ourselves that many of those movies cited above (there are 1,000s more) are in fact producer-led, studio-packaged movies. They're not *auteur* projects, where a director is 'expressing' themselves artistically. They are not originated by the director. And they are not written by the director. They are productions developed by film studios and film companies, as products to fill a schedule, to generate profit, to sell toys, and directors are simply one of many people hired to deliver the product.)

SIDENOTE ON JULIA KRISTEVA AND COMEDY.

Now for a complete change of pace!

If you *really* want to get intellectual – or, as they quip in comedies, I'm gonna get intellectual on your ass – here is a summary of Julia Kristeva's theory of abjection: Kristeva (a French-Romanian philosopher born in 1941) sees the artist's project as the purifying of abjection. Abjection lies behind the history of religions: the abject is simultaneously the 'land of oblivion' and that 'veiled infinity', the moment 'when revelation bursts forth', Kristeva remarked in *Powers of Horror* (9). For Kristeva, sociality and subjectivity are founded on abjection, on the expulsion of the unclean and the disorderly. But the abject can never be totally eliminated, and accompanies, in sublimated form, society. The abject is the borderland of ambiguity, a total subjectivity. Ironically, it is *jouissance* that

> alone causes the abject to exist as such. One does not know it, one does not desire it, one joys in it. Violently and painfully. A passion. (ibid., 9)

The abject is a 'space of simultaneous pleasure and danger', commented Elizabeth Grosz in "The Body of Signification" (1990, 94).

Food, urine, vomit, tears and saliva are the things that create abjection – associated with the orifices and body surfaces which later become the erotic zones. Abjection is linked to the body's waste fluids, to those materials which produce disgust (spit, shit, urine, mucus, blood). The fluids of abjection remind society of the body's limitations, its boundaries, its cycles and fatality. These excremental products signify 'the danger to identity that comes from without' (*Powers of Horror*, 71).

In fact – I don't even need to check – but I bet there actually are essays and articles somewhere on Earth which apply the theory of Kristevan abjection to contemporary movie comedies. After all, comedy is always using those body fluids, precisely because they are full of dramatic value. And, like the concept of abjection, comedy is always exploring the limits of what society deems 'acceptable' or assimilable.

No need to say any more: Kristeva + abjection + society + comedy is an essay or a riff that writes itself.

Premiere of Best Night Ever.

PART TWO

MOVIES

1

MAXIMUM RISK

Maximum Risk (1996) was a Jean-Claude van Damme action thriller directed by one of the geniuses of Hong Kong cinema, Ringo Lam (Lam Ling-tung, born 1955, and sadly died too young, in 2018, best-known for the *On Fire* films, and also *Full Contact* and *Burning Paradise*). At his best, as an action director, Lam is the equal of any film director from the history of cinema. Lam's action movies are sensational by any standards, burning up the screen in white heat. And they feature incredible performances by icons of Chinese cinema such as Chow Yun-fat and Simon Yam.[1] (I would highly recommend any of Ringo Lam's movies – start with *City On Fire* and move onto *Full Contact, Wild Search* and *Burning Paradise*. Lam is a total natural in cinema, a really compelling storyteller).

Moshe Diamant was producer for *Maximum Risk*, Roger Birnbaum was executive producer, Jason Clark was co-producer, Robert Folk (m.), Alexander Gruszynski (DP), Bill Pankow (ed.), Deborah Brown (casting), Steve Spence (prod. des.), Joseph A. Porro (costumes), Katalin Elek (make-up), and Nelson Ferreira (sound sup.). The stunt co-ordinators were: Patrick Cauderlier, Ted Hanlan, and Charlie Picerni, with car stunts by Rémy Julienne (very well-known in film circles). Released Sept 13,

---

[1] Van Damme, bless him, is not in that class, but his name helped to get many Hong Kong and Asian pictures made.

1996. 100 mins.

In the cast were: Jean-Claude van Damme,[2] Natasha Henstridge, Jean-Hugues Anglade, Zach Grenier, Paul Ben-Victor, Frank Senger, Stefanos Miltsakakis and Frank van Keeken. Filming took place in Nice, Paris, New York, Philadelphia, and Toronto. The budget was estimated at $25m (huge for a Hong Kong movie).

Maximum Risk was written by Jason Friedberg and Aaron Seltzer for producer Moishe Diamant, who has extensive credits in TV and cinema (it was Diamant who oversaw J.C. van Damme moving into Hong Kong cinema). Larry Ferguson, however, has the screen credit.

Ringo Lam recalled he was in Toronto visiting his parents when he received a call from a film producer in Hollywood to direct Jean-Claude van Damme in a movie. This would be his first American production. Lam had heard rumours about John Woo's trials with Van Damme during the making of *Hard Target*. Ultimately, *Maximum Risk* was a problematic movie for Lam: the studio had the film previewed (as usual), and the audience decided they didn't care for the character played by Natasha Henstridge. The studio wanted reshoots, which took place over three days, and altered the script. Lam felt it wasn't really his film anymore.

Maximum Risk was conceived as a vehicle for Belgian star van Damme, the 'Muscles From Brussels'. Jean-Claude van Damme (Jean-Claude Camille François Van Varenberg in Berchem-Sainte-Agathe),[3] born on October 18, 1960, Brussels, is a second tier action star in the West (like Steven Seagal and Dolph Lungren, with whom van Damme is often lumped). Van Damme moves well, is convincing and competent in fight scenes,[4] but always seems to be rather wooden in talky scenes. You wouldn't hire van Damme to play Oedipus or Othello, for instance! Like Christopher Lambert or Vin Diesel, van Damme is more like a coathanger on which a movie can hang its narrative elements, which it isn't really interested in.

(Prior to *Maximum Risk*, Jean-Claude van Damme was known for action movies such as *Universal Soldier, Replicant, Last Action Hero,*

---

[2] Curiously, van Damme plays the entire movie with a massive red bruise on his face (instead of the usual ploy of keeping an injury for a scene or two after a fight).
[3] His website is jcvdworld.com.
[4] Fight fans who don't like van Damme complain that he only has a few moves, which he uses again and again (like kickboxing).

Streetfighter, The Quest and *Kickboxer*.[5] He appeared in *No Retreat, No Surrender* (1986), produced by Ng See-yuen (one of the important producers in Hong Kong) and directed by Corey Yuen. Van Damme often played villains in his early films. One of his biggest hits was *Timecop* (1994), an amusing sci-fi actioner. He also appeared in *Death Warrant, Legionnaire, Derailed, The Order, Sudden Death, A.W.O.L. Black Eagle* and *Predator*. Van Damme's biggest successes were in the early-to-mid 1990s, after that, his movies received decreasing revenue, and some went straight to video).

Jean-Claude van Damme has also appeared in several Asian movies or for Asian film directors, including *No Retreat, No Surrender, Bloodsport* (1987),[6] *Knock-off* and *Double Team* (both directed by Tsui Hark), and *Hard Target* (1993) helmed by John Woo. Like those movies, in *Maximum Risk* there is a European star (van Damme), a Chinese director (Lam), an international cast, and filming in Europa as well as the U.S.A. (Europe acts as a kind of halfway point between China and America – *Knock-off* and *Double Team* also filmed in Europe).

•

Maximum Risk is a technically accomplished action thriller, the sort that Hong Kong cinema can churn out at a staggering rate (and better than anywhere else). It's a man-on-the-run movie, a wrong man movie, a twins/ doubles movie (and not the only one in van Damme's career), with one brother, Alain Moreau[7] (who just happens to be a military man and a brilliant fighter) being mistaken for his sibling, Mikhail Suvorov (who just happens to be a major gangster).

Maximum Risk gets going with a massive, crunching chase – on foot, across rooftops, and by car – and doesn't let up after that. Sure, many action movies and thriller movies are simply extended chases. *Maximum Risk* is no different: Alain is on the run from the villains (Russian mobsters), and also the Federal Bureau of Investigation. (His sidekick? Alex, played by Natasha Henstridge, a dancer/ waitress and former lover of the deceased brother Mikhail). So we start *Maximum Risk* in South France, head to Paris, then to Gotham.

---

5 The *Kickboxer* series, like the *Universal Soldier* films, continues to recent times, with movies in 2016 and 2017.
6 *Bloodsport* was filmed in Hong Kong at Clearwater Bay; it was produced by Cannon.
7 Presumably named after two icons of French cinema.

Car chases, chases in stairwells, chases over roofs (again), chases down back alleys – *Maximum Risk* has the lot. The filmmaking team headed up by Ringo Lam can deliver hi-octane, slambang action second to none (have a look at *Full Contact*, for instance). Lam is a major director of action, known for his tough, urban thrillers (which're tougher and coarser than many Hong Kong flicks – a cinema already out-there in terms of delivering loud, crude, flashy fare).

Not a deep, profound story, then, about theology and philosophy and the despair of modern life. No – it's cars hurtling down rainswept streets, it's sleazy bars and nightclubs (cue the nearly-nude dancers!), it's bang-bang-bang fire-fights, and it's men punching each other every which way. Glass shatters and fires erupt (as in every contemporary-set Hong Kong thriller ever made).

For the finale of *Maximum Risk*, it's back to La France, where the legendary Rémy Julienne and the car stunt team stage more mayhem (a massive car chase – if there's a car chase in a recent French movie, Julienne has probably done it). Narratively, there are no surprises – the villains are wasted, the heroes prevail – but the 1996 production continues to deliver high quality action. We end up in, of all places, an abattoir, amidst a forest of hanging carcasses (as if that isn't enough, there's also the sight of Federal Bureau of Investigation agent Pellman (Paul Ben-Victor) lurching after Alain with a chainsaw).

•

As to the input of Jason Friedberg and Aaron Seltzer – their work on the screenplay of *Maximum Risk* was rewritten. (It's likely that several writers worked on the script, as usual in Tinseltown). The gimmick of the New York taxi driver being a novelist (and a very wired, excitable personality), might've come from Friedberg and Seltzer. (So that he's using the escapades in the taxi as material for his novel).

The critical reception to *Maximum Risk* was the usual indifference to action movies coupled with suspicion about Jean-Claude van Damme as an actor. It's easy to lampoon van Damme (he is wooden, he is silly, he doesn't convince, etc), but exquisite acting abilities are not the only ingredient in the mix in movies like *Maximum Risk*. This isn't Chekhov or Ibsen. It's a thriller, an action movie, a commercial movie.

2

'YOU CAN RUN, BUT YOU CAN'T HIDE!': S*PY HARD*

Spy Hard (1996) was dir. by Jason Friedberg's father Rick, prod. by Rick Friedberg, Doug Draizin, and Jeffrey Konvitz, exec. prod. by Robert Rosen and Leslie Nielsen, and wr. by Friedberg and Seltzer, Rick Friedberg and Dick Chudnow. Friedberg and Seltzer also receive a 'story by' credit. Bill Conti (m.), John Leonetti (DP), Eric Sears (ed.), William Creber (prod. des.), William J. Durrell Jr. (art dir.), Tom Bronson (cost.), Ken Chase (make-up), Janice Alexander (hair), Mark Paladini and Fern Champion (casting), Fred Waugh (stunt co-ord. and 2nd unit dir.), and Gregory M. Gerlich (sup. sound ed.). Released May 24, 1996. 81 mins.

In the cast were: Leslie Nielsen, Andy Griffith, Marcia Gay Harden, Barry Bostwick,[8] Charles Durning, Nicollette Sheridan, John Ales and Stephanie Romanov. Plus cameos from Robert Culp, Hulk Hogan, Pat Morita, Ray Charles, Mr T., etc.

Spy Hard came about, Aaron Seltzer explained, as a youthful script spoofing *James Bond* and similar thrillers (Seltzer was 22 at the time). It wasn't written for a company, or as paid work. It's the product of movie fans, who'd seen *Airplane!* and other Zucker-Abrahams-Zucker movies, and *Saturday Night Live*, and *Wayne's World*, and all of the usual suspects. But Friedberg's Dad Rick showed it to Leslie Nielsen, with

---

[8] Barry Bostwick does a Kennedy impression. That perplexed some reviewers. They asked, 'why?' And the answer, in a comedy, is always: because it's funny!

whom he was making some parody golf instruction videos.[9] Nielsen liked it, and that started the ball rolling.

Spy Hard benefitted from being released a year after the revival of the *James Bond* franchise with 1995's *Golden-Eye*. Also, the *Die Hard* sequel was the top movie of 1995. And it was a year before the first *Austin Powers* flick (in 1997). Other comedies released theatrically in 1996 included *The Nutty Professor, Jingle All the Way, The Cable Guy, Mars Attacks!* and *Beavis and Butt-head Do America*. In that market, *Spy Hard* grossed a decent $84.1 million, placing it at no. 38 in the top-grossing movies that year.

Spy Hard features some iconic Los Angeles locations – the lovely Rose Garden downtown at Exposition Park (the start of the horse chase), Hollywood Boulevard (where Steele and Agent 3.14 climb aboard a bus), Disney Studios in Burbank, and the L.A. County Arboretum and Botanic Garden.

You can never under-estimate the talents of Leslie Nielsen (1925-2010) as a screen comedian. *Spy Hard* benefits immensely from the casting of Nielsen as Dick Steele, a.k.a. Agent W.D. 40. He is marvellous as an accident prone spy. We don't need much background or characterization for Steele, because Nielsen's casting does that for us. Nielsen can do physical comedy, intellectual comedy, tongue-twisting dialogue comedy, and everything else. He has the charm and nonchalance of a self-confident Bond character while also being a useless goof. It's funny too when stunt guys very obviously take over from Nielsen to ride a bicycle, or dive thru a window (*Spy Hard* is stuffed with stunts, as many comedy films are, including some amazing gags with vehicles.[10] 64 stunt people – a huge crew – are credited. The stunts were overseen by stunt co-ordinator Fred Waugh; he was also the second unit director).

For Leslie Nielsen (then 70), *Spy Hard* was a very physical role – he's riding horses, running alongside cars, jumping fences, taking falls, and doing some stunts.

•

Spy Hard draws heavily on the spoof movie format developed by

---

9 Golf appears in *Spy Hard* (Steele visits a golf club); Nielsen had filmed some comic golf videos for director Rick Friedberg.
10 Bill Young was vehicle stunt co-ordinator.

Zucker, Abrahams and Zucker – *Top Secret!, Police Squad, The Naked Gun* and the matchless *Airplane!* For ex, the extensive use of flashbacks as a way of introducing new genres to send-up. Flashbacks are not what comes to mind when considering a comedy script, where action takes place in an ever-lasting present tense (as with all movies). But the flashback device was honed to the level of genius by the Z.A.Z. team in films like *Airplane!*, where the lovers think back on their courtship. (In the golf club in *Spy Hard*, a flashback is simply the same shot but in black-and-white, to suggest the past. And there are so many flashbacks, Steele's Boss insists they haven't got time for any more, just as Steele is about to drift into another flashback).

Spy Hard is fond of the subjects it is lampooning – that comes across strongly. And it's the aspect of the cinema of Friedberg and Seltzer that film critics find lacking in their later work as movie directors. For the critics who loathe Friedberg and Seltzer with a passion, they are cynical hacks who deride the audience and the popular culture they consume. No. Friedberg and Seltzer are clearly *major* fans (and consumers) of all sorts of popular culture. It's just that their spoofs of it are cruder and more cynical than many of their contemporaries in the world of comedy.

And *Spy Hard* is very funny – it completely nixes the usual gripe of 99% of film critics who keep on insisting that Friedberg and Seltzer can't write comedy.

They can, and they did, with this 1996 movie.

•

For the critics who regularly complain that the films of Friedberg and Seltzer don't respect narrative structure, and that they use a story solely for humour-generating purposes (well, they *are* making comedies), *Spy Hard* replies with a strong narrative that is founded solidly on the hi-tech thriller format, and on *James Bond* and the numerous *007* imitators. You could take out the jokes in *Spy Hard* and play it straight – and you've got yet another contemporary thriller about nasty people who're going to use a nuclear missile (we've all seen too many movies like that. The mid-1990s, for instance, featured several. And years later, hi-tech thrillers with nuclear arms as the MacGuffin were still being churned out by film centres around the world).

The *James Bond* narrative framework has been used so many times, it's become so familiar and it's sort of unbreakable. You can take that story template and twist it and re-arrange it and it still works. Like a fairy tale, it's one of those narrative structures that works every time, and can be molded every which way.

Spy Hard hits all of the expected beats of a *James Bond*-style thriller story, and delightfully spoofs them at the same time. It features all of the ingredients: the opening teaser, the summoning to HQ, the reluctant hero, the gadgets in Q's laboratory, the flirtation with Miss Moneypenny (here Miss Cheevus – Marcia Gay Harden), several *Bond*-like women, the super-villain, the ridiculous schemes of the bad guy, and so on.

•

The reviews, as ever for comedies, were mixed. Leonard Maltin found *Spy Hard* patchy, and more like a series of outtakes from the *Naked Gun* films. Ditto with *Variety*. *Time Out* carped that *Spy Hard* thinks it's amusing just to evoke its target movies rather than doing something with those movies (this would be a recurring complaint with Friedberg and Seltzer's movies: critics carp that they just point to something, or include a reference to it, and expect that to be funny).

Critics have been making the same complaints about spoof movies since the Z.A.Z. movies of the 1980s, or the Mel Brooks classics of the 1970s. Like, critics gripe that spoofers seem to think it's enough simply to evoke a movie to raise a laugh. *Time Out* says that of *Spy Hard*.

Now this is surprising – hi-falutin' theoretical magazine *Diacritics* reviewed *Spy Hard*, and found it to be a searingly insightful, deliriously postmodernist and Gitanes-on-lip-quivering deconstruction of the U.S.A.'s troubled involvement with the Middle East. No. Just kidding.[11]

•

THE SPOOFS AND THE GAGS.

Spy Hard includes many spoofs – primarily, of the *James Bond* franchise, but it also takes in *J.F.K., Speed, Home Alone, True Lies, Jurassic Park, Planet of the Apes, E.T., Pulp Fiction, Mission: Impossible, Butch Cassidy and the Sundance Kid, Jaws* and *Die Hard*.

---

[11] It was *Cahiers du Cinéma*, not *Diacritics*.

The *J.F.K.* send-up has Dick Steele nearly killing the U.S. President thru his nervous over-reaction to loud, popping sounds from the crowd at a procession (including two cheerleader babes blowing bubblegum). The *Mission: Impossible* send-up features the famous self-destructing tape machine (it blows up the helicopter being flown by Mr T.). The *Speed* movie spoof features some spectacular vehicle stunts (with Ray Charles playing the bus driver), including a giant jump (across the full moon, *à la E.T. The Extraterrestrial*). On the shaking, rocking bus, a dentist and assistant tries to work on a patient, and a chef ices a giant wedding cake. For *Pulp Fiction*, Steele and the Russian Agent 3.14 appear as John Travolta and Uma Thurman in that vastly over-praised 1994 movie (a hapless guy in a 'I want to party!' Tee shirt gets shot, and is later used as a battering ram). The *Butch Cassidy and the Sundance Kid* parody focusses on the famous Burt Bacharach song and romantic interlude ('Teardrops Are Falling On My Head'),[12] with Nielsen in the Paul Newman role on a bicycle (Steele impresses his date with ridiculous, look-at-me bike acrobatics). For *True Lies,* Steele pops up in a Harrier jet. The *Home Alone* send-up features the bratty, know-it-all kid getting beaten up by Rancor's heavies. The heroes end up on the super-villain's tropical island, which leads to an appearance of the dinosaurs out of *Jurassic Park.*

The *James Bond* send-ups in *Spy Hard* are quite brilliant (yes, this *is* the screenwriting of Friedberg and Seltzer we're talking about!). *James Bond* is an easy target, and it was being spoofed many times already by the mid-1960s,[13] and continued to be parodied in the *Austin Powers* movies (which clearly drew on *Spy Hard*).

It's easy to send up *James Bond* for lots of reasons: everybody knows the movies, the films are full of iconic moments, music, props and sets, the characters are simple types, the narrative structure is set in stone (there are recurring scenes in every *James Bond* movie), the films are already very OTT, the situations are colourful and flashy, the films send themselves up, and the films are pure escapism.

The main titles of *Spy Hard* is a gloriously dopey and mischievous

---

12 That scene was itself a parody of *Jules et Jim*. And *Butch Cassidy and the Sundance Kid* was a major element in one of the greatest parody movies ever, *Blazing Saddles*.
13 For instance, in the *Carry On* film *Carry On Spying* (1964), the *Harry Palmer* films, *Agent 8 3/4* (1965), *Our Man Flint* (1966), and the over-blown *Casino Royale* (1967).

take on the famous Maurice Binder titles of the *Bond* films.14 Aided by Weird Al Yankowic (he also directed the sequence), the familiar slinky silhouettes of naked women swimming become fat women, a poodle, baby, a scuba diver, household objects, etc. The OTT song parodies 'Goldfinger', sung by Shirley Bassey.15 And at the end, Weird Al's head explodes. Meanwhile, Bill Conti composed a wicked send-up of the typical *James Bond* theme song (having also written the real thing himself, for the 1981 *Bond* movie, *For Your Eyes Only*).

The crude, *Carry On* innuendoes16 of the *James Bond* movies are irresistible for a comedy team – *Spy Hard* delivers several amusing riffs on the smutty dialogue between Agent 007 and his women (like the hands and things riff on the plane).

Q's laboratory includes the mandatory spoof versions of the famous gadgets in *James Bond* (there's a briefcase which is actually... just a briefcase); plus the mandatory appearance of Michael Jackson in a Friedberg -Seltzer script.

Disney produced *Spy Hard* – thru their Hollywood Pictures arm. (So we have the exterior of the secret headquarters being represented by the famous postmodern Disney building in Burbank. It's funny seeing guards armed with rifles outside the Disney building, and the pool swimming with sharks. That's what the front office of a Hollywood movie studio is really like!).

One of the great gags in *Spy Hard* doesn't make complete sense, but it's very funny: over a short shot of Los Angeles at dawn, we hear the music of an Arabic call to prayer (turning the skyscrapers of downtown L.A. into the minarets of Arabia). Is it funny because contemporary North America has spent a *lot* of time and effort in recent years tussling with the Middle East diplomatically, politically, ideologically and militarily?

There are numerous sight gags and signage gags in *Spy Hard* – the 'Intruder Entrance' at Rancor's compound, the photos at Steele's home

---

14 The *James Bond* title sequences (designed by Maurice Binder in the early films) famously involved images of semi-naked women in silhouette, large phallic guns, cars, jewels, and Bond in silhouette running or posing, all filmed in garish Sixties colours, pinks, purples, blues, reds. Though out-of-date by the early 1970s, the swirling, psychedelic title sequences continued to be a part of the Bond series beyond the 1990s.
15 *James Bond* songs were performed by acts such as Shirley Bassey, Frank Sinatra, Tom Jones, Paul McCartney, Lulu, Rita Coolidge, Carly Simon, Louis Armstrong, and later, pop performers such as Duran Duran, Sheryl Crow, Madonna and Sheena Easton.
16 It's a 'PG-13' rated movie, and it's a Disney movie, but plenty of risqué jokes are included in *Spy Hard* (sex, swearing, violence, etc).

(Steele with Kennedy, on stage with Madonna, etc), the blink-and-you-miss-it list on a secret dossier,[17] and this street sign on the taxi rank outside L.A.X. airport:

'YOU CAN RUN, BUT YOU CAN'T HIDE'

It's funny, but does it make sense? (No – but it's funny!). The idea that the city council would put up a sign welcoming visitors at an airport, 'You can run but you can't hide' is funny.

Many gags are sound gags – like the squeal of a cat when Steele stuffs some gear in the overhead lockers on the plane. And that staple of many comedy movies – the off-screen car crash, the cheapest (and funniest) way of suggesting mayhem.

Bill Conti provides some spoof music and songs for *Spy Hard*. Conti (*Rocky, Escape To Victory*) was a great choice – he composed the music for the 1981 *James Bond* flick *For Your Eyes Only* (with its Sheena Easton title song), so he knew all about how *Bond* movies use music.

Every Friedberg and Seltzer film script includes comedy gay characters – here, the waiter at the nightclub is an OTT Asian guy (a cameo from Pat Morita, the *sifu* in *The Karate Kid*).

One of the running gags in *Spy Hard* is a J. Edgar Hoover send-up featuring the head of the secret service. (Hoover is a gift to comedy writers – the gags write themselves).

Dick Steele's boss, the Director (Charles Durning), hides in an armchair in his office – a bizarre sight gag: did this influence J.K. Rowling for the book *Harry Potter and the Half-Blood Prince*? (where a very similar scene occurs, involving Professor Slughorn).

A giant chase begins in the Rose Garden at Exposition Park with Dick Steele, improbably, on horseback, being chased by one of Rancor's very persistent hoods driving (what else?) a lawnmower. The chase enters silent comedy territory – into a hotel, up the elevator, and onto the roof, with several pay-offs (diving into a swimming pool, and Steele menacing the heavy in a jumpjet, *à la* Arnold Schwarzenegger in 1994's over-blown thriller *True Lies*).

---

[17] This movie was surely filmed with an eye for a home video release – as some of the jokes are on screen for a very short time.

3

THE *SCARY MOVIE* SERIES

The first movie in the lucrative *Scary Movie* franchise was produced[18] by Gold/ Miller Productions/ Wayans Bros./ Brad Grey Pictures, prod. by Eric Gold, Keenan Wayans, Marlon Wayans, Shawn Wayans,[19] and Lee Mayes, exec. prod. by Cary Granat, Brad Grey, Peter Safran, Peter Schwerin, Bob Weinstein, Harvey Weinstein, and Bo Zenga (15 producers in all!), wr. by Jason Friedberg, Aaron Seltzer, Buddy Johnson, Phil Beauman, Marlon and Shawn Wayans, dir. by Keenan Wayans, with David Kitay (m.), Francis Kenny (DP), casting: Denise Doyle, Anne McCarthy, Christine Sheaks and Mary Vernieu, Robb Wilson King (prod. des), Darryle Johnson (cost.), Sandy Berman (sound des.), J.J. Makaro (stunt co-ord.), and Mark Helfrich (ed.). Released July 7, 2000. 90 mins.

In the cast were: Anna Faris, Regina Hall, Shawn Wayans, Marlon Wayans, Shannon Elizabeth, Jon Abrahams, Lochlyn Munro, Dave Sheridan, Cheri Oteri, Kurt Fuller and Carmen Electra. In the soundtrack were Tupac Shakur, Black-eyed Peas, Top Dogg, the Ramones, Bender, Public Enemy, and Silverchair.

The *Scary Movie* movies had some recurring cast members, such as Anna Faris, Regina Hall, Charlie Sheen, the Wayans brothers, Leslie

---

[18] Dimension released the movie (part of the Miramax group, run back then by the legendary Weinstein brothers).
[19] The Wayans were uncredited as producers.

Nielsen, Kevin Hart, Chris Elliott, Carmen Electra, and Molly Shannon.

The *Scary Movie* franchise peaked with the first movie in 2000, with a box office gross of $330 million in 2005 dollars, from a budget of $21.5 million in 2005 dollars. The 2nd movie dropped substantially, with $159 million in 2005 dollars from a budget of $49m in 2005 dollars.

Among the spoofs unrolled in *Scary Movie* were: *Buffy the Vampire Slayer, Dawson's Creek, The Sixth Sense, I Know What You Did Last Summer, The Shining, The Usual Suspects, Amistad, The Matrix* and *The Blair Witch Project*.

Jason Friedberg and Aaron Seltzer had written a send-up of horror movies entitled *Scream If You Know What I Did Last Hallowe'en*. It was sold to Dimension Pictures (part of Miramax) in 1998 by producer Peter Safran; Dimension put other writers on it, and the Wayans brothers also co-wrote the script. But the premise, the characters, and most of the situations come from Friedberg and Seltzer.

However, as we know, writers are far down the pecking order in terms of influence on a movie production – compared to film producers, big stars, important investors, toy manufacturers, studio executives and directors. Writers are commonly hired and fired like it's nothing. So once producers such as Eric Gold and Lee Mayes came on board, and the Wayans family, and the script was sold to Dimension, the Friedberg and Seltzer project became something else.

But some observers have wondered just how much of the script of *Scary Movie* written by Friedberg & Seltzer made it into the final film. Some have suggested that two scripts were being developed – one by Friedberg and Seltzer and one by the Wayans brothers. Miramax might've bought up the Friedberg-Seltzer script to keep it off the market, so that they could concentrate on the Wayans brothers' script (it's common practice for movie companies to buy up competing projects if they can, sometimes just to bury them so their own productions won't be affected). The Wayans later claimed that most of *Scary Movie* was derived from *their* script, and not much of the Friedberg and Seltzer script ended up in the movie (however, Friedberg and Seltzer have claimed that some of their jokes *did* appear in the final cut).

Anyway, the Writers' Guild decided that, yes, Friedberg and Seltzer *did* contribute significantly enough to *Scary Movie* to be given credits. (You can find the rules of credits and arbitration online). It does seem as if the first *Scary Movie* is more a Wayans brothers movie than a Friedberg & Seltzer movie; however, the approach to spoofs and jokes is very similar, and clearly draws on the Zucker-Abrahams-Zucker model (indeed, David Zucker directed two of the *Scary Movie* sequels, and produced the fifth one. Zucker also brought in many of the regular contributors to the Zucker-Abrahams-Zucker movies, in the cast as well as the crew).

The *Scary Movie* franchise began by spoofing the *Scream* franchise, which had been launched in 1996 with *Scream* (also produced by Dimension/ Miramax); but ended up going far beyond that, with multiple send-ups of numerous recent (mainly) North American movies. Of course, *Scream* (directed by veteran Wes Craven) was itself a knowing, postmodern and ironic deconstruction of the horror movie genre, and in particular recent horror movies (and director Craven had already unpacked the horror movie genre in a *Nightmare On Elm Street* film produced in 1994 called *New Nightmare*). Incidentally, the Kevin Williamson-scripted *Scream* was originally called *Scary Movie,* and the second sequel also appeared in 2000 (and it was helmed by Craven again).

Even as it sent up horror movies, *Scream* also presented a horror movie of its own, starring Neve Campbell as the 'final girl' evading a serial killer. *Scream* was a Hallowe'en party for people who'd attended too many trick or treat party nights, for teens who loved horror so much but were also bored and jaded by 'serious' or 'straight' horror flicks.

But even *Scream* (and its sequels) was somewhat smug and smart, still too 'look at us, aren't we clever?' – and it was ripe for spoofing. Enter the Wayans brothers,[20] a team which had already appeared on U.S. TV (they had their own sit-com, for ex).[21] And, like the best of the low budget horror flicks that they spoofed, the *Scary Movie* flicks were hits at the box office, with grosses of $190m, $200m, etc (when they hit big,

---

[20] Shawn Wayans (b. 1971) and Marlon Wayans (b. 1972)
[21] The Wayans' clan includes Keenan Wayans, Damon Wayans, Michael Wayans, Cara Wayans, Kyla Wayans, Kim Wayans, Shawn Wayans, Marlon Wayans, Nadia Wayans, Damien Wayans, Elvira Wayans, Chaunté Wayans, Craig Wayans, Summer Wayans, Vonnie Wayans, and Greg Wayans.

comedies, like horror movies, often have a strong cost-to-profit ratio that studios and producers find very appealing. However, with actors of that calibre, plus plenty of location shooting, visual effects, pricey music rights and high production standards, the *Scary Movie* productions weren't cheap – $19m, $40m, and $45m were some of the movies' individual negative costs).

The Wayans brothers (Shawn and Marlon) were key players in the first two *Scary Movie* pictures – they co-wrote as well as appeared in the movies, with their brother Keenan Ivory Wayans directing. However, the *Scary Movie* series was very much a collective effort as far as the writing went (which's common in American comedy television).

The Wayans had already explored spoof movie territory with films such as *Don't Be a Menace To South Central While You're Drinking Your Juice In the Hood* (Wayans/ Island, 1996). After *Scary Movie*, the Wayans continued to work in the spoof movie genre, with films such as *Dance Flick* (2009), *A Haunted House* (2013), and a *Fifty Shades of Grey* parody, *Fifty Shades of Black* (2016).

Guest stars and cameos were another staple of the *Scary Movie* franchise: Pamela Anderson, Denise Richards, Queen Latifah, Simon Cowell, Dr Phil, James Earl Jones, Lindsay Lohan, Snoop Dogg and Mike Tyson. They also drew on a group of established comedy actors, including Charlie Sheen, Leslie Nielsen and Tim Curry.

An important element in the *Scary Movie* series is the generous amount of screen time it gives to female characters and female comics. With American comedy in the 1990s and 2000s still dominated by men (Jim Carrey, Tim Allen, Robin Williams, Will Ferrell, Eddie Murphy, Martin Lawrence, Woody Allen, Ben Stiller, Adam Sandler, and Larry David), it was striking just how much of the *Scary Movie* franchise is given over to female characters.

The *Scary Movie* series was essentially part of the 'gross-out' style of comedy which developed in the late 1990s (*Road Trip*, *There's Something About Mary* and *American Pie*), combined with the Zucker-Abrahams-Zucker style of movie pastiches (*The Naked Gun*, *Hot Shots!*, *Mafia* and the genius comedy that trumps almost all other comedies since 1980: *Airplane!*). You could also detect Mel Brooks in there, Woody

Allen, the Marx Brothers, Richard Prior, *The Simpsons,* and of course *Saturday Night Live.* The *Scary Movie* series was thus also a *History of Comedy.*

The *Scary Movie* flicks were out-size, crude, fantastical, and very silly. They had a fabulously wild approach to comedy – it seemed as if the filmmakers would try *anything* to get a laugh, no matter how crazy. That devil-may-care, in-your-face attitude, combined with incredibly detailed, multi-layered (and very clever) deconstructions of favourite movies and favourite genres, made for a very appealing – and, crucially, very funny – series of movies.

Because often you didn't know where the movies were going to go, and that's a very rare thing in contemporary American cinema (except straight for the laugh, every time, of course). Let's face it, within ten minutes of most movies (no, five – no two), you know exactly what you're going to get, who the characters are, what they want, and how the story will play out.

In other words, *you've already seen this movie! Thousands of times!* The great thing about comedy, when it's working at its finest, is that sometimes you *don't* know where it's going. The scenes will be pushed to the limit, and then developed even further. There's a feeling of *freedom,* and of *danger.* Which, in terms of storytelling (which's what movies boil down to in the end), is exhilarating.

The *Scary Movies* combined dead simple, age-old slapstick comedy right out of silent comedies 80 years old, with ultra-smart, wise-ass humour of the *Saturday Night Live/ National Lampoon/ Simpsons* variety. And yet, like all great comedies, there is a carefully worked-out story, with characters and situations that have to follow the genre. Altho' the *Scary Movies appeared* to be free-form and scattershot, they were actually constructed along classical lines, with plots that took up regular narrative forms, and each script was rewritten numerous times. Even scenes which came over as stand-alone skits, like something from an anthology TV show or a TV special, were woven into the fabric of the overall concept and story

The DVD commentaries for the *Scary Movie* series are highly recommended. They offer, as with *The Simpsons'* commentaries, a workshop in comedy writing. Listen to how fast the writers and producers come up with quips and counter-quips, how quickly they put down someone else's idea ('it stank!', 'not funny!'), and how quickly they invent other ideas.

At the centre of the first four *Scary Movie* flicks was a sensational lead turn from Anna Faris (b. Nov 29, 1976, Baltimore). *Scary Movie* was one of her first roles. Faris throws herself into the movies with total committment – as you really need to do with this kind of film (why hold back? The films don't!). You have to trust the filmmakers and the (many) writers that they know what they're doing, and that it's going to be funny (film director David Zucker told his actors to be straight, not to try to be funny, and to let the comedy come out of the characters, the material, and the situations. Many comic filmmakers, such as Mel Brooks, have said the same thing).

Anna Faris isn't bothered at all about looking completely stupid (tho' she always looks gorgeous). In the first movie of 2000, Faris, only 24 at the time, displays a genius sense of comic timing combined with a wide-eyed, enthusiasm and cuteness worthy of Diane Keaton in Woody Allen's finest movies of the 1970s.

Looks easy, doesn't it? It isn't! Just as Diane Keaton (or Katy Hepburn or Margaret Dumont) made comedy acting look as if they were sailing thru it all breezily, without a care in the world, there's plenty of hard work, intuition, rehearsals, timing and great screenwriting in those roles. Everybody praises the Meryl Streeps and the Halle Berrys when they deliver a piece of 'Great Dramatic Acting', worthy of Academy Awards. (How often does the Oscar go to a comedy star, in a comedy movie?) But Anna Faris in the *Scary Movie* series is easily the equal of any of the 'Great Dramatic Actresses' of recent times (and she is a *lot* funnier, too!).

As everybody who's had a go at it knows – and if you think about it for even a milli-second you will realize – that the key to a great comedy movie is the writing, the writing, the writing. Of course, having terrific performers helps enormously (and the *Scary Movie* series certainly have that), and directors who understand both comedy and the genres and movies they're spoofing (and directors who keep the set-ups simple, and don't get too fussy). But at the heart of it all is *the writing*. This's where the concepts are hammered out, where writers and producers toss around ideas until they've come up with something that works, fits in the movie, and is amusing.

There's no formula, no secret recipe, and no quick and easy way of doing it. You have to rely, ultimately, on what makes *you* laugh. And that comes across very strongly in the *Scary Movie* flicks: you can see that the writers had a great time coming up with those preposterous concepts and scenes, and the filmmakers had a ball shooting them. These are movies made by movie *fans*; you can feel the enjoyment that the filmmakers have for movies in general, and for the movies they're spoofing in particular, all the way through.

SCARY MOVIE 2

Scary Movie 2 (2001) was backed by Dimension Films/ Brillstein-Grey/ Gold/ Miller/ Wayans Bros./ Brad Grey Pictures, prod. by Eric Gold, exec. prod. by Rick Alvarez, Tony Mark, Lee Mayes, Peter Schwein, Lisa Strode, Marlon Wayans, Shawn Wayans, Bob Weinstein, Harvery Weinstein and Brad Weston, dir. by Keenan Wayans, and wr. by Thomas Craig, Greg Grabianski, Alyson Fouse, Dave Polsky, Michael Anthony Snowden, Craig Wayans, Marlon Wayans and Shawn Wayans. Released July 4, 2001. 84 mins.

In the cast were: Anna Faris, Regina Hall, the Wayans brothers, James Woods,[22] Tim Curry, Tori Spelling,[23] Veronica Cartwright, Chris Elliott, Chris Masterson, Kathleen Robertson and David Cross.

(The Wayans family felt they were rushed into making *Scary Movie 2*, with the backers (including Dimension) demanding a movie too soon; the first outing had been amazingly successful, and the money-men saw

---

22 Woods was apparently paid $1 million for four days work. Marlon Brando had already filmed for one day, but left due to illness.
23 Daughter of Aaron Spelling.

dollar ign with a franchise. The experience soured the Wayanses, and they didn't return for the second sequel, *Scary Movie 3*).

Among the spoofs in *Scary Movie 2* were *The Exorcist, The Haunting, The Amityville Horror, Beetlejuice, The Legend of Hell House, Poltergeist, Hannibal, Hollow Man* and *The Changeling*. The movies were selected partly because they were based around the horror movie genre of the haunted house[24] (and the variants in horror flicks, such as Dracula's castle, the isolated Summer Camp, the remote shack in the woods).

The haunted mansion concept was aligned with a ghost hunter plot – Professor Oldman (Tim Curry) gathers together a bunch of youngsters at Hell House, in order to monitor the paranormal activity there. This supplies sufficient pretext for bringing together a range of characters, headed up by Anna Faris's clumsy, naïve, winsome girl-next-door character, Cindy. Marlon Wayans plays one of his familiar stoner, hip-hop idiots; his brother Shawn is a gay jock type. There's a paraplegic geek, an over-eager loser, and Regina Hall's excitable, scarily belligerent neurotic. But it's Chris Elliott as the caretaker Hanson who steals the movie with an over-the-top turn as a truly gross, pervy creep (with shades of *Beetlejuice*), along with the ever-dependable Anna Faris (many of the jokes need Faris's wide-eyed, innocent Cindy to work. Faris has got the air-head ditz persona spot-on).

The Exorcist (1973) is a movie that was 28 years old by the time of *Scary Movie 2*, but it's iconic, and everybody's seen it (and it's a fantastic blockbuster of a horror movie). *The Exorcist* had already been parodied in several movies (including *Repossessed*, 1990. Ironically, *Repossessed* was apparently reworked after previews because teenagers didn't get the references to the 1973 demonfest. But *The Exorcist* is one of the ten most significant horror movies in the history of the genre, along with *Nosferatu*, 1922, the 1931 *Dracula*, the 1931 *Frankenstein, Psycho*, 1960, and *Night of the Living Dead*, 1968).

The Exorcist spoof of course focusses on the demon-possessed girl in

---

[24] Later, the Wayans clan produced *A Haunted House* (2013), which was co-written and co-produced by Marlon Wayans and Rick Alvarez for I.M. Global/ Baby Way/ Endgame/ Automatik, and dir. by Michael Tiddes. In the cast were Wayans, Essence Atkins, Cedric, Nick Swardson, David Koechner, Dave Sheridan and Affion Crockett. Released Jan 11, 2013. 86 mins.

the bed, the spinning head, the crude insults and the inevitable vomiting (the scene degenerates into a vomiting contest). James Woods hams it up in the Max von Sydow role (as Father McFeely), eventually shooting Megan Voorhees in the face with a handgun, which closes the scene.

Apart from James Woods, among the cameos in *Scary Movie 2* were Veronica Cartwright (Cartwright's best-known role in horror movies is the hysterical astronaut in *Alien*, 1979; she was also one of the children in *The Birds*, 1963). Matt Friedman provides the voices of a foul-mouthed parrot in a cage.

The *Charlie's Angels* skit is a much-needed riposte to that cretinous movie franchise (inevitably, it's the martial arts fights that are spoofed. The girls in *Charlie's Angels* didn't convince on any level as warriors, and *Scary Movie 2* shows why). Marlon Wayans has his skull cut open *à la Hannibal* only to find rapper Beetlejuice from the Howard Stern Wack Pack inside (*Hannibal* is a truly horrible waste of money and time that cost an astonishing $87 million!). The *Hollow Man* send-up sees Tori Spelling enjoying a blowjob from the invisible phantom Hugh Kane (Richard Moll). The parody includes the gag from, of all things, the Fred Astaire movie *Royal Wedding* (1951), where Astaire danced on the walls and the ceiling. In *Scary Movie 2*, it's a girl and a ghost doing the nasty (while Hugh hollers over-the-top encouragement).

Along with the handjob jokes, there are girls pissing jokes, gay rape jokes (Ray takes the Clown), and more getting head jokes (this time in a car). A stupid bit with a puppet is mandatory in a spoof movie – here, it's Anna Faris duking it out with a cat.

Scary Movie 2 is one of the weaker installments in the franchise. The mix of movie parodies within the background context of the haunted house and this particular group of characters doesn't quite gel. But it is very funny in many scenes.

SCARY MOVIE 3

Scary Movie 3 was wr. by Pat Profit and Craig Mazin, prod. by David Zucker and Robert K. Weiss, and dir. by Zucker. Released Oct 24, 2003. 85 mins.

The up-for-it cast included: Anna Faris, Simon Rex, Charlie Sheen, Leslie Nielsen, Anthony Anderson, Kevin Hart, Camryn Manheim, George Carlin, Pamela Anderson, Jenny McCarthy, Queen Latifah,[25] Drew Mikuska, Jianna Ballard and Denise Richards.

Scary Movie 3 was a hit – $220 million gross from a budget of $48 mil. To widen the audience, the film rating was lowered to 'PG-13' from the 'R' rating of the previous two *Scary Movies*.

The Weinsteins at Miramax invited David Zucker to helm the third *Scary Movie* installment. He couldn't refuse – as he put it, he didn't want to wake up with a horse's head in his bed (exactly! – who wants to wake up like that?!). Of course, the *Scary Movie* series drew heavily on the model provided by the Zucker, Abrahams and Zucker movies, so Zucker directing seemed like a natural fit. (The Wayans fell out with the studio, Dimension, apparently – they felt they had been badly treated with the first *Scary Movie* sequel. Thus, a new team was put together to make the second *Scary Movie* sequel).

Leslie Nielsen appeared in *Scary Movie 3* as an idiotic U.S. President. You just have to look at Nielsen and you start laughing. Directing Nielsen was like driving a Lambourgini, David Zucker remarked.

Scary Movie 3 spoofed *A Beautiful Mind* (Ron Howard, 2001), about mathematics genius John Nash, played by Russell Crowe), *8 Mile* (the Eminem flick about a white rapper in Detroit), *The Matrix, Signs* (and other M. Night Shyamalan pictures), and movies such as *Jaws* and *The Ring* (the Japanese horror flick about a killer video tape, which was remade in the U.S.A. in 2002). And, in an abandoned ending, *The Hulk* (you can see this ending on the DVD, where David Zucker remarks that spoofing a movie that people *didn't* like is not a good place to start! But the abandoned ending does have many amusing bits in it).

---

[25] There's a 'rap battle' in *Scary Movie 3*, featuring many real rap artists (such as Macy Gray, Raekwon, Fat Joe, Redman and Method Man).

Scary Movie 3 benefitted greatly from the dreaded preview process. Most filmmakers absolutely *loathe* the Hollywood studios' insistence of putting their movies before suburban audiences, to test their reactions, with score cards and comments. In the case of a comedy movie, it can help: you never know if something's going to play and be funny until it's actually screened before an audience (the Zucker-Abrahams-Zucker team employed previews to polish their films). So the filmmakers were able to go back and not just tweak the movie, but cut out whole swathes of it, and replace it with about a third of new material. That meant substantial rewrites[26] and reshoots (far, far more than on most movies). But it worked. Out went the Incredible Hulk vs. the aliens ending, the extended *Matrix* fights, our heroes battling nasty aliens, Denise Richards as Charlie Sheen's wife cooking in the kitchen (and having sex using the front end of a truck),[27] and plenty of other scenes (despite some of the material being very funny).

If you read the interviews and listen to the audio commentaries about *Scary Movie 3*, you'll hear about the writers trying all sorts of things to get a laugh. Concepts were hashed out, developed, but then ditched. Scenes were shot then dropped. A whole new ending was written and filmed. The writers are very quick to acknowledge anything that didn't work, and they are savage in their dismal of anything that doesn't raise a laugh: 'it stank', 'it sucked', 'it didn't work'. These comments come up all the time in the filmmakers' audio commentary as the deleted scenes play in *Scary Movie 3* (and some of the scenes in the finished movie!). On the plus side, you can feel the pride when something *did* work, which the writers *did* find funny.

With the advent of DVD and home entertainment formats, those deleted scenes and unused endings could be enjoyed. You can see how the scenes are both skits that work on their own, but how they are also part of the overall structure. It's a big mistake to regard a comedy movie as simply a series of comical sketches put end-to-end. No. The scenes are also part of a story, they are placed within the structure carefully. They are discussed and analyzed at length in the editing process (which in comedy

---

26 The actors recalled the movie was being rewritten all the time.
27 This is a sort of extended run on the scene in *Top Secret* where Omar Shariff is imprisoned in a car that's been thru a compactor. As a woman leans over him and presses her cleavage in his face, the car's aerial extends.

is absolutely ruthless: if it doesn't get a laugh, out it goes! Even scenes that the filmmakers and writers lavished weeks on writing and shooting are jettisoned if they don't generate laughs).

SCARY MOVIE 4

The credits: produced by Dimension Films/ Miramax/ Brad Grey Pictures, Robert K. Weiss and Craig Mazin (prod.), Jim Abrahams, Craig Mazin and Pat Profit (wr.), David Zucker (dir.), Craig Herring and Tom Lewis (eds.), James Venerable (m.) and Thomas Ackerman (DP). Released Apl 14, 2006. 83 mins.

Scary Movie 4 continued the delightful parody series of the *Scary Movie* franchise, with the amazing Anna Faris again back at the top of the cast (which included cameos and turns from Carmen Electra, Regina Hall, Charlie Sheen, Leslie Nielsen, Chris Elliott, Kevin Hart, Cloris Leachman, Shaquille O'Neal, Molly Shannon, Michael Madsen, Anthony Anderson, Bill Pullman, Dr Phil and, incredibly, Mike Tyson. James Earl Jones also shows up at the end, as the serious narrator).

Among the parodies in *Scary Movie 4* were *War of the Worlds* (the desperately serious and straight Steven Spielberg remake of the 1950s classic science fiction movie), *The Village* (another dreadfully earnest and seriously dreadful 'thriller' or 'mystery' directed by M. Night Shyamalan), *The Grudge, Million Dollar Baby, Hustle & Flow, The Oprah Winfrey Show, King Kong, Saw, Final Destination, Deuce Bigalow: European Gigolo, Scooby Doo* and *Brokeback Mountain*.

Again, the attention to detail and the care with which the movie parodies were staged was so impressive. The filmmakers took the time to include so many aspects of the originals, as to be virtual copies. Except the people in the stories are very dumb. Plus some send-ups of cinematic conventions. That's how the production team approached their movie: it wasn't a political satire of some Big Issue, it was movie spoofing).

Providing one of the main spines of the story of *Scary Movie 4* was *War of the Worlds*: *Scary Movie 4* reproduced the 2005 sci-fi/ disaster movie extraordinarily accurately, sometimes barely having to deviate from the original to create laughter. The visual effects and practical effects were very effective, one could intercut the shots with the 2005 movie and not notice the difference. Again, the parody of *Scary Movie* revealed just how delightfully *moronic* these big blockbuster movies are – movies that are taken so seriously and literally. The movie closed with a terrific send-up of Tom Cruise's insane performance on *The Oprah Winfrey Show*.

The Village (2004) was a very silly movie: the concept, the characters and the scenario was tailor-made for the *Scary Movie* writing team to parody. The po-faced earnestness of M. Night Shyamalan's movies (as well as some of Steven Spielberg's work) was ripe for sending up. Bill Pullman played the patriarch of the *Village* community, with Carmen Electra providing a wonderfully ditzy turn as a blind woman.

Meanwhile, Anna Faris's Cindy Campbell, the star of the *Scary Movie* series, hooked up with Regina Hall's Brenda to explore the village (the two stories – *War of the Worlds* and *The Village* – fuse at the beginning, but then diverge, because the *War of the Worlds* narrative doesn't have a place for a young female star in its later stages).

One of the most amusing scenes in *Scary Movie 4* is very simple: two people talking in a room. It's a variation on the subtitles gag (which Woody Allen used so brilliantly in *Annie Hall*), as Cindy rattles off a list of Japanese brand names and famous phrases to the boy ghost spooking the house, and he replies in kind: Fujitsu, tsunami, etc (meanwhile, the subtitles translate along the lines of, 'what makes you think I give a shit what you're saying?').

There's a terrific send-up of *Brokeback Mountain*, as CJ and Mahalik camp out in a tent (very camp!). Out comes the vaseline, the baby oil, the rubber gloves, the shin pads, the battery (for electric shocks), and the gerbil.

Again the DVD commentary for *Scary Movie 4* is very funny (it featured David Zucker, Bob Weiss and Craig Mazin), and offers plenty of amusing insights into how the film was made. And the deleted scenes – never meant to be seen! – demonstrate the writers and filmmakers trying out things that didn't, in the end, prove to be so amusing. They are, again, very dismissive of their own efforts.

Part of the problem with writing/ making comedy is that you don't know *for sure* what will make an audience laugh – until it's there, in front of the audience. You write what makes *you* laugh, and hopefully the audience will like it too. But you never know *for certain* (altho' there *are* some mainstays of comedy, as there are in any genre. Filmmakers know that certain things usually work. But with laughter there's no guarantee!). Hence, the previewing process, where many comedy filmmakers have refined their works.

SCARY MOVIE 5

Scary Movie 5 was prod. by David Zucker and Phil Dornfeld for Brad Grey Pictures and Dimension Films, wr. by Pat Profit and David Zucker, and dir. by Malcolm Lee, with Sam Seig (ed.), Steven Douglas Smith (DP), and James L. Venable (m.). Released Apl 12, 2013. 86 mins.

In the cast were: Ashley Tisdale, Simon Rex, Erica Ash, Molly Shannon, Heather Locklear, J.P. Manoux, Jerry O'Connell, Charlie Sheen and Lindsay Lohan, with cameos from Mike Tyson, Snoop Dogg, Usher, Terry Crews, Tyler Perry and Big Ang.

Scary Movie 5 was filmed in Georgia (Atlanta) and Los Angeles (the Sunset Gower Studios) on a budget of $20 million. It grossed $78m.

The parodies in *Scary Movie 5* included: *Black Swan, Mama, Sinister, Rise of the Planet of the Apes, Inception, Fifty Shades of Grey, Ted, Saw, The Ring, Evil Dead, Paranormal Activity, The Cabin In the Woods, Insidious, 127 Hours, The Day the Earth Stood Still* and *The Help.*

Altho' *Scary Movie 5* was written by two terrific comedy writers who have made millions of people laugh – David Zucker and Pat Profit – it didn't quite work. Maybe it was exhaustion for the audience – we have seen this movie before, and it was the fifth installment in a series. Certainly the direction (by Malcolm Lee) isn't as punchy as the previous entries. And the casting lacked something – we miss Anna Faris in the lead role; her replacement, Ashley Tisdale (a Disney graduate), is not in the same league (and her eye-rolling becomes irritating). Similarly, Simon Rex, playing the well-meaning but useless husband, is not as entertaining as some of the previous cast members.

But parts of *Scary Movie 5* were funny. The skit where 100s of home appliances have a pool party was terrific – vacuum cleaners snorting bleach and drinking was a suitably ridiculous notion (it's the dream/nightmare of the Mexican home help, Lidio Porto). Having a toy car driving along a garden path at night instead of the usual flashy helicopter shot (while the characters speak in voiceover) was amusing. Snoop Dogg has a speech that's bleeped out with every other word.

The opening skit of *Scary Movie 5* featuring Charlie Sheen and Lindsay Lohan sending up their hellraiser/ law-breaker media personas was good fun (an entire wall of Sheen's bedroom is set up with video cameras, and the other wall a library of sex tapes).

There were plenty of very crude jokes in *Scary Movie 5*, as we've come to expect from the franchise. In the *Planet of the Apes* scenes, for instance, there's a lengthy run of super-racist jokes likening black men to apes and gorillas. That was part of the ideological project of the original *Planet of the Apes* movie of 1968, of course, but in *Scary Movie 5* it's completely turned around. (But Caesar is right – humans are a pathetic race. That observation must've come from Pat Profit).

A lengthy riff on lesbian sex between Kendra and Jody features some classic, Zuckerian gags, including a twist on one of the stand-ins for sex in movies – a train entering a tunnel. This time, it's two tunnels bashing into each other – plastic tunnels from a toy train set.

Much of the humour comes from the multiple cameras set around the house, and recording everything, apeing shows like *Paranormal Activity* (which had been spoofed in *A Haunted House*, released the same year, 2013, and starring Marlon Wayans). *Scary Movie 5* milks the CCTV motif as much as possible, including speeded-up replays which echo one of silent cinema's regular comedy routines.

The twaddle of *Inception* is spoofed in a series of dream sequences: this is a gift to Zucker and Profit (they have used the structure before): it means they can have the dreamer thinking of all sort of scenarios (they used it in *Airplane!*, for example). One is the house party of the pool cleaners; another has Jody humping a microwave in bed (and a potted plant – 'that explains the ivy'); another has Jody being inducted into the S/M realm of *Fifty Shades of XXXX*.

Of course, film critics loathed *Scary Movie 5*: 'flatlines right out of the gate' (*Toronto Star*); 'faintly amusing' (*New York Times*); 'the pacing alternates between frenzied and stoned' (*L.A. Times*); 'barely a single laugh' (*Movie Nation*).

Maximum Risk (1996).

Spy Hard (1996), this page and over.

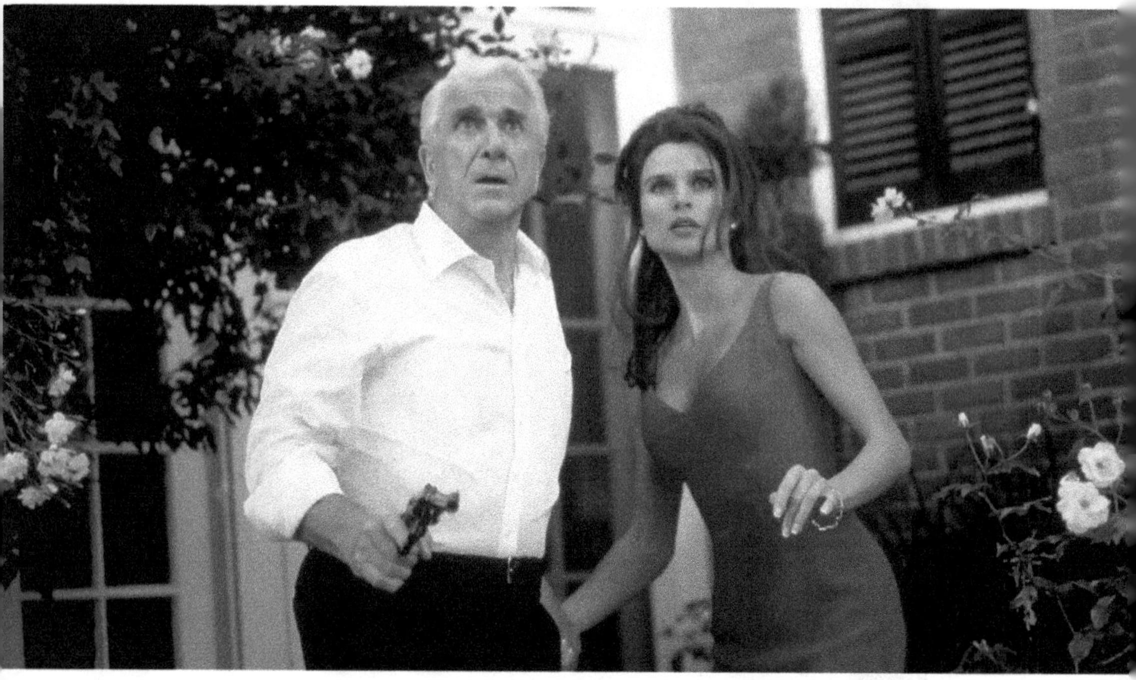

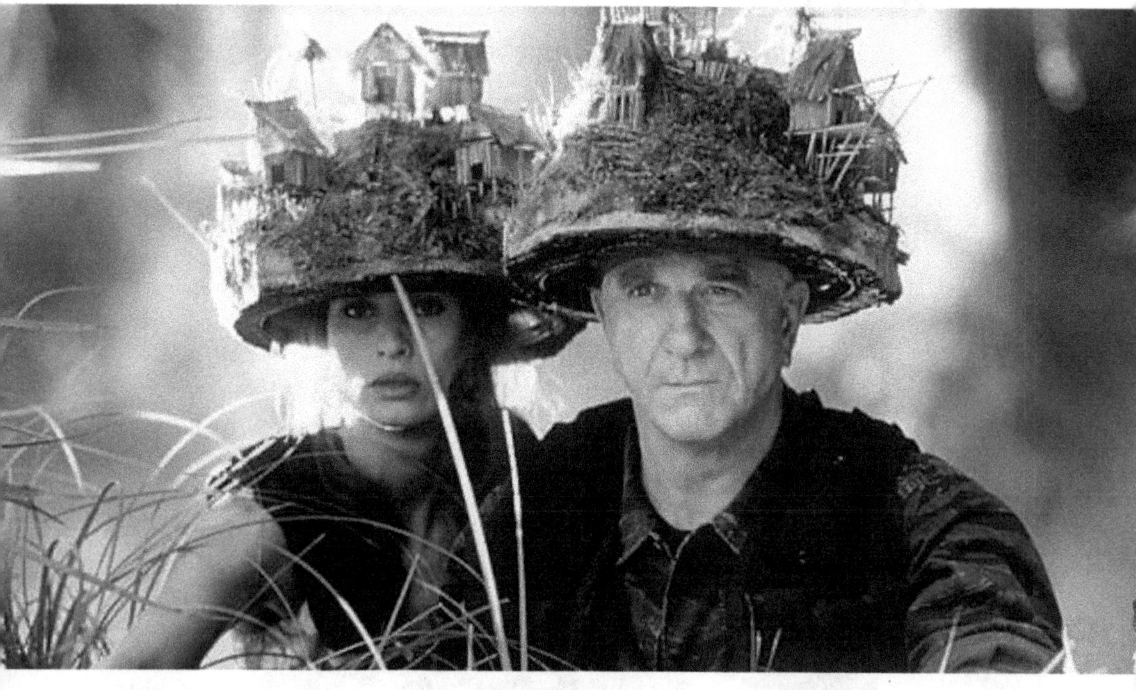

Scary Movie (2000), this page and over.

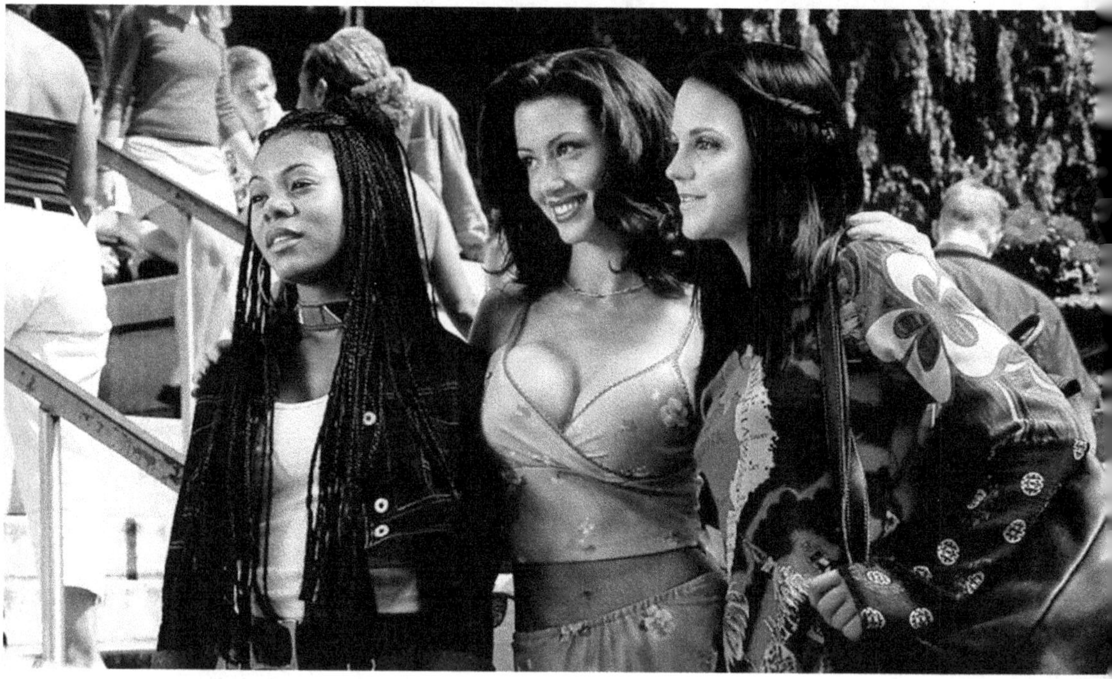

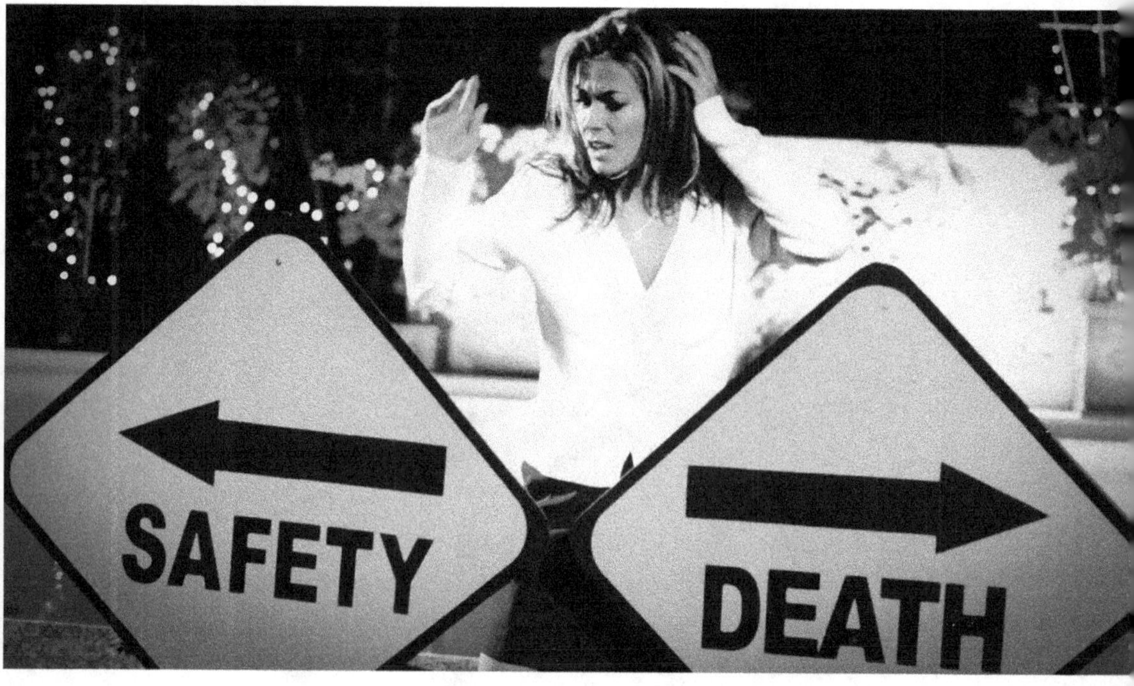
SAFETY
DEATH

Scary Movie 2 (2001), above. Scary Movie 4 (2006), below.

4

DATE MOVIE

Produced by Regency Enterprises/[1] Epsilon Motion Pictures/ New Regency, the crew of *Date Movie* (2006) included: Arnon Milchan (exec. prod.), Paul Schiff, Jack L. Murray and Jason Friedberg (prods.), wr. and dir. by Aaron Seltzer and Friedberg, David Kitay (m.), Shawn Maurer (DP), Amanda Harding and Amanda Koblin (casting), William A. Elliott (prod. des.), Daniel A. Lomino (art dir.), Alix Friedberg (Jason Friedberg's sister, costumes), Rebecca Alling and Debbie Zoller (make-up), Candace Neal and Teressa Hill (hair), Terry Leonard (2nd unit dir.), Hal Olofsson (1st A.D.), Anna MacKenzie (supervising sound editor), Keith Adams (stunt co-ordinator), and Paul Hirsch (ed.). Released: Feb 17, 2006. 83 mins.

In the cast were Alyson Hannigan, Carmen Electra, Josh Meyers, Adam Campbell, Meera Simhan, Marie Matiko, Judah Friedlander, Tony Cox, Mauricio Sanchez, Fred Willard, Jennifer Coolidge, Eddie Griffin and Aussie super-model Sophie Monk.

Jason Friedberg and Aaron Seltzer (then 36 and 32) apparently got the gig of directing *Date Movie* because Regency Enterprises couldn't attract a director to sign up.[2] This happens more often than one would

---

[1] The other films released by Regency in 2006 were: *The Fountain, The Sentinel, Deck the Halls, Just My Luck, Big Momma's House 2* and *My Super Ex-Girlfriend.*
[2] Friedberg and Seltzer pitched themselves to the company as directors with storyboards and ideas.

think in the film industry: there might be 3,000 film directors clamouring for only 70 directing jobs (a rough estimate from the 1980s/ 1990s), but not every director is available for every movie, or the schedules don't match – there are any number of reasons. (Scheduling and availability account for a good deal about whether movies get made – it's not only being the right person for the job, or having experience or talent, or being the right price, or even knowing the right people. And *Date Movie* was a very particular kind of movie – a parody comedy, and in the rom-com genre. That would automatically put off many film directors).

Date Movie was filmed mainly in L.A., including the backlot at Fox, and locations such as a house on Wilshire, a garage on La Cienga, and Rodeo Drive. The schedule was short (32 days), and the budget was low ($20m). (However, shooting in Tinseltown meant that the production could secure some impressive crew members, such as Bill Elliott and Paul Hirsch, so they could travel from home, rather than on location, as Friedberg and Seltzer point out in the audio commentary).

Shooting their first movie as directors was a blast, as Jason Friedberg said:

> For us, who had only been writers for years and years, to actually hear actors saying our lines and see our characters living and breathing, and seeing what you've created on a blank page is thrilling and still is thrilling.

Alyson Hannigan (b. 1974, Washington, DC) is best-known for playing Buffy's b.f. Willow in *Buffy the Vampire Slayer* and the long-suffering girlfriend and Band Camp geek Michelle Flaherty in the wonderful *American Pie* movie series (one of many forerunners of the Jason Friedberg and Aaron Seltzer comedies, which they refer to). Hannigan has also done tons of television (*How I Met Your Mother, Penn & Teller: Fool Us, Veronica Mars,* etc), and many other movies.

Alyson Hannigan has a charming 'girl next door' quality; she's a good comedienne (great at playing straight and sweet), and has a kilowatt smile that lights up the screen. In every scene, she is adorable. This is Hannigan's movie, and she's happy to try anything (and to look completely ridiculous in numerous scenes). Friedberg and Seltzer say they sort of wrote the movie with Hannigan in mind; there are other actresses who could've played Julia Jones, but Hannigan is perfect casting.

Adam Campbell as Grant Fockyerdoder does a terrific Hugh Grant turn (tho' he's much funnier than the terribly over-rated Grant, one of the poorest exports Great Britain has ever made). Campbell is happy to try anything, and doesn't hold back. He is given some of the movie's funniest moments.

Eddie Griffin is scary as Julia Jones's possessive, domineering dad, who's keen to have her marry the hopeless, grubby slob, Nicky (Judah Friedlander), rather than Grant (because Nicky is Jewish, Greek, Japanese, Indian and American). Griffin delivers his comical lines in a deadpan manner, which makes them funnier (Griffin had already appeared in parody movies, such as *Coneheads* (1993), the *Scary Movie* series and *Undercover Brother* (Malcolm Lee, 2002), an under-rated and wonderful comedy with a similar approach as the Friedberg-Seltzer movies).

Jennifer Coolidge delivers a terrific, very funny Barbara Streisand caricature (and frightening Jewish Mom), complete with the nose and the hair (and Streisand is a juicy target for parody; here, Coolidge's Roz Fockyerdoder utters meaningless, momsy, Yiddish spiel, is alarmingly upbeat, and gives outrageous sex therapist tips). Fred Willard[3] is great, as ever, as Grant's liberal, old-but-still-cool father, Bernie Fockyerdoder. The film sends up the couple as faddish New Agers.[4] Meera Simhan is solid as Julia's Indian Mom, prim and quirky. Tony Cox, who became a regular in the F.-S. troupe, is very funny as the love therapist Hitch; Cox has several scenes with Alyson Hannigan in the fat suit – they make a delightful odd couple. And there are the usual lookalikes in a Friedberg and Seltzer outing: Michael Jackson,[5] Britney Spears, Napoleon Dynamite, Ben Stiller, Owen Wilson, Gandalf and Frodo,[6] etc.

Jason Friedberg and Aaron Seltzer are dubbed the 'worst directors in the world', but the 'worst directors in the world' certainly would *not* be able to hire a legendary editor like Paul Hirsch. One of the three editors of the original *Star Wars* movie of 1977 (for which he, Marcia Lucas and Richard Chew rightly won an Oscar), Hirsch (b. 1945, New York City)

---
[3] Both Willard and Coolidge ad-libbed some of their lines.
[4] Though they have a luxurious home in what looks like Beverly Hills.
[5] Seen in the background trying to pick up a young boy.
[6] Selling the One Ring in Tiffany's for 50 bucks.

has an incredible resumé of top movies which includes: *The Empire Strikes Back, Ferris Bueller's Day Off, Ray, Planes, Trains and Automobiles, Lake Placid, Mighty Joe Young, Footloose, Falling Down, Hard Rain, Phantom of the Paradise, The Secret of My Success, Steel Magnolias,* and *The Mummy.* Hirsch is best-known for his collaborations with Brian de Palma (11 features – including *Carrie, The Fury, Mission Impossible* and *Obsession*).

Date Movie is a parody of the romantic comedy, the 'rom-com' or 'chick flick'. We've all sat thru them – the masterpieces (*Annie Hall, Bringing Up Baby, His Girl Friday*), the so-so ones *(When Harry Met Sally,*[7] *Pretty Woman, Sleepless In Seattle*), and the dreadful ones (*Bridget Jones Diary, Notting Hill, Music and Lyrics, About a Boy, Four Weddings and a Jerk*). Some of the main plot of *Date Movie* derives from *My Big Fat Greek Beheading, Bridget Jones's Friary* and *Meet the Parents* (but it is also an all-purpose, all-terrain romantic movie plot).

The critics panned it, but many cinema-goers went to see *Date Movie* (to the tune of $79 million gross theatrically. And over a million DVDs were sold). But spoof movies are not made for crrritics! They are for mass audiences in multiplexes, and for folks watching at home or on airplanes or in hotels. (Frederic Jameson, postmodern theorist supremo (*Postmodernism, or the Cultural Logic of Late Capitalism*), found *Date Movie* 'an exhilarating celebration of the implacable bitter-sweetness of Western, consumer capitalism'. I kid).

I liked *Date Movie*. It was fun, it was upbeat and amazingly optimistic, it was gross in parts, it had a winning performance by Alyson Hannigan as Julia Jones, a talented supporting cast, and it delivered plenty of successful movie spoofs. True, *Date Movie* wasn't the funniest comedy, or the most entertaining spoof movie, but did it really deserve the bile it generated among film critics? (Some walked out, some complained there wasn't a single laugh, some sued Regency Enterprises and 20th Century Fox for $10 million, etc).

The vitriol that *Date Movie* received from some viewers was scary in its intensity. Online user reviews (at Internet Movie Database, Metacritic,

---

[7] A Woody Allen clone in many respects.

Amazon, etc) lay into *Date Movie* as if it's Nazi propaganda calling for the extermination of all non-Ayrans. A sensitive, vulnerable filmmaker might give up and go home after reading some of the reviews of their first movie as a director.

Repeatedly, viewers who hated the movie objected to (1) paying for it, and (2) for the movie wasting their time. The issue seems to be primarily that *Date Movie* is not what viewers were expecting. It wasn't funny, and they were expecting a comedy.

Complainers can be louder than those who enjoyed a movie (the *Star Wars* franchise is the obvious case for attracting *really* loud complainers): it's surprising just how many viewers have added their ten cents of gripes to websites and the like that feature user reviews. But *Date Movie* was certainly enjoyed by many, too: the viewers who appreciated *Date Movie* advise the grumblers to lighten up.

How can you not enjoy a movie where the grossly overweight heroine (dressed top to toe in bright pink) goes to a relationship advisor who turns out to be a black midget called Hitch, and his first words when he sees her fat, pink form looming over him are: 'oh, hell, no!' (Tony Cox is a delight in his scenes with Alyson Hannigan. The 'krumping' scene is amazing – especially in the expanded scenes).[8] Hitch helps the love lives of celebrities (Brad and Angelina, Tom and Katie, Miss Piggy and Kermit, etc). In the scene where Julia tries out kissing with Hitch, disastrously (to the music of Barry White, of course), there's a bizarre cut to a photo of Tom Cruise and Katie What's-her-name.

It's typical that the first movie helmed by the Jason Friedberg and Aaron Seltzer duo should be in the romantic comedy genre, should focus on a young woman, and should include several musical numbers. *Date Movie* opens with a big musical sequence, and features dancing[9] in many scenes (such as in Hitch's office). It's typical for Friedberg and Seltzer, but it's unusual as a first movie (some film directors in their whole career never put a young woman in the leading role. And many of the most celebrated directors in film history have never attempted a full-on comedy movie. And plenty of macho directors would die rather than feature girls

---

8 The long wig helps to disguise the other dancers who performed the scene (one was Allison Kyler), as well as the sudden appearance of face make-up.
9 Travis Payne was choreographer.

dancing in pink costumes their films).

Set in a bright, colourful, chocolate box New York City,[10] *Date Movie* pivots around the chief desire of all romantic comedies: finding a mate. It's announced in the opening scene, introducing us to Julia Jones as she dreams of marriage[11] (the first shot of *Date Movie* is of Julia in a white wedding dress in a sunlit park: this is how she imagines herself). The dream (featuring the first gag in *Date Movie*), functions exactly the same way as in a straight rom-com movie: it delineates the gulf between the heroine's dreams and her reality. (The joke – that the hoped-for wonderful man turns out to be a ditz (in the form of Napoleon Dynamite) – is also tied to the key goal of *Date Movie*: where can our heroine find a decent man? Can she find true love?).

Some viewers griped that *Date Movie* was merely thirty or more spoofs of movies strung together. No. Not even close. *Date Movie*'s script is actually carefully worked out structurally, and the film hits all of the expected beats in a romantic plot. For example, it creates multiple obstacles for the heroine, includes reflective, doubtful moments for her, features narrative devices such as flashbacks, changes (reversals) of fortune, unexpected twists, and so on.

Thus, *Date Movie* – despite what film critics say – *is* a solid script, structurally – it opens with a scene of the heroine fantasizing about finding true le*rrr*ve; and when she wakes, we see she's not the princess she'd like to be, and the gulf between that is part of the narrative engine that drives the piece.

And *Date Movie* takes up one of the most common, the most loved, and the easiest of scripts to write: a romance. Here's the formula:

1. You create a heroine.
2. You create desire/ longing/ yearning in the character.
3. You introduce her to an object of desire (or several choices).
4. You fashion a convincing means of keeping them apart.

This last mandate is the most important bit – you can keep them apart using gimmicks such as: two warring families (*Romeo and Juliet*), different social classes (*Tess of the d'Urbverilles*), or even different

---
[10] Yet *Date Movie* doesn't go for the lyrical views of Gotham of the typical New York-set rom-com. So we don't have Central Park, the Hudson, the Empire State Bldg, and all the Gotham sights.
[11] The dream in the deleted scenes includes Julia disastrously riding a horse.

species (vampires and humans – *Twilight*). Or, he's gay, he's dead, he's a squirrel, etc.

Date Movie uses the differences in class and family for one of the obstacles (the gulf between the down-to-earth New Yorkers and the New Agers on the West Coast Julia reckons is too much for her to overcome).

Other hurdles for Julia's quest for happiness through love is her father Frank Jones: he's determined that she will marry super-slob Nicky. This subplot is woven into the movie at intervals (for example, Nicky joins the Joneses visiting the Fockyerdoders,[12] where Daddy presents Nicky again to his daughter). The subplot is played out in full in *Date Movie*. Frank persuades Julia to accept Nicky after things have gone South with Grant Fockyerdoder, and it goes as far as a wedding ceremony.

Act two of *Date Movie* introduces the formidable threat of the Ex-Girlfriend From Hell, Andy. Impossibly beautiful, with a super-model body (and a girl who can fashion miniature carousels from cherry stalks in her mouth), it seems as if Julia doesn't have a chance. And Julia has doubts about herself several times – she's haunted by her former fat self, for example, in the mirror (her father appears there, too).

The 2006 movie ends happily ever after, of course[13] – the wedding is the 'simple but elegant' ceremony that Julia Jones asked for. It is filmed in the same sunny location as the dream sequence (so our girl gets her dream).

Romantic comedies have been one of the staples among film genres since the silent age of Hollywood. Every year a new batch is released. The term 'romantic comedy' is a misnomer, of course, for romantic comedies from the 1960s to today: most of these movies are *not* comedies. Nor are they especially 'romantic'. A more accurate term is a relationship movie with a few jokes added. Or a melodrama (or soap opera) with some humour added. The *comedy* aspect of the genre 'romantic comedy' really means a lighthearted approach to a romance/ relationship story. That is, it won't be a romance where the heroine viciously kicks a down-and-out guy on the ground – that occurs in spoof romances like *Date Movie*.

12 By travelling *Cape Fear*-style, underneath the R.V.
13 The end credits include outtakes.

Thus, *Annie Hall* can be properly classed as a romantic comedy because it is (1) very romantic, and (2) very funny. But *Bridget Jones's Diary* is *not* a romantic comedy, no way, nohow, because it is (1) not romantic, and (2) not funny. At all.

Rom-coms are also cheap to produce, like urban thrillers – it's two pretty people in a contemporary setting. And most of the scenes comprise two people talking. Occasionally kissing. Often arguing. Mix and repeat the formula (adding obstacles as necessary) until the final clinch in the final reel.

Date Movie exposed the smugness of pretty much every recent romantic 'comedy' movie – that self-satisfied, self-righteous self-absorption, where middle-class characters in nice, middle-class homes (which're always luxurious, yet they never seem to work)[14] in nice, middle-class cities (curiously devoid of crime, poverty or sleaze), swoon and simper and chatter and feel smug about their relationships. You want to punch the stars of rom-coms: Renee Zellwegger, Meg Ryan, Helen Hunt and bloody Julia Roberts, and their beaus: Hugh Grant, Adam Sandler, Owen Wilson, Tom Hanks, Mel Gibson and Colin Firth.

Romantic comedies are Hollywood cinema at its most conservative, self-righteous and conceited – yet also Hollywood cinema at its best (when it works). *Date Movie* doesn't seriously challenge the rom-com movie genre, but it does draw attention to the disturbing self-satisfaction and narcissism of rom-coms, where characters are obsessed with their own petty lives and exclude everything else.

As usual in a Jason Friedberg and Aaron Seltzer movie, there is a ton of music in *Date Movie* – existing pop/ rock/ hiphop music, that is, in addition to the incidental music (written by David Kitay, the composer of *Scary Movie*).[15] The amount of music, and how it's presented, reminds us that the spoof/ parody movie is very close to the musical movie genre in form: the short, stand-alone sequences (the comical skits), the variety of music, the exaggerated presentation, characters as types, and even the primary theme of musicals – romance.

---

14 The production design in the home of the Joneses was perfect in its starched bourgeois atmosphere. But for folks who run a diner, it was a swanky home.
15 Dave Jordan and Jojo Villanueva were music supervisors; Michael T. Ryan was supervising music editor; William Levine was orchestrater.

Many of the skits in *Date Movie* required a particular piece of music to make them really work (and some gags are based around a certain song: for instance, the kissing scene with Barry White; Grant and Julia singing their favourite song to each other; the opening musical/ dance number; Grant holding up a ghetto blaster to woo back Julia; the ensemble song in the engagement party; and the cheesy scary music in the *Kill Bill* spoof.

Date Movie includes music by Soundmaster, Richard Wagner, the Pussycat Dolls, Kelis, Roy Orbison, Burt Bacharach, 50 Cent, the Lovin' Spoonful, Player, Alana D., Quincy Jones, the Perfectionists, Dieter Reith, Classic, Sparklemotion, Barry White, Pitbull,[16] Jack Trombey, Ennio Morricone, Daniel May, Ixya Herrera, Latisha Bonita, David Kitay, Nick Haydn, Twista, Fili Style & Tenashus, Todd Schietroma, Michael T. Ryan and Journey.

★

There are Latino elements in *Date Movie*, as in most Jason Friedberg and Aaron Seltzer movies: Eduardo the Fockyerdoder's housekeeper, for ex (Mauricio Sanchez), and Jell-O (Valery Ortiz as J. Lo). Even more Hispanic actors were cast in subsequent movies by the directors.

The look of *Date Movie* (courtesy of Shawn Maurer, DP, Bill Elliott, production designer, Daniel A. Lomino, art direction, Teresa Visinare, set decoration, and Alix Friedberg, costumes), captures the impossibly positive and upbeat quality of the feel-good romantic comedy picture. Blue skies, pink tracksuits, and sunny, flowery settings (for the wedding) predominate. This is New York City at its Disney theme park chintziest, far away from the sleazy, crime-ridden streets of urban thriller movies.

Date Movie included plenty of stuntwork, as in the rest of the movies of Friedberg and Seltzer, and in parody/ spoof movies in general (Keith Adams was stunt co-ordinator). Some of the stunts were dangerous – like a stunt person being yanked back a long way on a wire, with a harness (in Julia's bedroom).[17]

★

Date Movie on DVD contains three commentaries. The writer-directors (Jason Friedberg and Aaron Seltzer) are pretty straightforward;[18]

---

[16] Lil Jon has a cameo.
[17] Stunt guys have had their legs broken doing this stunt.
[18] Friedberg and Seltzer even worry about how their audio commentary will be reviewed – after having their movies slated.

and, no, they are not comedy terrorists (the Zucker-Abrahams-Zucker team have recalled how they would go to press conferences, and journos would expect them to be wildly funny. But they weren't. Actually, that's not true: the audio commentaries to the Z.A.Z. movies are great!). However, in between the bleeps and meanderings, there are some nuggets in the commentary. (Like, Friedberg and Seltzer were buzzed to have veteran editor Paul Hirsch chose to edit their movie. Like, the schedule of 32 days was very tight.)

The second DVD commentary for *Date Movie* is the actors (with giggly accounts of on-set goings-on – it was often cold, or too hot,[19] and the night shoots went on forever). But *Date Movie* is very unusual in featuring an 'anti-commentary' from two L.A. critics, Scott Foundas (*L.A. Weekly*) and Bob Strauss (*Los Angeles Daily News*). They had both trashed the movie in print, but were invited to provide a commentary! (Not many filmmakers would go for that!).[20]

I have to admit to listening to only about ten minutes of it: the commentary reveals why film critics and spoof movies do not mix. For instance, during the opening musical number of *Date Movie*, the critics wonder if fat people are funny. Well, *duuuh*! Yes, fat people *are* funny! In fact, they've been a staple of comedy for at least two thousand years! And the guy that everybody agrees is the Greatest Writer In History Ever, William Shakespeare, created comedies about fat people: Falstaff in the history plays, and in *Twelfth Night*.

And yet – once again, in the face of the ire of the film critics – *Date Movie* did actually deliver a carefully worked-out story, hitting every beat of the typical romantic comedy. The puerile plot points, the cute meeting, the too-obvious reversals of fortune, the anxiety over rivals in love, the stupid set-backs before the final reunion, the conservative ideology, and of course the dumb-as-concrete dialogue, with its sickly platitudes and home-spun, down-home philosophy – these're all ingredients of your average rom-com outing.

The casting of Alyson Hannigan, and the way that Hannigan inhabits

---

19 It always is during filming. And it's always cold when it's a Summer scene, and too hot when it's a snow scene.
20 Actually, tho', it might be entertaining hearing famous hacks like Pauline Kael or Roger Ebert ripping apart movies they've loathed for 80 minutes.

the role of Julia Jones (so sweet, so adorable!), indicates as soon as we meet her that everything will turn out all right. Nobody could possibly injure Hannigan and get away with it – they would be hunted down and slaughtered with samurai swords.

But that's the way with all rom-com movies – as soon as Meg Ryan, J. Lo, Liv Tyler or Julia Roberts appears in their first, glowing close-up in a romantic comedy, we know all will be well.

On the down side, some of the staging, direction and editing of the scenes seemed off in *Date Movie*. Some scenes were milked (!) for every ounce of humour, way beyond the usual requirements: the cat puppet Jinxers shitting on the toilet, for instance, or Sophie Monk's entrance as 'Andy' at the swimming pool.[21] Meanwhile, some great concepts were not exploited fully: for instance, the idea that Julia Jones has Greek, African American, Jewish, Japanese and Indian elements in her family.

THE SPOOFS.

Date Movie managed to squeeze in many spoofs: of *Bridget Jones Diary, When Harry Met Sally,*[22] *Pretty Woman, The Princes Diaries, Wedding Crashers, The Wedding Planner, The Seven Year Itch,*[23] *What Women Want,*[24] *Sleepless In Seattle, You've Got Mail, One Night At McCool's,* the *Meet the Parents* movies and *My Big Fat Greek Wedding.* And even more send-ups: *King Kong, The Lord of the Rings, Cape Fear, Hitch, Along Came Polly, Kill Bill,* and *Star Wars.* (Much of the story structure comes from the *Meet the Parents* films, *Bridget Jones's Diary* and *My Big Fat Greek Schlong*).

Like *Austin Powers* (1997), *Date Movie* opens with a big dance number. Well, only Julia Jones dances, primarily – but she is very big! Filmed on the Fox backlot with Alyson Hannigan in a giant fat suit[25] (plus a dance double), it was an enjoyably fluffy and upbeat way of starting a picture. She wiggles for firemen – they turn the hose on her; she waggles for road workers – they nail-gun themselves dead. It wasn't a

---

21 There's even more in the deleted scenes! More banana close-ups and spraying with milk.
22 The pantomimed orgasm scene of course – tho' the filmmakers gave it to a guy.
23 Julia stands over a grating in the opening musical number, *à la* Marilyn Monroe.
24 Julia can hear what people are thinking.
25 The fat suit was made by W.M. Creations. Fat suits were a bit of a fad in movies at the time, with the *Big Momma* movies starring Martin Lawrence.

satire of any particular movie, but a celebration of movies in general. Seeing Hannigan in a fat suit is entertaining. Friedberg and Seltzer are very fond of dance numbers – they appear throughout their movies (*Disaster Movie* has an amazing send-up of *High School Musical*).

I guess you can't have too much of British-born, Australian, super-gorgeous super-model Sophie Monk – eating a banana (in giant close-up), spraying milk on her face, taking a shower, swinging her long hair, bouncing about with a pneumatic road drill, eating a burger, cleaning a car *à la* Liv Tyler in *One Night At McCool's* and Paris Hilton in the car wash ad, etc.

This is actually a mini-movie within *Date Movie*: it last some three minutes, with slow motion and heightened visuals (backlighting and golden colour grading to make Andy look even more gorgeous). As a rival for Grant's affections, Sophie Monk's Andy is formidable – a million-dollar body designed to make Julia feel as ugly as Betty (Andy is, improbably, Grant's best man at the wedding. And if she is a super-model, she's probably got more $$$$ than Julia).

Why is the introduction of Andy such a long scene? Partly because it's amusing, partly because the movie and the producers know that some of its target market is very fond of beautiful, young women, but it's also to promote Andy as a powerful obstacle for the path of True Lerrrve. The scene's like the introduction of the villain in an action-adventure movie: typically, they look mean, chew the scenery, and do something bad (like kill someone). They have to represent a significant challenge for the heroes. That's also why Frank Jones and Nicky are kept in the mix, with Frank's project of marrying off his daughter to Nicky. Remember the romance plot formula: obstacles all the way!

I loved the *Kill Bill* spoof in *Date Movie*, partly because I loathed the *Kill Bill* movie (another of those movies that film critics go nuts over – I would recommend watching any Hong Kong martial arts movie[26] instead. *Kill Bill* was terrible!). The *Date Movie Kill Bill* spoof was an editor's joke: the same over-stylized and narratively empty pieces of footage were replayed again and again (with a red wash over them. That was editor Paul Hirsch's idea). The scenes just happen to include Andy washing the

---

[26] Friedberg and Seltzer are fans of Hong Kong action films; they often send up Chinese martial arts, and have written a script for Jackie Chan.

car. The recycled footage played in several character's mind-screens, including a passer-by (but he gets the same visions of Andy soaping up that car) The music was especially amusing in this skit. It was a pity we didn't get to see Alyson Hannigan and Sophie Monk in a full-on duel.[27]

I loved the send-up of *Cosmopolitan* magazine and its stuck up, self-obsessed dating articles about, 'how I messed up my relationship with my girlfriend'.[28] And the screenwriting is certainly dramatically inventive here, in the way that it employs the *Cosmo* article as a plot device to get Grant directly interacting with Julia (using photographs and voiceover, which becomes somewhat argumentative, when Grant and Julia disagree about where to meet).

The parody of *Bridget Jones's Diary* included Julia writing in her diary,[29] with the text appearing on the screen. In Julia's digs there are joke self-help books: *The Fat Girls' Guide To Life* and *Marriage For Morons*.

The *Pretty Woman* spoof (complete with Roy Orbison on the soundtrack), featured, in a humorous and pleasing reversal, Grant in drag as a hooker *à la* Julia Roberts on Rodeo Drive. Andy, driving up in her limo as a bigshot, asks how much Grant would charge to let her fuck him anally.

In the *What Women Want* send-up, Julia discovers she can hear people's thoughts, as if she's in that cruddy Mel Gibson movie[30] (she overhears a small kid with his Mom thinking he'll jam his lollipop up his Mom's butt). In the world of Friedberg and Seltzer, it would be *very* scary if you could hear what other people were thinking! (The gag played into the rivalry with Andy – Julia can hear Andy's schemes).

I loved the streetwise cue cards that Julia shows the little boy they're looking after in the R.V.[31] (about how pimps deal with crooks and ho's). And the kid speaks his first word, 'bee-atch'; Julia and Mrs Jones look on fondly like proud mothers.

In the *Star Wars* skit, Julia appears as Darth Vader in the rebirth sequence from 2005's *Revenge of the Sith*. (It's set in the transformation-

---
27 Their swords clash, break and fly off.
28 Here, Grant has (probably) authored an article on being a jerk boyfriend.
29 As soon as she wakes up.
30 Friedberg and Seltzer often kick Mel Gibson.
31 Why are they travelling in an R.V.? Because they live in New York and they're visiting Grant's folks on the Coast.

of-Julia scene, which comes, very improbably, from a bunch of mechanics in a garage[32] (it's Hitch who takes her there; Hitch appears as Yoda). This is a send-up of the makeover scenes in reality TV and rom-coms (such as *Pimp My Ride*, 2004-09) – and it's a staple of women's magazines such as *Cosmopolitan* and *Elle*. The version in *Date Movie* is gross – body hair, fat, and more fat).

In the *When Harry Met Sally* skit, the faked orgasm scene is of course the one picked for satire: here, Grant runs thru some ridiculous bits of business as he sits at a restaurant table with Julia (Adam Campbell is great in this scene). This is the sort of scene that critics deride – it seems to merely quote from *When Harry Did Sally*, without doing anything else. Sure. Maybe. But it's funny!

Adam Campbell excels again in the send-up of *Mrs and Mrs Smith* (2005) when he mimes beating up his girlfriend, and smothering her with a pillow – while Alison Hannigan's Julia sits uncomfortably next to him.

Jennifer Lopez, famous for her rear, is parodied in *The Wedding Planner* skit: you have to enjoy a movie where Jell-O (skilfully played by Valery Ortiz) has an enormous ass which she wiggles in the face of the stunned couple: the heiny waggles towards the camera in a low angle, threatening to demolish all in its path. (And this is after Jell-O has stripped down to a gold lamé bra-and-pants get-up;[33] she's the wedding entertainment, she says. In the deleted scenes, she's joined by some dancers, in gold hot pants).

Yet another TV game show spoof in Jason Friedberg and Aaron Seltzer's comedies brings together the reborn Julia with Grant Fockyedoder: the dating show *Extreme Batchelor, Desperate Edition* (where Grant is invited to blow away all of the other contestants he doesn't fancy banging with a shotgun (as the host quaintly puts it). Misogynist aggression in a Friedberg and Seltzer movie? Surely not!).

Critics don't like the violence in the comedies of Jason Friedberg and Aaron Seltzer, but as Friedberg and Seltzer have pointed out, the portrayals of violence in the movies that they are sending up are far, far worse. Oh yes – not only in 'PG-13', but also in 'PG' movies, there are astonishingly calamitous scenes with body counts running into the

---

32 Filmed in a garage down on La Cienga.
33 A great choice by costume designer Alix Friedberg.

hundreds (or, if it's the *Star Wars* franchise, millions).

Again, this is a *category* error – spoofs can't be compared in the same way, using the same criteria: a parody movie is *not* the same sort of movie as a straight movie! Not the same as a drama such as *War of the Worlds* or *The Lord of the Rings*, where literally 100s of people die on screen.

The cat – Jinxers[34] – is another of Jason Friedberg and Aaron Seltzer's mad puppets: introduced on the throne (the loud sound fx of farting and shitting do the work here),[35] it becomes a running gag in *Date Movie* (humping Mr Jones's momma's corpse, and getting freaky with the crazy, old bat next door (played by Beverly Polcyn). The later scene of Jinxers with the old woman, in a dinner suit and smoking, is very strange).[36]

In the *King Kong* sketch, the heroes film a victim tied to posts on the island (where they go for their honeymoon – this was 2006, a year after the release of the lousy, interminable, cack-handed and imaginatively bankrupt *King Kong* movie). It features Carmen Electra as Anne Darrow[37] (the inhabitants chant, 'Carmen Electra!', as well they might, and cheer when Kong rips off her clothing to reveal a leopardskin bikini. (If only Electra had appeared in *King Kong*). From this movie onwards, Electra became part of the regular troupe in Friedberg and Seltzer's movies).

PETER JACKSON'S KING KONG VIDEO DIARY.

The DVD release of *Date Movie* includes a mini-spoof segment called *Peter Jackson's King Kong Video Diary*. It's linked to the parody of *King Kong* (2005) that *Date Movie* used to portray the wild honeymoon of the golden couple, Julia and Grant.

Peter Jackson (director of *The Lord of the Rings, The Hobbit* and *The Frighteners,* b. 1961) is the most over-rated film director of recent times,[38] *and* the film director most aggressively sold by publicity and marketing departments as this amazing, 'master' filmmaker (the term

---
[34] By Creature Effects; puppeteer: Mark Rappaport.
[35] This scene looks like it might've been extended after it did well during previews.
[36] All the more so because it is directly contrasted with Julia feeling miserable after her failed wedding.
[37] A decided improvement on Naomi Watts.
[38] Guy Ritche, Quentin Tarantino, Robert Rodriguez, Shawn Meadows, and Christopher Nolan are also contenders.

'master' was often used at the time. But only for 'master' directors, of course – 'slave' directors went unnoticed, as usual). So it's a delight to see Jackson taken down a few notches. Adam Campbell does a fine job depicting Jackson as the geek of all geeks, the amateur, Super-8 wannabe director.

In *Peter Jackson's King Kong Video Diary,* we see Peter Jackson pontificating to camera about his amazing opus (as Jackson has done in numerous 'documentary' featurettes on the *Lord of the Rings, King Kong* and *Hobbit* home releases and online. For fellow filmmakers, for real filmmakers, Jackson's video diaries are smug and irritating). And we see that his long-suffering A.D. (Alexandra) is the person actually directing the movie (Jackson seldom strays from the monitor, where he asks for sandwiches).

Meanwhile, *Peter Jackson's King Kong Video Diary* cleverly cuts together on-set footage of the filming of the *King Kong* spoof in *Date Movie* featuring Carmen Electra with Adam Campbell as Jackson as if he's directing the godawful 2005 *King Kong* movie. (Several sections were left out of *Date Movie*, which appear in the *King Kong* diaries spoof – Electra being doused in green goo, and Kong hurling Electra at Julia and Grant).

5

'I HATE THOSE FUCKING KIDS!'

EPIC MOVIE

Epic Movie was made by Regency Enterprises/ New Regency/ Schiff, dis. by Fox, prod. by Paul Schiff, exec. prod. by Arnon Milchan, Rodney Liber, Friedberg and Seltzer, wr. and dir. by Friedberg and Seltzer; Edward Shearmur (m.), Peck Prior (ed.), Shawn Maurer (DP), William Elliott (prod. des.), Amanda Harding and Amanda Koblin (casting), Daniel A. Lomino (art dir.), Frank Helmer (costumes), Keith Adams (stunt co-ordinator[39] and 2nd unit dir.), Anna MacKenzie (sup. sound ed.), and vfx by Digital Dimension, Creature FX, Amalgamated Pixels, Pixel Magic and Handmade Digital. Released Jan 26, 2007. 85 mins.

In the cast were: Kal Penn, Adam Campbell, Jennifer Coolidge, Jayma Mays, Faune Chambers, Crispin Glover, Tony Cox, Héctor Jiménez, Carmen Electra, Jim Piddock, Kevin Hart, Katt Williams, David Carradine and Fred Willard. Plus the usual retinue of dancing girls, pretty girls, nuns, lookalikes, puppeteers, and midgets. The storybook narration (which takes care of the exposition) is courtesy of Roscoe Lee Browne, the folksy narrator of the *Babe* films.

Appearing as 'themselves' in *Epic Movie* were Puff Daddy, Mel

---

[39] And a huge team of 43 stunt people.

Gibson,[40] Flavor Flav, Paris Hilton, Ashton Kutcher, Samuel L. Jackson, and of course Jason Friedberg and Aaron Seltzer's go-to quick laugh (hell, *everybody's* go-to for instant humour): Michael Jackson. Harry Beaver was a puppet (Friedberg and Seltzer are very fond of puppets. Twelve puppeteers are credited in *Epic Movie*, with Mark Rappaport as the supervising puppeteer. There are several animatronic creatures, too, plus special make-up, prosthetic make-up, etc).

Locations included San Pedro (for the pirates), the Veluzat movie ranch, New Jersey and second unit material filmed in Paris. *Epic Movie* grossed $86m from a budget of $20m (placing it at number 60 in the global box office).[41] There's an unrated cut released of *Epic Movie* – with some nudity and swearing.

The home release of *Epic Movie* features an impressive group of extras: a commentary by the directors, humorous interviews with the cast (and Mr Beaver), a Fox special with Fred Willard, extra footage of the babes in the movie, an alternative ending, outtakes and more extras.

★

The 2007 spoof *Epic Movie* drew on some promising targets: *Charlie and the Chocolate Factory*, the awful *Narnia* series, and *Harry Potter*.

Other items spoofed in *Epic Movie* included *Superman Returns*[42] (the ill-judged reboot), *Nacho Libre, The Da Vinci Code, Pirates of the Caribbean, The Fast and the Furious* (which Friedberg and Seltzer would take on later in *Superfast!*), *Rocky, Mission: Impossible 3, Harold and Kumar, Click, Star Wars, Casino Royale* (the moronic *James Bond* flick), *X-Men, Snakes On a Plane, Borat, Scarface, Punk'd*,[43] etc.

One of the stars of *Epic Movie* was undoubtedly production designer Bill Elliott and the art department and set decorators (A. Lomino was art dir., Teresa Visinare was set dec.), for recreating (on a low budget) lavish settings such as Willy Wonka's Chocolate Factory, the Louvre Museum, and the Winter wonderland of Gnarnia. (The impressive sets, filled with individual props, too, are an amazing accomplishment on a reported budget of $20 million. That's $20m for the whole movie, not just the

---

40 Edward meets a drunken Mel Gibson in jail.
41 Not near the top, of course, but way above the 600 or more movies below it.
42 Peter imagines himself as a useless Superman – facing a villain on the rooftops, he tumbles over the edge after being shot in the eye.
43 Ashton Kutcher from *Punk'd* is thumped by Edward after irritating the hell out of him. (Edward also attacks Mel Gibson and other charas).

sets!).

And composer Edward Shearmur delivers a send-up of the floaty, choral cues that Danny Elfman is a master of (listen to the opening cues of the Chocolate Factory sequence, with a choir trilling in the schmaltzy, Hollywood manner of Elfman). Once again, the score of a spoof movie was very impressive (yet very few critics referred to it – again, as usual).

As with all of the films of Friedberg and Seltzer, *Epic Movie* is filled with songs created for the movie, along with existing songs or recordings bought for the show (such as 'Promiscuous' by Nelly Furtado, 'Ms New Booty' by Bubba Sparxxx', 'Let's Get Dirty' by Tika Rainn, 'Fergalicious' by Fergie, 'My Block' by 'Cham Pain, 'Art of Wars' by S.W.J., 'Waiting For a Girl Like You' by Foreigner, 'Eye of the Tiger' by Survivor, and 'Kung Fu Fighting' by Carl Douglas).

There's plenty of dancing in *Epic Movie* (as in *Date Movie*, Stacy Walker was choreographer): Willy Wonka performs several dances in the Chocolate Factory sequence (to 'Fergalicious' by Fergie); the *Pirates of the Caribbean* skit has two dances (including 'Lazy Pirate Day') – the pirates (who break-dance), and the showgirls.

★

Plot-wise, *Epic Movie* employs the over-arching narrative of the *Narnia Chronicles* films, with the White Bitch as the primary antagonist. But because the dwarf, Bink (played by Friedberg and Seltzer regular Tony Cox), is useless as a henchman, for that role we have the mad monk from *The Da Vinci Code*, Silas (seen in the opening *Da Vinci Code* skit).

Splitting the heroes into four in *Epic Movie* cleverly allowed for multiple parodies as each chara was introduced in their own movie spoof. Each send-up ended with the discovery of the Golden Ticket, the entry to Willy Wonka's Factory. Thus, we're in Paris and the Louvre Museum for the first send-up – of the smug, costly and truly dreadful *Da Vinci Code* movie – as still-born as a movie could ever get (despite the quality of the talent involved). 'A humourless drudge of a movie, endured by most audiences rather than enjoyed', as Mark Kermode put it.[44]

So Lucy (Jayma Mays) is the dopey, perky, innocent orphan[45] (a kind

---

[44] M. Kermode, 2013, 278.
[45] May plays the wide-eyed innocent with a quirky charm – the little laughs and 'huhs' she makes seem affected but funny.

of Anna Faris role from *Scary Movie*), who encounters the insane, self-flagellating monk Silas and her break-dancing adopted daddy, David Carradine (while she tries to discover the mystery of her naked father lying in the middle of the deserted museum at night). The scene introduces the first of many scenes featuring dancing in *Epic Movie*. Again, it's a favourite form of dance in the Friedberg and Seltzer movies – break-dancing.

Snakes On a Plane[46] is the parody setting for the intro of Susan (Faune A. Chambers): following the inevitable appearance of Samuel L. 'Motherfucking' Jackson,[47] Susan is thrown from the airliner (landing on Paris Hilton exiting a swanky store and snaffling a Golden Ticket from her purse). A scene of panicking people on an airliner can't help but be (in part, at least) an *hommage* to the All-Time Number One Parody Movie, *Airplane!*

In the send-up of *Nacho Libre*, Edward (Kal Penn) is holed up in a monastery in Mexico (he's portrayed as completely grumpy and fed up. Edward functions as the sarcastic, cynical character in the group in every Friedberg and Seltzer film). In a fight (with a kid), where he is soundly beaten, he is hurled thru a window, snatching a Golden Ticket on the way from a monk.

In a parody of the *X-Men* series, the hopeless, cowardly Peter (Adam Campbell, returning from *Date Movie*) is introduced: we're back at high school (or, rather, at a Special Academy), where mutants rule the corridors. As well as Wolverine (Vince Vieluf), there's an appearance by parody movie regular Carmen Electra in a blue bodysuit and make-up as Mystique (Electra and her astonishing physique provides the mandatory inclusion of T. & A. early on in a Jason Friedberg and Aaron Seltzer picture).

Peter's mutant ability? A pair of feeble chicken's wings sprouting from his back, a great joke about cinema's obsession with flying angels and superpowers. The chicken wings emerge during the face-off between Peter and the X-Men in the school corridor.

The multi-racial elements among the lead characters of *Epic Movie* are

---

46 The spoof includes many real snakes, plus the mandatory puppets.
47 Jackson delivers his joke line at least five times – a classic example of Friedberg and Seltzer pushing a joke beyond its limit.

a world away from the strictly white bread of Oxford don C.S. Lewis and his *Narnia* books. (Two of the four are white). The Pevertskis are all cast older than the teens in the *Narnia* books and in the movie adaptations (as usual with casting teenage characters). And, in customary parody movie style, they don't look at all like siblings.

★

★

Epic Movie shifts next into an extended send-up of a movie that's self-consciously already beyond parody, a movie that deliberately contains its own parody: *Charlie and the Chocolate Factory* (2005), the picture where many reckoned that Tim Burton and Johnny Depp had gone too far into the Wacky Wierdo Zone (which Burton and Depp are famous for. But this time, it was seen as too much).

Crispin Glover (who appears in *Alice In Wonderland*, another Tim Burton production (of 2010), as the Knave of Hearts), delivers an amusing send-up of Willy Wonka in *Charlie and Chocolate Factory* (altho' Johnny Depp's characterization of Wonka is so out-there already, and contains, like many of Depp's other recent turns, its own commentary about itself).

The big factory floor set in *Epic Movie* isn't as enormous as the one built on the 007 Stage at Pinewood Studios in England for *Charlie and the Chocolate Factory*, but it does the same job. There's plenty of room, for example, for Willy Wonka to dance. (And of course the chocolate river is inevitably revealed as sewage, and the fat boy – here it's Edward – eats a turd).

To hide from the creepy Willy Wonka (who wants to play hide-and-seek), our heroes find sanctuary in the magical wardrobe of C.S. Lewis and the *Narnia* books, and we enter the familiar snowbound realm of Gnarnia. The *Narnia* movies were very expensive turkeys – *The Lion, the Witch and The Wardrobe* cost $180m, *Prince Caspian* cost $200m and *Dawn Treader* cost $155m, truly shameful wastes of money and resources. (The *Narnia* films were marred by elements such as the incredibly irritating cast of snooty Brits, pointlessly complicated plots, and over-long running times. The short children's books published in the 1950s were turned into prestige-length movies, running to two-and-a-half hours).

Playing the wicked queen in *The Lion, the Witch and The Wardrobe* was one of the most over-rated and tiresome British actors of recent times – Tilda Swinton. So thank the Gods that Jennifer Coolidge[48] (another Jason Friedberg and Aaron Seltzer regular), steps in as the White Bitch, in a ravishing, Raquel Welch-ish diva costume and make-up (with a series of furry animals around her shoulders). The White Bitch is a proper movie villainess.

Lucy Pervertski encounters Mr Tumnus in Gnarnia first – in the 2005 version of *The Lion, the Witch and the Wardrobe*, this was a creepy section where an under-age girl spent a lot of time with a half-naked man. In the version in *Epic Movie*, this is where Tumnus (winningly played by Héctor Jiménez), introduces Lucy to his hi-tech crib[49] ('Gnarnia Hills, California' – inhabited by a bevy of beautiful women (the 'Crib's Fauns' in the credits) – all of them're half-human-half-goat like Tumnus[50]). North America's all-out obsession with television[51] is sent up with Tumnus installing plasma TV sets everywhere in his funky pad (including the toilet bowl and the top of the head of one of his babes when she's kneeling down to... polish his hooves).

Scarface is a funny spoof of an older but much-revered movie (among people who love gangster flicks). But this is *Scarface* with Mr Tumnus played Tony Montana; that doesn't make sense, but it's funny (it's the scene with the machine gun, of course).

The *Narnia* films feature a beaver as a minor character, who helps out the plucky teen heroes. That's a gift to a spoof movie, and *Epic Movie* features several scenes with Mr Beaver (voiced by Katt Williams). Any legitimate means of getting the word 'beaver' into a movie will be taken by comedy writers (like the 'nice beaver!' gag in *The Naked Gun*, which revolves around a stuffed animal. As producer Robert Weiss remarked, when he read that gag in the *Naked Gun* script, he knew the movie would work. It got a big laugh at the previews).

There's a mid-film dance/ musical number ('Lazy Pirate Day'), as usual in Jason Friedberg and Aaron Seltzer's parodies – this one's led by

---

48 There's a joke about M.I.L.F.s when we meet the White Bitch – Coolidge played the Mrs Robinson character of Stifler's Mom in *American Pie*.
49 A spoof of *MTV Cribs*.
50 But they're clad in slinky clothes revealing lots of skin, and're more appealing than Mr Tumnus.
51 Four hours at least are watched daily on average in the U.S.A.

Captain Jack Swallows, another impossible-for-parodists-to-resist character (Captain Jack springs Edward from prison, where he's held by the White Bitch). It's a goofy pirate number on a ship, accompanied by bikini-clad showgirls and crusty, street-tough pirates (a bit like the daily stage show at Treasure Island Casino in Las Vegas). It's not one musical number, but two, segued together (and back again).

I wish the filmmakers had tackled a whole *Harry Potter* parody: the *Barry Trotter* series is crying out for a spoof along the lines of *Vampires Suck*. But this stuff isn't cheap – to recreate the wizarding world and Hogwarts would prob'ly be pretty darn costly.[52] With a knocked-up, farting, smoking Hermione (played by Crista Flanagan, one of Friedberg and Seltzer's regulars), an ugly, pimply, bald Ron, and a far-too-old-to-play-fourteen Harry Potter, the send-up of J.K. Rowling's phenomenally successful fantasy novels begged for a more extensive and merciless savaging. (*Epic Movie* shifts into *Rocky* mode for some training exercises, with the heroes accidentally nobbling other *Harry Potter* charas as they fight, such as Dumbledore and Hagrid).

Fred Willard steals the second half of *Epic Movie* with his turn as Aslo, the ageing half-man/ half-lion. Inevitably, Aslo's first encountered in bed with a babe – and soon he's tupped the heroes (as the price for them asking for his help). Aslo is portrayed as a weary, playboy type, who'd prefer to drink and smoke rather than act heroically (he listens to the earnest explanations of the heroes – yadda, yadda – with a tired resignation).

Edward is sprung from prison in the White Bitch's Castle (by Captain Jack), but Aslo is dispatched by Her Royal Nastiness[53] (after fighting with Silas the mad monk). During the smackdown, there's a reprise of the motorcycle stunt gag in *Date Movie*,[54] where the stunt guy looks nothing like the main actor. As it's a martial arts duel, Aslo is played by an Asian stunt guy, in a costume from a knock-off version that you're supposed to examine too closely. The duel is a riff on Jackie

---

[52] Compared to *Harry Potter*, the *Twilight* series, after all, boils down to three actors – if you forget about ultra-expensive digital wolves, locations, etc.
[53] No Christian Resurrection in *Epic Movie* – when Aslo's killed by the White Bitch, he isn't reborn.
[54] There's a stunt where Julia rides a motorcycle in *Date Movie*: like the Zucker, Abrahams and Zucker team, Friedberg and Seltzer enjoy moments where the stunt guy is definitely not the star.

Chan's action scenes).

THE FINALE.
Another musical number occurs on the eve of the big battle – because a movie called *Epic Movie* has to have a Big Battle, right? So the charas party (cue rock band – Eagles of Death Metal (playing 'Don't Speak'), cue scenes of beer drinking, and Susan projectile vomiting several times. Vomit is always a surefire laugh).

Mystique seduces Peter in a tent (paying off the scene earlier at the Mutant Academy, when he approached her and was dismissed with a scornful 'as if!'). The joke here is that no one would want to change the million-dollar body of Carmen Electra, but when she straddles Peter and offers him her magical transformation skills, he asks her to turn into a gross creature with a single eyebrow, flabby, chicken wing arms, and fat everywhere. The transformation occurs in stages, with Peter getting more excited as his grotesque fantasy woman materializes.

Next day, everyone's fled (handily reducing the need for extras by half), and the foursome face the White Bitch and her horde of heavy metal devotees alone. Before hostilities commence, there's time for another music-and-dance segment (more hiphop music, with the White Bitch inexplicably becoming Davy Jones from *Pirates of the Caribbean*).

Handily, Peter has a special remote control (from *Click*) which can freeze time, heal his buddies, and allow the heroes to triumph. The remote control is an artificial, all-purpose gimmick that enables the group to conquer their rivals: with the enemies frozen, Peter, Edward, Susan and Lucy set about them exactly like you'd expect kids to do (Peter runs with his sword held out to slice thru multiple victims; Lucy, using her *Harry Potter* wand, holds her hand over her eyes and blasts the soldiers away).

To demonstrate how the remote control works (just so the audience gets it), there's a very typical gag from the Friedberg and Seltzer School of Comedy: Peter points the device at three passing joggers, to slow their movements down (it's the comedy rule of three, folks!): the first (the set-up, you might say), is a young woman whose breasts bounce in slo-mo (it's a Zucker-Abrahams-Zucker type of gag); the next jogger is the main joke, a fat guy who jiggles by; the twist is a younger guy, with the camera tilting down to reveal show his crotch (each of these gags are accompanied by suitable sound effects).

Epic Movie closes with several lazy flicks of the wrist; it seems as if finishing the narrative off satisfactorily is too much work. So the White Bitch is (apparently) killed by the wooden water wheel Jack Swallows is running atop (a very complicated and expensive set-piece in the second *Pirates of the Caribbean* picture of 2006, *Dead Man's Chest*. Here, it's a much cheaper joke). The Wheel of Doom also wastes the four heroes, after they've emerged from the magical wardrobe, back in Willy Wonka's place (sudden, unexpected violence – a baseball bat, a shotgun – or instant death – a bus, or, as here, a mill wheel – is a recurring gag in the films of Friedberg and Seltzer; it's their all-purpose means of closing a scene. When in doubt, *kill the fuckers*. If you don't know how to end a scene: *waste them*). The final shot of *Epic Movie*? Borat (Danny Jacobs) delivering one last joke, turning, and slapping his naked butt (as if the filmmakers are inviting the film critics: *kiss this*).

★

Let's side with the crrritics for a moment here (what?! Really?!).

Altho' it contained some amusing moments, very much in the *Airplane!/ Naked Gun/ National Lampoon/ Scary Movie* type of parody and comedy, parts of *Epic Movie* were somewhat lame ('lame' like Tom Hanks's hair in the museum). The quality of writing wasn't as strong as some other recent parodies (or some other Jason Friedberg and Aaron Seltzer scripts), and the casting and the performances seemed a little off the mark. There's a wonderful feeling of *play* in the *Scary Movie* and the *Naked Gun* parody flicks which was lacking in *Epic Movie*. It's as if the performers weren't really enjoying themselves, or weren't engaged fully with the material.

For instance, you'd think that the four insufferably prissy, stuck-up, smart-ass English brats that headline the *Chronicles of Narnia* series would be perfect fodder for parody (those spoilt kids are, I reckon, a chief reason for the *Narnia* movies being so disappointing, irritating and utterly unmagical ('Once a Jerk of Narnia, Always a Jerk of Narnia', as C.S. Lewis's novels put it). I *loved* the *Narnia* books as a child, but the movies *stink*. As the White Bitch puts it in *Epic Movie*: 'I hate those fucking kids!'). The irony is that altho' *Epic Movie* mocked the kids, they were also the heroes of an action-adventure-type narrative, so they still had to carry the plot along. Thus, there was always a point where the script was obliged to pull back from the mockery and have them drive the narrative.

But altho' *Epic Movie* based its central narrative around *The Lion, the Witch and the Wardrobe*, somehow it fell flat. The writers (Aaron Seltzer and Jason Friedberg) seemed to have squeezed everything they could think of out of the C.S. Lewis Hollywood adaptations, and there was nothing more that was funny. But still the narrative struggled onward.

Epic Movie was one of those comedies that was well-lit and in focus, like all professional movies, and the dialogue was well-recorded and audible, there was music, a script, costumes, vfx, sets, and all the rest.... but ultimately, some of it wasn't very amusing.

The violence of the reaction of some film critics to *Epic Movie* was scary: it's as if the movie jumped off the screen and beat the critics round the head with a baseball bat. But not every critic slammed *Epic Movie* – the *New York Times* said 'the humor is coarse and occasionally funny'; and *Entertainment Weekly* reckoned there were 'tasty tidbits' in the film (Owen Gleiberman was one of the few film critics would enjoyed Friedberg-Seltzer's work).

★

Now let's side with the audience, and with the filmmakers. Yes, *Epic Movie* is very funny in many sections – any scene with the White Bitch, the pirate dance number, Silas the crazy monk, Willy Wonka, Mystique seducing Peter, group sex with Aslo, Tumnus's crib, etc.

And it really is amusing to see those movies which're so earnest, so desperate to be liked, or so self-important and smug, or so hungry to be seen as cool, take a kicking – *X-Men, The Da Vinci Code, The Fast and the Furious, Mission: Impossible, Casino Royale,* etc. (Many film critics slated *Epic Movie*, but some of its targets were true trash: *The Da Vinci Code* and *Casino Royale*, for example).

Jason Friedberg and Aaron Seltzer rarely gave interviews, and preferred to stay out of the public eye. They didn't answer critics, get into arguments over their movies, or do much publicity to promote them. (However, they recorded some audio commentaries for home releases of their movies, such as *Epic Movie*. In a typically antsy move, however, they deliver mindless technical guff and wittering about porn which has nothing to do with the movie. Their commentary also isn't funny – but, as already noted, it's not essential for comic filmmakers to be funny themselves. It sounds like it was recorded elsewhere, from scripted notes, and added to the DVD release).

But they did appear on camera for 'making of' interviews to promote *Epic Movie* – true recluse artistes would never do that (detractors wonder if Friedberg and Seltzer even exist – well, guys, they're in a video interview on the *Epic Movie* DVD). And they recorded another audio commentary with the cast for *Date Movie*. And Friedberg and Seltzer appear on set in some of the clips used in the promotion of their movies, and in many photographs. (But they're not talking to camera in on-set interviews – their opinion of video diaries is expressed in their send-up skit entitled *Peter Jackson's King Kong Video Diary*).

EPIC MOVIE IN 2007.

2007 was the year of *Pirates of the Caribbean 3, Harry Potter 5, Spider-man 3, Shrek the Third, Transformers, Ratatouille, I Am Legend, The Simpsons Movie, National Treasure 2* and *300* (that's the top ten movies at the global box office). Mostly they are sequels (including remakes), and nearly all made from existing properties, with a few adaptations. (Friedberg and Seltzer have spoofed four of those movies).

There were many great movies released in 2007: *Sweeney Todd, Paprika, The Warlords, Youth Without Youth* and *The Simpsons Movie,* and some patchy but entertaining ones: *Bridge To Terebithia, The Golden Compass, Vexille, Rush Hour 3, Beowulf,* and *Pathfinder* (plus some of the top ten movies, such as *Pirates of the Caribbean 3, Harry Potter 5* and *Ratatouille).* Among the dreadful films of 2007 were: *Music and Lyrics, In the Name of the King* and *La Vie en Rose,* and some misfires: *Next, Cassandra's Dream* and *There Will Be Blood* (and those duds were directed by celebrated directors: Woody Allen, Paul Thomas Anderson, Lee Tamahori, etc).

EPIC MOVIE VERSUS *THERE WILL BE BLOOD*.

How about comparing *Epic Movie* with *There Will Be Blood,* another movie released in 2007? They are very different movies, a comedy and a drama – but let's compare them in terms of the critical reaction. One was slammed by most film critics; the other was a critical hit (mostly), winning an Academy Award for its star.

There Will Be Blood was produced by D. Lupi, S. Rudin, E. Schlosser, D. Williams, J. Sellar and P. Anderson for Paramount/ Miramax/ Ghoulardi, directed and written by Paul Thomas Anderson from Upton Sinclair's 1927 book *Oil*! It cost $25 million. Released: Dec 26, 2007. 158 minutes.

Film critics[55] (in the main) raved about *There Will Be Blood*, calling it a masterpiece (or a flawed masterpiece). It's not. It's like watching someone dying.

There Will Be Blood was written (partly) for Daniel Day-Lewis, with director Paul Thomas Anderson hoping that the famously idiosyncratic and difficult-to-please actor would for go it. He did: *There Will Be Blood* is largely *The Daniel Day-Lewis Show,* a vehicle for the Day-Lewis bag of actorly tricks. Day-Lewis for me is an actor who has a big neon sign floating above his head which announces: 'YOU ARE WATCHING A DANIEL DAY-LEWIS PERFORMANCE' (© and ™ Day-Lewis, Inc). And you are encouraged to sit back and gasp and applaud the intricacies, the detail, the grandeur of the Daniel Day-Lewis™ Performance. (Day-Lewis duly won an Oscar for this movie, and lots of other awards).

You get bored with seeing another scene open with (1) a close-up of Daniel Day-Lewis™ in his Freddie Mercury[56] moustache looking dour, or (2) a drifting[57] tracking shot of the Texan scrubland/ desert. And in each scene, nobody says anything until Day-Lewis™ starts the scene; Day-Lewis™ also leads most of the scenes; and he closes them, too.

So *There Will Be Duds* isn't a very interesting story, and it's not told in a particularly interesting way. It's empty (*much* emptier than *Epic Movie*). Oh, it's 'worthy', it's technically impressive, and it's delivered in

---
55 Critics admired the exploration of capitalism, of greed, of ambition, of obsession, etc. Of course – *There Will Be Blood* has got 'desperate-to-be-a-masterpiece' written all over it.
56 Oh, if only Freddie could pop up in this movie dressed in silver satin atop a grand piano and belt out 'Killer Queen'!
57 Even a would-be great director like Paul Thomas Anderson has succumbed to the disease in Hollywood cinema of slow tracking/ zooming camerawork.

a suitably 'serious' tone, but are the characters that compelling? No. Is the story that gripping? No. Does it tell us anything we didn't already know or feel? No. Is it entertaining? Not especially. *Epic Movie* is far more entertaining.

One of the biggest sins of *There Will Be Blood* is its length: at 152 minutes, it is far too long. It has already made most of the points it's going to make, and shown most of the sort of scenes it's going to show, by – what? – 30 minutes, 50 minutes into the piece. (By contrast, the Friedberg and Seltzer films are all three-act movies of 80-90 minutes. There is no justification whatsoever for a five-act movie of 152 minutes like *There Will Be Mud* <u>if you have nothing of any interest to say</u>).

But we do learn two important lessons from *There Will Be Guff*:
• never go down a mine.
• never go near a mine or a drill and rig.

Because something heavy will fall on you and you will die in a splurge of b-l-o-o-d.

And here endeth the lesson from the 945,136th chapter of the Great American Dream.

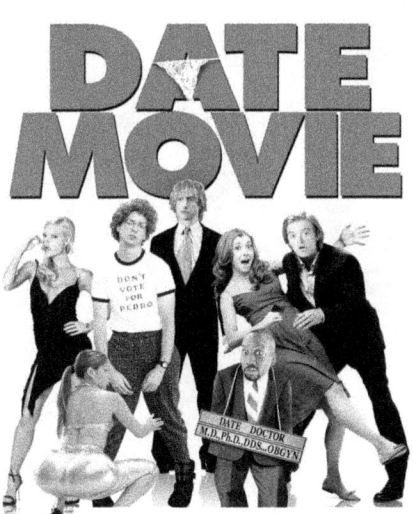

Date Movie (2006), this page and over.

UNA LOCA PELÍCULA ÉPICA

Epic Movie (2007), this page and over.

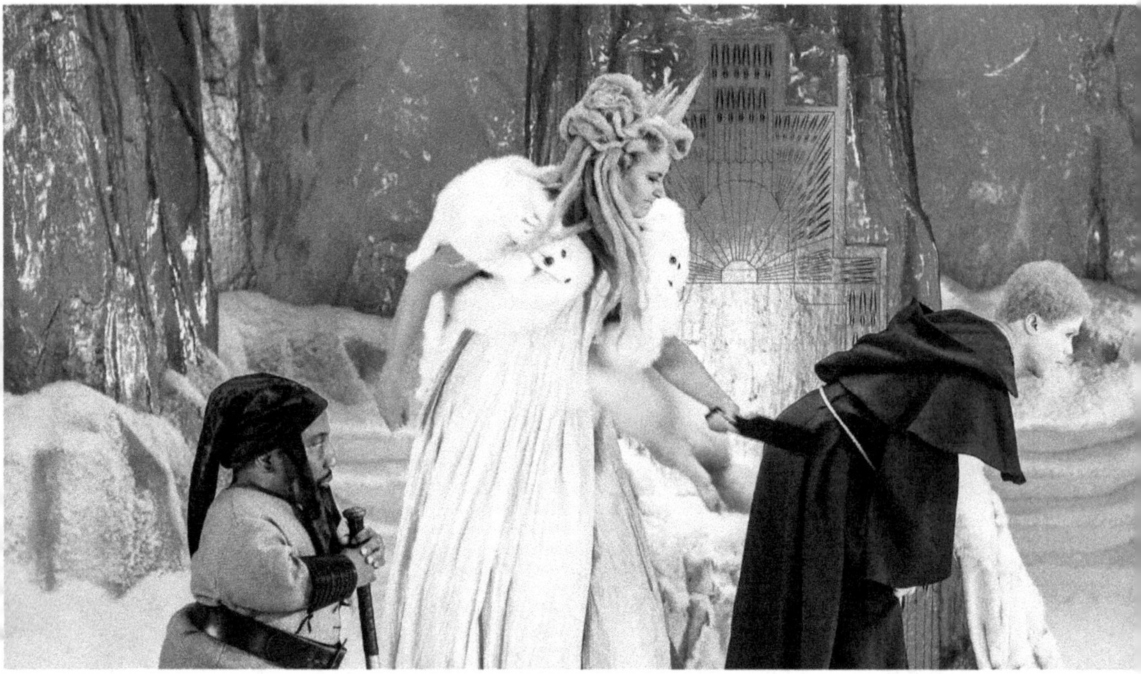

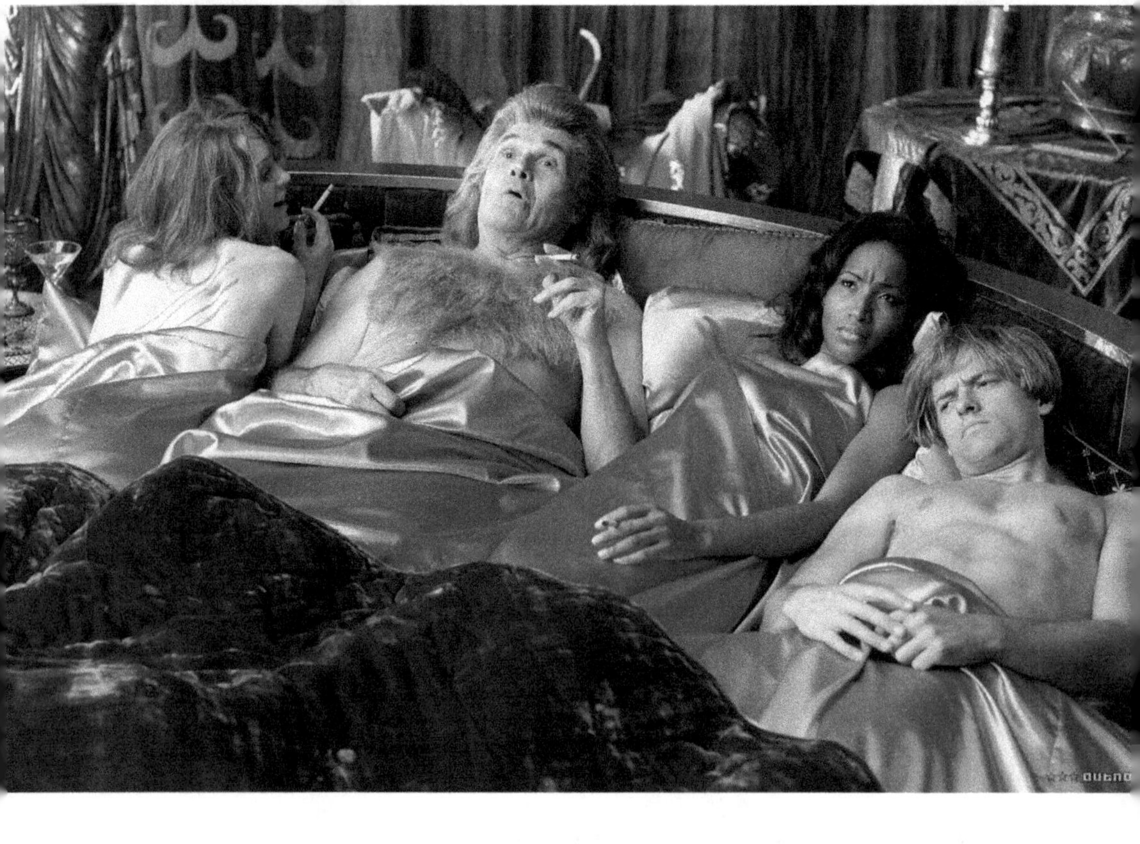

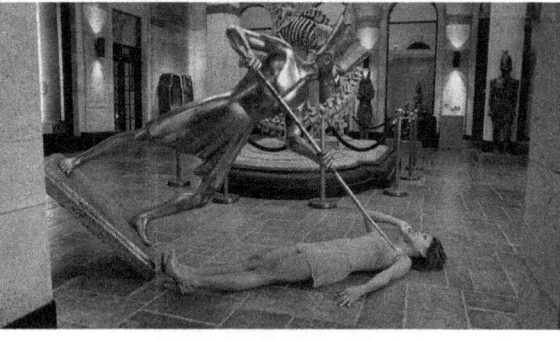

6

'MR. WAR-MONGERING LATENT HOMOSEXUAL!'

MEET THE SPARTANS

Meet the Spartans (2008), the third feature from Friedberg and Seltzer, was made by Regency/ New Regency/ 3 In the Box, dis. by Fox, exec. prod. by Arnon Milchan, prod. by Peter Safran, Jason Friedberg and Aaron Seltzer, co-prod. by Hal Olofsson and Mark McNair, and wr. and dir. by Friedberg and Seltzer. With Eyde Belasco and Lisa Mae Fincannon (casting), Christopher Lennertz (m.), Shawn Maurer (DP), Peck Prior (ed.), Frank Helmer (cost.), William Elliott (prod. des.), William Ladd Skinner (art dir.), Anna MacKenzie (sup. sound ed.), Douglas Noe (make-up), Mishell Chandler (hair) and Keith Adams[1] (stunt co-ordinator). Many in the crew were regular collaborators in the Seltzer-Friedberg Circus. Released Jan 25, 2008. 83 mins.

In the cast were: Sean Maguire, Carmen Electra, Kevin Sorbo,[2] Nicole Parker, Ike Barinholtz, Diedrich Bader, Travis Van Winkle, Ken

---

1 Keith Adams' stunt team is huge (some of the stunt guys worked on *300*), and *Meet the Spartans* is stuffed with stunts, like most spoof movies.
2 Kevin Sorbo was perfectly suited to this movie, being known for TV's *Hercules* (which is of course referenced in *Meet the Spartans*). *Hercules: The Legendary Journeys* ran for 111 episodes in the 1990s, and included several movies.

Davitian, Jim Piddock, Crista Flanagan, Dean Cochran, Phil Morris, Method Man, Hunter Clary, and Jareb Dauplaise (many were by now regulars in the Friedberg and Seltzer Travelling Carnival). Narrated by Robin Atkin Downes.

None of the actors in *Meet the Spartans* are big names, and Carmen Electra is about the most well-known performer (she is second-billed, and prominent in the marketing, along with Sean Maguire).

Meet the Spartans was filmed in New Orleans,[3] and almost entirely in the studio (on sets designed by William Elliott, art directed by William Ladd Skinner, and dressed by Teresa Visinare). As with *300*, the sets in *Meet the Spartans* are very stylized versions of the ancient world (*300* was based on a comic, after all). Instead of providing naturalistic-looking settings, Elliott and co. went for a bright, clean look (aided by Shawn Maurer's lighting, which emulated the light of Greece). A hot, sunny look not only fits the epoch and the film it's spoofing, it also helps the comedy (there's no tricksy lighting to get in the way of the humour. As comedy director David Zucker repeatedly puts it, can I at least see the joke?). Elliott remarked:

> We tried to keep the sets grounded in reality and let the laughs come from the script and the actors. The sets and locations were there to give them a good, firm foundation in which to work.

As Friedberg commented, Elliott and Maurer,

> pulled off an amazing feat in getting so close to the look of *300*. We told them what we wanted, what we were thinking and how much money we had – and those guys just made it happen. They're the real studs of the movie.

2008 saw the Jason Friedberg and Aaron Seltzer Joke Machine churning out two spoof movies in a single year (the other one was *Disaster Movie*, released on Aug 29, 2008).

Meet the Spartans features a funny audio commentary by the cast and crew on the DVD release – Jason Friedberg and Aaron Seltzer are joined by many of the key actors (Maguire, Sorbo, Parker *et al*). Contrary to the

---

[3] Friedberg and Seltzer continued to film in Louisiana (for *Vampires Suck* and *Disaster Movie*, for example).

notion that Friedberg and Seltzer are 'reclusive', or don't exist (!), they happily chat and joke about making the movie with the actors (and they've recorded several audio commentaries).

And of course the film critics loathed *Meet the Spartans*. Yet it was number one at the box office on its opening weekend – January 25, 2008 (gross: $18.5 million). (Of course, not a single critic offered to rewrite the script, or to suggest ways of improving the movie, or even, in amongst their 500 words of bile, to add a joke or two that could fit into the film).

•

If ever a movie begged – nay, <u>pleaded</u>, *by the Gods!* – for a send-up, it was the fascist claptrap of *300* (2007). And yet – *by Zeus!* – *300* is so insanely over-cooked, so camp, so silly, it's almost beyond parody (and it contains its own satire within itself). In the press kit of *Meet the Spartans*, Aaron Seltzer said: 'The characters in *300* take themselves very seriously. Their humorless natures gave us a lot to explore.'

Meet the Spartans was unusual in a Jason Friedberg and Aaron Seltzer movie in using a single film – *300* – for most of the plot. (See the appendix for more on *300*.) But of course *Meet the Spartans* also sent up many other movies, TV shows, and pop culture items.

300 is a cinch to parody – *by Hera!* – and has been parodied many times in popular culture. *301: The Legend of Awesomest Maximus Wallace Leonidas* was a movie parody in the pipeline from Universal.

Meet the Spartans laid into the creepy depiction of homoeroticism of the *300* movie, the fake tans, the painted-on six packs,[4] and the controversial links between gay sexuality, brotherhoods, male bonding and war-mongering (there's a great song about latent homosexual war-mongerers: it's sung while Leonidas and his army look very embarrassed: 'Today, we salute you, Mr. Warmongering Latent Homosexual').

Friedberg and Seltzer were fans of *300,* and saw plenty of potential for parody. According to Friedberg (in the press kit):

> We liked the movie and how it was so committed to the world of violence and leather underwear... The characters are overly macho – and the film is rife with homoerotic undertones.

---

[4] Actually, with very expensive visual effects, six-pack bodies have been added to Hollywood stars in other movies.

Emphasizing the homoerotic undercurrents of *300* was fair game for Friedberg and Seltzer – and besides, many reviews of *300* drew attention to them. Friedberg said: 'But it's never meant to be mean-spirited, all in fun.'

It's of the same order as a running gag in *The Naked Gun 3,* where ageing actors are mercilessly sent up at the Oscars ceremony in the finale, with one of the burly actors from the 1960s (such as Kirk Douglas or Charlton Heston) appearing on stage in a wheelchair to accept a Lifetime Achievement Award. The actor's films include several ridiculous sword-and-sandal epic movies from the 1960s with titles such as *Sweaty Boat Men, The Leather-Clad Centurion, Sandal and Loin Cloth* and *Big Shiny Spears.*

Meet the Spartans is an entertaining parody of one of the subtexts that Hollywood cinema pretends doesn't exist – the disturbing links between masculinity, narcissism, brotherhoods, aggression and war. In selecting *300*, *Meet the Spartans* chose a film that explicitly fuses those issues with male sexuality (in particular, homosexuality) and the cult of the body beautiful.

Hollywood action movies, superhero movies, war movies, and gangster movies glorify brotherhoods of men bonding in violence and bloodshed, elevating their cause with notions of 'heroism' and 'sacrifice', and then pretending that the homoerotic subtext isn't there.

Meet the Spartans is a parody of a war movie, after all – the films of Friedberg and Seltzer have taken on action movies before for shorter parodies, but this is a whole story based around mass conflict between groups of men. And, inevitably, Friedberg and Seltzer exaggerated what was already present in *300* – focussing on the male sexuality issue, and the links between it and aggression, with jokes about homosexual stereotypes and gay lifestyles. (King Leonidas: 'That is how *men* greet each other in Sparta: high-fives for the women and open-mouthed tongue kisses for the men'.)

The 'Mr. Warmongering Latent Homosexual' song[5] is one of the funniest segments of *Meet the Spartans*, ruthlessly attacking the subtext of violence in contemporary cinema:

---

5 A spoof of a beer-drinking commercial, for Buttmeister Beer.

Wearing nothing but leather underwear and a cape, you charge your enemy like an oiled-up hairless wonder.
Sure, there's danger – charging rhinos, stampeding elephants, and that cute toga-wearing guy named Chad.
Your keen instincts tell you to cut, slice, and chop every man you see. But enough about your career as a hairstylist. Let's talk war.
So this Butt's for you, King Leonidas! Because when the going gets tough, the tough go antiqueing.

•

Meet the Spartans featured the usual mix of Jason Friedberg and Aaron Seltzer delicacies:

• ultra-violent humour – numerous *bête noires* are kicked into the pit of death (Tom Cruise,[6] U.S. Presidents, the American Idol judges, Britney Spears, etc);
• a sexy dance from Carmen Electra (while old men ogle her);
• grotesque body shapes;
• gross-out body humour (vomiting, penguin doo, cat doo);[7]
• musical numbers and dances;
• a break-dance competition;
• pop music quotations;
• stupid signs;
• U.S. television send-ups, including several game shows;[8]
• and there's the usual collection of celebrity lookalikes, including Lindsay Lohan, Donald Trump, Tom Cruise, Rocky, President Bush, Tyra Banks, Twiggy, Dane Cook, Angelina Jolie, Randy Jackson, Simon Cowell, Paula Abdul, Ghost Rider, Britney Spears, Ellen DeGeneres and Paris Hilton (played by Nicole Parker).[9]

Among the spoofs in *Meet the Spartans* were: *American Idol,*[10] *Rocky, James Bond, Star Wars, Spider-man 3, Alexander, Troy, Grand Theft Auto, Transformers, Shrek, Ugly Betty* and *Happy Feet*. No dancing, singing puppets in *Meet the Spartans* – but we did have a guy in a penguin suit (played by Marty Klebba, the little guy[11] (he's 4'1") from *Pirates of the Caribbean*).

---

[6] Come on, it *is* funny seeing Tom Cruise being pushed into oblivion.
[7] And lots of jokes about balls – including a spoof of one of the creepiest scenes in the recent *James Bond* flicks, where Bond's naked and being tortured.
[8] *Deal or No Deal, American Idol, America's Next Top Model* and *Dancing With the Stars.*
[9] Parker's Britney Spears impersonation went down well at test screenings – at one point, it was going to be dropped because it was deemed out-of-date.
[10] There are send-ups of the judges on shows such as *American Idol, America's Next Top Model* and *Dancing With the Stars.*
[11] Friedberg and Seltzer are very fond of little people – they're in every movie.

THE CINEMA OF FRIEDBERG AND SELTZER ♦ 150

And *Meet the Spartans* is funny. Leonidas training his son violently while mom looks on proudly is funny.[12] Leonidas getting his butt kicked by a giant penguin (*Happy Feet*) is funny (and having to lick the penguin's balls).[13] The pit of death is funny. Leonidas as James Bond being tortured is funny (more testicles jokes). The painted-on abs[14] are funny. Leonidas meeting the envoys from Xerxes is funny (he can't understand their wry comments about the 'free' society of Sparta, or references to San Francisco and West Hollywood).

Somehow the celebrity culture and the TV talent shows were a good fit with the ancient world vaudeville of *Meet the Spartans*. *300* was partly about the obsession with possessing a perfect, gym-honed body. And the ideals of beauty and health were also a part of Nazism in the 1930s – the notion of a 'pure' form of humanity, and the mythology of the Nietzschean 'Superman'.

There's a lot of nudity in *Meet the Spartans* – tho', very unusually for a Hollywood flick, it's male nudity (as with *300*). Even with the painted-on abs, it still meant hours in the gym for the lead actors. Carmen Electra performed one nude scene (bar some sliced vegetables and a piece of pizza on her crotch).

Carmen Electra noted:

> I'm usually the one who's hardly wearing anything in a film, but in *Meet the Spartans* the guys are actually a bit more naked than I am – which is kind of nice for a change. It was cute the way some of them were so shy they kept trying to cover themselves up.

Sean Maguire was terrific as King Leonidas, at times uncannily like the preposterous characterization of Gerard Butler in *300*. (Maguire recalled that the filmmakers wanted a British actor for the role (they apparently met 100s of actors for Leonidas). Maguire added a little Scottish to his accent, as Butler had done in *300*). Maguire could step into any regular ancient world epic movie and be right at home; Maguire really sells the role of an Ancient Greek king who's honest and true but very dim (and he delivers the cod-ancient dialogue of epics, too). The

---
12 She suggests using the pile-driver.
13 The penguin scene includes a song translated into Greek which has the lyrics: 'The great hero falls and is asphyxiated by Penguin testicles'.
14 Leonidas: 'The Oracle also said that our painted-on abs look fake! But I beg to differ!'

directors said that Maguire played the role straight, sometimes as if he didn't realize he was in a comedy.[15] And Maguire is up for it: he doesn't seem bothered about looking very silly.

Even without the jokes and the slapstick, without the spoofing and the fooling around, *Meet the Spartans* demonstrates just how mindless movies of this kind are, and how silly characters such as King Leonidas are in *300*, and how they're played so earnestly and pompously. Sean Maguire alters the performance style a little – too loud, too camp, too histrionic – and reveals the lunacy in historical movies.

Meet the Spartans generously gives a significant amount of screen time to Carmen Electra; she is Queen Margo, wife of King Leonidas, and she actually affects the plot (unlike girlfriends or wives of the hero in most movies of this kind) – she persuades the Council to send more troops to aid Leonidas, and exposes the traitor, Traitoro (Diedrich Bader). Electra is delightful in *Meet the Spartans*, beginning with her introduction in schoolgirl bunches with a lollipop and developing into the sort of imperious royal figure that Monica Bellucci or Angelina Jolie might play at the time. As with Sean Maguire, Electra only needs to nudge the performance of a character a little to reveal how fake and really stupid characters in historical movies are. Electra was happy to spoof her media image from aerobic videos in the *House* TV show or the *Scary Movie* series.

The way that the role of Queen Margo is written, plus the casting of Carmen Electra, is shamelessly chauvinistic: Margo uses her charms to seduce Traitoro, and she persuades the council of Sparta to send more troops by dancing sexily in front of them. In a send-up of the troubled *Spider-man* sequel (rumoured to have cost more than the health budgets of 50 nations), Margo dons the black Spidey costume and attacks Traitoro.

Meet the Spartans is about a bunch of white Greeks, right? Yes – but Friedberg and Seltzer still manage to incorporate 100s of references to contemporary, African American culture – from the voice of the giant penguin to the break-dancing and name-calling scenes.

Nicole Parker is also given a lot of screen time: Parker is brilliant at

---

[15] Maguire said he was paying homage to Gerard Butler as Leonidas, not doing a send-up.

depicting women going to pieces; she provides several examples here: Britney Spears, Paula Abdul, and Paris Hilton. In the world of Friedberg and Seltzer, female celebrities are stupid, superficial and shamelessly shallow.[16]

During the filming of the orgy at Xerxes' palace, of course every electrician and grip in the studio just happened to turn up, as they often do when women are disrobing on set. (But the orgy of course focusses on Paris Hilton and her grotesque hump and arm, rather than the beautiful, slinky extras).[17]

The filmmakers were once again skirting carefully around the 'PG-13' classification, always pushing it towards the 'R' rating. The home releases included material that had to be snipped for the theatrical release.

300 was idiotic, but it did present the makers of *Meet the Spartans* with a simple, clear and bold plot upon which to hang their comedy: Sparta fends off thousands of Persians. *Meet the Spartans* employs the same narrative structure, so that, yes, it does tell a story, even if that is not the main goal.

Meet the Spartans reminds us that contemporary actors dressing up in togas and sandals and pretending to be characters from the ancient world is completely idiotic (or, rather, that audiences buy that is idiotic). It was stupid in the Golden Age of Hollywood (1930s-60s), it was stupid in *Intolerance* in 1917, and it was stupid back in the Shakespearean era on the Elizabethan stage (1590s-1620s).

The actors in *Meet the Spartans* also send up the pompous performance style of historical dramas – Sean Maguire isn't only parodying (or homaging) Gerard Butler in *300*, but the histrionics of many an ancient world flick ('We'll funnel the Persians in where their numbers won't count for shit!').

Frank Helmer did a great job with the wardrobe for *Meet the Spartans*, putting the Spartan warriors in ridiculous leather shorts and scarlet cloaks. That, plus the spray-on abs, were amusing riffs on the foolish costumes and toned bodies in *300*. (The costumes are brilliant – they deliver so much humour on their own. Every time the film cuts to

---

[16] Women (usually out of control celebs) splaying their legs with mosaics over their crotches is a recurring gag in *Meet the Spartans*.
[17] There are a host of extras in *Meet the Spartans* called on the credits 'Pretty Girl' or 'Hooters Girl' or 'Hot Orgy Girl'.

group shot of the 13 Spartans, it's funny).

300 featured silly gouts of blood spraying from bodies tricked in with animation. When you get slashed on the shoulder with a sword, it sprays with blood, right? *Meet the Spartans* responded in true spoof movie fashion – with the customary gallons of gunk, spit, shit, snot and piss. These are the liquids that spoof movies regularly employ for laughs (they appear in every Jason Friedberg and Aaron Seltzer movie). Oh yes, you *could* be very smart and link the blood, mucus and sperm in parody movies with Julia Kristeva's concept of abjection, but that would be going *too* far! (See the side-note on Kristevan abjection earlier).

The super-stylization of the *300* movie suited *Meet the Spartans* just fine – actors in a studio filmed against blue and green screens, with a vivid comicbook[18] visual approach that was fun to emulate because it was so extreme. (And *Meet the Spartans* included just that – a big blue screen carried in behind the front row of soldiers, to indicate the vast army that would be snuck in later by visual effects).

So, yes, thousands of extras fighting was outside the budget of *Meet the Spartans*. The solution? Have them dancing instead (the grossly stereotypically gay attributes of the Spartans had already been established in the early scenes, so the next step – a break-dancing competition – wasn't such a stretch). In the finale, the action included a name-calling competition,[19] a video game spoof, and a parody of slow motion violence.

The dance competition isn't a short, throwaway skit, either – it's a full-on dance number which runs thru several beats (it's the climax of act one of *Meet the Spartans*, in the usual place for a big action sequence). Choreographer Stacy Walker comes up with some impressive break-dancing moves but also some moronic shtick that the warriors can perform (this is a comedy, after all). Once again, we're struck by just how much *dancing* there is in the filmic output of Seltzer and Friedberg.

Wait a second, though – the budget of *Meet the Spartans* was apparently $30 million! Not such a low budget, then (*300* cost $65 million). In Hong Kong cinema, for example, you most certainly *could* stage a gigantic battle for 30 million U.S. dollars in 2008. For example,

---
18 An edition of the comic is shown on screen.
19 'Your mama's so hairy, the only language she speaks is Wookiee!'

the incredible action-adventure movie *Detective Dee and the Mystery of the Phantom Flame* (2010), a far, far, bigger production than *Meet the Spartans*, cost U.S. $20 million. But then, it was made in Mainland China, and it was directed by Tsui Hark, for my money the greatest action director in the world.

The pit of death in the *300* movie – and the bit where King Leonidas kicks the emissary from Xerxes into it (what schmuck put a pit of death right there in the palace?!) – was fully exploited in *Meet the Spartans*: indeed, the device was a gift to Jason Friedberg and Aaron Seltzer, who like nothing better'n kicking their cultural targets very hard. Even better if they can send them to their death, too! It's a movie set in the ancient world, right? So you can legitimately have characters acting in a brutal manner. (And if the victims included in the main body of the movie of *Meet the Spartans* were not enough, more were featured in scenes playing during the end credits).

Yes – a *Pit of Death* movie: you could have an entire Jason Friedberg and Aaron Seltzer movie of celebrities being pushed into the Abyss of Doom (they would have no shortage of victims they'd like to see tossed to their death). Or you could have that bit lasting 40 minutes, and the other 40 minutes being a series of break-dancing routines.

Leonidas explains his battle strategy to the sniggering Oracle, using crude drawings in the sand: 'I'm assembling an army to go to war with Persia. I'm going to take them in the rear, and then I'm gonna reach around, and I'm gonna take them again from the front!'

The battle at the Hot Gates ('this way for slaughter'), shifts through several spoofs, including an extended video game (a send-up of the San Andreas edition of *Grand Theft Auto*), jokes about vast armies added in with digital effects on blue screens, and a delightful riff on the endless and tiresome slow motion shots of duelling warriors from *300* and similar movies (instead of the creepy and improbable spurts of red stuff of *300*, we have nipple tweaking, wet towels, and wedgies).

Slow motion: recent Hollywood directors pretend they're Sam Peckinpah or John Woo (when they're so obviously *not*),[20] and *Meet the Spartans* sends up the over-use of slo-mo. And not only in the action

---

[20] Peter Jackson and James Cameron are some of the worst offenders – particularly of forcing slow motion to evoke 'meaning' or 'emotion'.

scenes, but in scenes such as Leonidas vs. the Penguin.

•

Once again in a Jason Friedberg and Aaron Seltzer movie, it seemed as if the filmmakers were desperate to transfer everything to Broadway, and turn their wacky spoofing into Broadway musical theatre. Dance is everywhere in *Meet the Spartans* – the battles are presented as dance competitions (with break-dancing a favourite, once more).[21]

The 13 – not 300 – Spartans go to war to the sounds of the iconic 'It's Raining Men' (by Dino Fekaris and Freddie Perren, sung by the cast) The movie runs out of story prior to the usual running time (around 70 minutes), and shifts into another *American Idol* skit, this time as a full-on musical number over the end credits. 'I Will Survive' provides the soundtrack for this all-out dance number, staged now in a television studio setting (but with the actors still in costume). It's a great curtain call for *Meet the Spartans* (which would make a terrific comedy musical).

Why the big dance number? And why 'I Will Survive'? Partly because the story of *300* ends on such a downer! Everyone dies! Sparta loses the war! ('We may have won the battle, but they will win the war!' as Leonidas puts it).

MUSIC.

Meet the Spartans is stuffed with music in its 83 minute running time. David Jordan and Jojo Villanuevea were the music supervisors, J.J. George was sup. music ed., and Rebekah Touma was music co-ordinator. Christopher Lennertz provides the suitably epic, dramatic score, and Ali Dee Theodore and a group of co-songwriters composed many pieces, including 'Supa Da Fly', 'O.M.G.', 'Amazing', 'Give It 2 Me', 'Spartans vs. Persians', 'Raw Dawg', 'Make It Bueno', 'Oh Gawd', 'Old Man Watching', 'Ripper', 'Bounce Back', 'Get Down', and 'Break It Down'.

Other songs in *Meet the Spartans* include 'The Bomb' by Ak'Sent, 'Dig In' by Bud Guin, 'Humpty Dance' by Parliament (performed by Digital Underground), 'Mer Ibrium' by Kirsty Hawkshaw, 'Good To Go' by Daniel May, 'We Gotta Party' by Jag Team, 'La Cucaracha', 'Barbie Girl' by Aqua, and 'D.A.N.C.E' by Justice. 'I Will Survive'[22] was given

21 Stacy Walker was choreographer.
22 The 13 (not 300) warriors skip to war singing, 'I Will Survive'.

the Ali Dee and DeeTown treatment for the finale (and performed by the cast).

One of the stand-out elements in *Meet the Spartans* is the score by Christopher Lennertz (of course, no film critic mentioned it, but they very rarely mention music anyway. Dialogue, yes, but music and sound, no). It is a straight score, not a parody (there is plenty of pop music to provide that). Lennertz approached the movie as if he were scoring a serious drama. Indeed, the score for *Meet the Spartans* contains many of the expected sounds of an ancient world epic movie in the manner of *Gladiator*, including brassy cues for the battles, amazing choral effects, and the famous plangent, female vocals from *Gladiator* (in that 2000 movie, they were sung by Lisa Gerrard and composed by Hans Zimmer. After *Gladiator*, every 'epic' movie had to have a bit of 'ethnic', female warbling for the sad, slow scenes). There are also Arabic motifs, world music percussion, a *doudouk*, and electric guitars.

Christopher Lennertz recorded the score with the 94-piece Belgrade Film Orchestra and an 80-voice choir. As well as *300* (by Tyler Bates), the score of *Meet the Spartans* is comparable with Hans Zimmer's for *Gladiator* and Nathan Furst's for *Dust To Glory*.

In Filmtracks,[23] Christian Clemmensen commented on the score by Christopher Lennertz:

> The scope of the work is massive... *Meet the Spartans* competes favorably with 2008's most dramatic action scores... the score excels in its instrumental creativity, mostly tonal constructs, and occasionally triumphant fanfares like the choral and brass outburst in 'He's Got a Huge Package.' The large scale expressions of heroics are led by the monumentally rendered 'Land of Sparta,' 'A King Returns,' and 'A God King Falls,' each exploding with harmonic resonance that is actually easier to handle than Bates' *300*.

Clemmensen concluded:

> if you take the circumstances that Lennertz faced with this production, from the obvious stupidity of the film's haphazard, shifty plot to the limited budget and the employment of song placements throughout the narrative, you can't help but admire the resulting score.

---
23 Filmtracks.com, Feb 3, 2009.

MEET THE SPARTANS AND ZUCKER-ABRAHAMS-ZUCKER.

Critics compared *Meet the Spartans* unfavourably with the spoof stylings of the Zucker, Abrahams and Zucker team, pointing out that Z.A.Z. carefully construct their comedy and pay attention to detail in the recreation of their spoof movies, but Jason Friedberg and Aaron Seltzer don't seem to bother (Zucker-Abrahams-Zucker are well-known for being meticulous craftsmen when it comes to comedy cinema).

Actually, *Meet the Spartans* features numerous gags that are *exactly* like those of the Zucker, Abrahams and Zucker team (Friedberg and Seltzer are big fans of the comedies of Zucker-Abrahams-Zucker, as we all are – they're geniuses). For example, when Queen Margo receives an ultra-violent massage, from a stern, Asian masseuse, it's pure Z.A.Z. material – the crunching on the back, the stepping on the head, and finally the use of dummies for the closing gag of the masseuse landing on the Queen from on high. Plus the gratuitous nudity – from their first movie, *Kentucky Fried Movie*, Abrahams and the Zuckers have included nude or near-nude scenes. (And having that slapstick comedy occurring during an exposition scene is also pure Zucker-Abrahams-Zucker: they would often alleviate the boredom of having to deliver explanations in a film with comedy).

Friedberg and Seltzer employ many of the comical techniques of the Zucker, Abrahams and Zucker team, but they put their own spin on them; the comedy in the films of Friedberg and Seltzer, for example, *seems* cruder and more violent than Zucker, Abrahams and Zucker's works (a common complaint by film critics about Friedberg and Seltzer). But that's not true, if you go back and look at the films of Zucker-Abrahams-Zucker. They feature outrageously violent gags in their movies (for ex, the character Nordberg in the *Naked Gun* movies (played by O.J. Simpson) is repeatedly shot, beaten, and thrown around).

In *Meet the Spartans* alone, there are numerous gags in precisely the same style as the output of Zucker, Abrahams and Zucker: the joke signs ('Hot Gates: Gas, Food, Slaughter'); the tattoo list of the Queen's lovers; the Asian masseuse; Traitoro carrying a *Traitors For Dummies* book, etc.

However, Zucker, Abrahams and Zucker wouldn't extend the gag of the pit of death in *Meet the Spartans* so long (there are even more examples in the outtakes!). Or maybe they would, if they saw that the audience was laughing at the preview screenings (Zucker, Abrahams and Zucker would preview their films three or four times, and adjust the jokes accordingly).

300

300 was based on the comic[24] by Frank Miller and Lynn Varley, which in turn was inspired by the 1962 movie *The 300 Spartans* (an excellent movie, by the way). It was published in the U.S.A. by Dark Horse in 1998.

Frank Miller's *Dark Knight* graphic novels of the mid-1980s had inspired the *Batman* movies of 1989 onwards.[25] Miller's (b. 1957) other comics work included the *Ronin, Daredevil, 300* and *Elektra* series (many of which have been filmed); he also worked on the scripts for the *RoboCop* films (tho' he hadn't enjoyed the experience).[26]

300 took a famous event in (military) history (the Battle of Thermopylae in 480 B.C.), and did what it liked with it: this is historical fantasy, or fantastical history. It's not intended to be 'accurate', it's not a documentary. It's a comic! *300* is one of those movies that's so over-the-top, frantic and heightened, it's already a parody of itself.

300 starred Gerard Butler, David Wenham (as the narrator), Lena Headey, Giovanni Cimmino, Dominic West, Tom Wisdom, Andrew Pleavin, Andrew Tiernan, Rodrigo Santoro, Stephen McHattie, Michael Fassbender, Peter Mensah and Kelly Craig.

Gianni Nunnari,[27] Mark Canton, Bernie Goldmann and Jeffrey Silver produced, written by Kurt Johnstad, Michael Gordon and Zack Snyder, and Zack Snyder directed for Legendary Pictures/ Virtual Studios/

---
24 A copy of the comic appears in *Meet the Spartans*, the object of a throwaway gag (a literal throwing gag).
25 And also the work of Alan Moore, Dennis O'Neal and Neal Adams.
26 Later, Miller's work was made into films such as *Sin City* (2005).
27 Nunnari had secured the rights to Frank Miller's 1998 book, after failing to obtain the rights to *Gates of Fire* by Steven Pressfield.

Atmosphere Pictures/ Hollywood Gang Productions. Prod. des.: Jim Bissell. Vfx supervisor: Chris Watts. Music:[28] Tyler Bates. DP: Larry Fong. Editing: William Hoy. Released Mch 9, 2007. 117 mins.

300 was filmed mainly in Montréal, with a budget of $65 million. It was a massive hit, with a global gross of $465 million.

Fox was planning to remake its own *The 300 Spartans* (1962), around the same time as Universal was preparing *Gates of Fire*, based on the same story of Thermopylae (from Steven Pressfield's 1998 novel, with a script by David Self, direction by Michael Mann, production by George Clooney, and possibly Bruce Willis to star). Both *The 300 Spartans* and *Gates of Fire* bit the dust, and *300* emerged as the frontrunner for a film about Thermopylae.

The extensive post-production period gave *300* an impressive comicbook look, replacing green screens and blue screens with ancient world vistas, and a glowing, textured storybook look.[29] Every sky was moody and brooding (no blue skies in Ancient Greece!), in high contrast, with a palette given over to gloomy browns, beiges, whites, greys and yellows.

The costumes in *300* combine Las Vegas flamboyance, fetish gear, and contemporary wrestling outfits with nods towards 'historical' accuracy. (Frank Miller acknowledged that he took plenty of liberties with history – he took off the helmets, for instance, so you could see the characters). *300* also added many elements that were there to look cool – such as creatures like elephants and rhinos, and nasty fantasy beasts.

Gerard Butler is certainly a strong, charismatic performer – he'd make a great Othello or Macbeth, or an Indiana Jones (as *Nim's Island* demonstrated). And he can play warrior leaders terrifically, as *Attila* (a.k.a. *Attila the Hun*, 2001) showed. There's an element of danger or unpredictability about Butler – you don't quite know what he's going to do (he's like a Scottish Russell Crowe in this respect, tho' he doesn't have so many of the irritating quirks that Crowe uses).

•

Two aspects of the *300* movie strike you immediately. (1) Violence.

---

[28] The score was subject to copyright issues – claims were made that the score lifted from *Titus* (1999) and *Troy* (2004).
[29] Some of the props were re-modelled from *Troy* and *Alexander*, two big ancient Greek movies of 2004.

(2) Homosexuality. Altho' I guess audiences responded to *300* as (1) an action movie, and (2) as a digitally-dominated comicbook/ video game movie. Let's take the gay issues first. Despite some strong contenders – such as Frodo and Sam in the *Lord of the Rings* movies, or the 1990s *Batman* movies, or any superhero or band of brothers movie – *300* is without doubt the gayest and the campest movie of recent times in Hollywood cinema. It's so camp in an over-the-top manner, you can't believe it! Rarely have so many near-naked male bodies been displayed so openly in a big, Hollywood action movie. (The bodies are also, of course, the product of many weeks in the gym – reflecting the drive in Western lifestyle towards health and fitness taken to scary extremes. Now we're into protein shakes and two-hour work-outs to achieve that to-die-for body, with its toned abs and bulging biceps. And some of the bodies were augmented with digital trickery).

300 refers of course to the 300 Spartans at the Battle of Thermopylae (who have already been the subject of a few movies, including a hugely enjoyable 1960s flick). And that story, as we also know, is a supremely gay moment in history, as well as an iconic event in gay culture. The 300 Spartans is also an ultimate story in war history, when a tiny band of brothers battled overwhelming odds (it's the model, really, for all of those subsequent tales, including numerous movies).

The recent ancestors of the violence, blood and gore in *300* are movies such as *Saving Private Ryan*, *Gladiator*, and Hong Kong action cinema Going back further, there is of course Sam Peckinpah and *The Wild Bunch,* and *Bonnie and Clyde.*

To make sure that the heterosexual, conservative segments in the global audience don't freak out when they see all of those oiled torsos on display in *300* – and to ensure that guys on dates watching the movie don't go home with Dave or Miguel instead of Sally or Anna, the girls they came to the theatre with – the filmmakers include a Big Sex Scene in the first act. Here, King Leonidas tups his wife Queen Gorgo (Lena Headey) before going off to battle! Yes, my dears, King Leonidas is *not* gay! No he isn't! He has a wife, but she isn't no wife for pretence, or for political or courtly reasons. No! He lerrrves her, and he'll make lerrrve with her, too! (Meanwhile, the Athenians are derided as 'boy-lovers').

But when he goes to war, like most armies in the entire history of the world, King Leonidas is a guy among the guys. No women. No. Altho' Hollywood movies insist on placing women in amongst the armies of history, they simply weren't there in most instances. Altho' Hollywood comes up with silly reasons or tricks for putting women into battles and armies (cross-dressing, disguises, etc), it very rarely happened.

So at least the filmmakers of *300* stuck to history a little, and left the women at home. But they did make sure there was at least one significant part for a woman in *300*, and that was King Leonidas's wife Gorgo. So the Big Sex Scene is an attempt, too, to heterosexualize or normalize a very homosexual-inflected story, as well as to include some female roles.

Because *300* is a *very* masculinist and patriarchal movie. Yet, of course, some of the male characters are feminized, and there are hints of homosexual relationships amongst the warriors (and this movie also took up a stereotypical treatment of homosexual relations, where one guy is the feminized, more passive partner).

300 does include some other parts for women. But, what a surprise!, they too are eroticized: they're hookers in the court of the Big Villain, God-King Xerxes (Rodrigo Santoro).[30] Sticking with the sexualizing of the characters theme – the menagerie that surrounds King Xerxes is depicted with erotic undertones. And, because he's the villain, the kind of sex that Xerxes enjoys with his harem is twisted and creepy – in contrast to the good, healthy pleasure that King Leonidas has with his wife Gorgo.

But, come on, *300* isn't about sex or homosexuality, is it? It's about action! And it contains some of the creepiest, most sickening violence in recent cinema. *300* is a movie with a high visual effects budget, where much of the movie was created in computers by a bunch of highly-paid vfx wizards (from ten or so visual effects houses). Instead of blood squibs for wounds, *300* added sprays of blood which erupt like 100s of come shots from pornography, creating a new, digital pornography of violence.

Well, I guess it had to happen – that filmmakers would employ computer-aided imagery to portray excessive violence. It's stylized to the

---

[30] King Xerxes is depicted as a mysterious, formidable giant who sports improbable body piercings, bizarre make-up and a bald pate. He might've stepped out of an upmarket tattoo parlor and sauna in Beverly Hills, or a pro-wrestling show in Atlantic City.

point of near-abstraction, self-consciously anti-naturalistic. The blood and gore is part of the comicbook approach to the visuals: in a printed comic or *manga*, tho', such sprays of blood have a different impact and aesthetic (they are a staple of Japanese samurai stories, for instance). *300* is like a Japanese *manga* product, but with a twisted emphasis on violence and suffering which misinterprets the Japanese code of the samurai (*bushido*).

Despite its flashy, gimmicky, digital trickery, its lovely, oiled, male torsos, and its glossy, comicbook sheen, there is a desperate, wounded feeling of depression and negativity in *300,* as if its relentless emphasis on pain and violent slashes and gouges crushes everything to the point of decline and death. No life, no hope – just swords whipped across the body to elicit another spray of digital blood. It's 'torture porn' again.

As Danny Fingeroth points out in *The Rough Guide To Graphic Novels*:

> Critics found fault with the film's broad strokes, its moral ambiguity and xenophobia, its lack of sophisticated characterization, its excessive violence versus plot – in short, its being all style and dubious substance. (270)

300 was controversial politically, as critics and audiences in certain parts of the world objected to the depiction of, for instance, the Persians (the movie was publicly denounced in Iran). So it's the West versus the East, yet again. In this respect, *300* was no more controversial than, say, some *James Bond* movies, or *True Lies.* So you can see *300* as another post-9/11 movie – tho' this time it replays the Gulf War, Afghanistan and the 'War On Terror' as a camp passion play done over in a heightened, comicbook fashion.

However, *300* is creepy and disturbing ideologically: after watching *300* you'll be tempted to invade Poland. The Nazis would love it. *300* definitely does flirt with fascism – or, hell, it's a two-hour advert for fascism. *300* does come over as a replay of American conflicts such as the Vietnam War – yes, the Yanks lost, but they lost heroically! – like the Spartans at Thermopylae. (Altho' some critics pointed out that *300* was about a small country (Sparta) taking on a mighty empire – Persia – so it couldn't be aligned with the U.S.A., there's no doubt that in *300,* as in pretty much every action and blockbuster movie to come out of Hollywood and North America, that it is really about contemporary America).

7

'HELL, NO!'

DISASTER MOVIE

INTRO.

Disaster Movie (2008) continued the run of spoof movies helmed by Jason Friedberg and Aaron Seltzer. It was prod. by 3 In the Box/ Safran Company/ Grosvenor Park, and backed by Momentum/ Lionsgate. It was wr. and dir. by Seltzer and Friedberg, prod. by Peter Safran, Jerry P. Jacobs, Friedberg and Seltzer, exec. prod. by Hal Olofsson, with Christopher Lennertz (m.), Peck Prior (ed.), Shawn Maurer (DP), William A. Elliott (prod. des.), Daniel A. Lomino (art dir.), Frank Helmer (costumes), Anna MacKenzie (sup. sound editor), and Keith Adams (stunt co-ord.). Released: August, 29, 2008.[31] 87 mins.

In the cast were Matt Lanter,[32] Carmen Electra, Vanessa Lachey (a.k.a. Minnillo), Gary 'G Thang' Johnson, Crista Flanagan, Nicole Parker, Tony Cox, Tad Hilgenbrink, Nick Steele, John Di Domenico, Valerie Wildman, Kim Kardashian and Ike Barinholtz.

The cast of *Disaster Movie* includes characters called (in the credits) Bikini Girl, Hot Girl, Party Girl, Bloody Pedestrian, Cowboy Fan, and a

---
31 Only 7 months after *Disaster Movie*.
32 He was Edward in the subsequent *Twilight* spoof, *Vampires Suck*.

host of Cheerleader Dancers. Plus lookalikes for Flava Flav, Jessica Simpson, Hell-Boy, Batman, Prince Caspian, Kung Fu Panda, Hancock, Justin Timberlake, the Hulk, Iron Man, Indiana Jones and Dr Phil.

Like many film productions of the 21st century (including *Jurassic World* and the *Twilight Saga* movies), *Disaster Movie* took advantage of the economical benefits of filming in Louisiana.

According to Wikipedia online, *Disaster Movie* is regarded as one of the worst movies ever! So? Who cares? What rubbish! I want to *see* the movies that are treated with such contempt! I'd rather watch 1,000 *Disaster Movies* than many of the movies dubbed 'classics' or 'masterpieces' that come out of the North American entertainment industry.

But *Entertainment Weekly*'s critic Owen Gleiberman enjoyed *Disaster Movie:*

> The movie is merciless sending up *Juno*'s selfsatisfied hipster gobbledygook, and it's quite funny to see *Hannah Montana* still promoting her tie-in products as she lies crushed and dying under a meteor.

The ensemble playing is delightful in *Disaster Movie,* as the group of characters gathered around Will (Matt Lanter) rush about while an unnamed North American city is decimated by meteorites, big freezes and twisters. The charas include: Nicole Parker, Vanessa Lachey, Kim Kardashian, Gary 'G Thang' Johnson and Crista Flanagan. Will is the main character in *Disaster Movie,* but this is a team outing, with the characters playing off each other continually. Johnson is Calvin, Will's friend, who's dating Lisa (Kardashian); Amy (Lachey) is Will's on-off girlfriend; Juney winds up with their group;[33] and the Enchanted Princess (Parker) is also part of the gang.

Juney, a spoof of Juno MacGuff, is a wonderful turn by Crista Flanagan[34] as the incredibly irritating teenage mom from the movie *Juno* (2007), who can't help commenting on everything with a smug, flip, desperate-to-be-hip remark ('I speak in overly written, clever-for-clever's sake quips'). Juney is given several runs of gags, the sort of jokes that

---

[33] Having smashed her boyfriend over the head with her guitar.
[34] Flanagan also plays Hannah Montana.

authors like to craft, because they're meant to be self-consciously witty, the product of a teenage Dorothy Parker who wallows in self-loathing: 'Take a Xanax, Fabio. You're wriggling harder than a smack addict at an Iggy show circa '73... I haven't seen a six-pack like that since I shotgunned Molson Golden at Lollapalooza.'

Calvin has a cute girlfriend, Lisa, played by Kim Kardashian: it's a somewhat unlikely pairing (but parody/ spoof movies are full of such couples). Kardashian exits the show halfway thru, squished by a falling meteor, in the midst of a panicky debate about What To Do. Calvin's shock and distress doesn't last very long, because the Enchanted Princess grabs his attention as soon as she clambers out of the sewers.[35]

How does the 2008 movie cram in so many movie spoofs? Simple, it uses the narrative device of dreams: so it's Will who's dreaming of a caveman from 10,000 B.C. being chased by some beasties (which, in the usual cheapo manner of lower budget movies, don't turn out to be million-dollars-per-minute C.G.I. monsters, but an actor – Nicole Parker as Amy Winehouse).[36] Will continues to dream, and the movie continues to dream up spoofs. (Also, characters have daydreams – which worked so well for Woody Allen in his 1970s films. *The Simpsons TV* series uses daydreams all the time, as Lisa or Homer or whoever drifts off into Fantasy Land).

The basic narrative structure of *Disaster Movie* is a typical disaster flick, with a bunch of characters dealing with a catastrophe. As in *The Towering Inferno, The Poseidon Adventure* or *Armageddon*, they are picked off one by one as they struggle thru the increasing chaos. The model for *Disaster Movie* is partly *The Day After Tomorrow* (2004),[37] a movie set mainly in Gotham,[38] which's hit by tidal waves and a big freeze.[39]

THE MAIN PLOT AND THE SUB-PLOT.

Disaster Movie is happy to kill charas regularly: so Kim Kardashian

---

[35] The cod fantasy movie lingo of the Princess and the Prince is amusing: they call Calvin, who's black, 'that Moorish ruffian' and 'dark peasant'.
[36] Amy Winehouse is the very unlikely prophetess predicting the End Of The World on August 29, 2008 (when *Disaster Movie* was released).
[37] And *Twister*.
[38] We are once again in North America in the present-day.
[39] The vfx budget runs to suggestions of freezing, but not *tsunami*.

is flattened by a meteorite (as is Hannah Montana); Juney is eaten alive by chipmunks; Calvin and the Enchanted Princess are sliced with a sword; and Carmen Electra's Beautiful Assassin is hit by a rogue bullet.

It's not until past the halfway mark of the first act of *Disaster Movie* (around twenty minutes into the picture), that the primary story, the disaster movie plot, kicks in, with the meteor attack. This occurs at the tail end of the *High School Musical* number. (Just as Amy Winehouse predicted!).

Before that, following the *10,000 B.C.* skit, there are scenes establishing Will's character. Breaking up with his girlfriend Amy introduces the romantic subplot, a staple of most mainstream movies (particularly the ones that *Disaster Movie* is spoofing – it's the subplot of an overwhelming proportion of action-adventure movies, and thrillers, and comedies, and so many other genres). The relationship break-up automatically suggests that a re-union will occur later on – how can it not, when Matt Lanter and Vanessa Lachey are so cute? (Even if she's been doing Flava Flav (Abe Spagner) and takes their midget mascot Jojo (Lloyd Arnold II) with her when she storms out).

The romantic subplot provides part of the dramatic structure of *Disaster Movie:* Calvin is all for fleeing the city (as everybody else seems to be doing – who wouldn't?). But Will wants to find Amy – he's heard from her at the museum[40] (where she works). That quest gives the characters a goal (Calvin goes along with what Will wants to do).

Spoof movies don't spoof other spoof movies, but they do steal other movies' jokes! (all comedians do it! Well, you can't copyright a joke!). When Amy huffs off from the Sweet Sixteen party, her parting shot is that she thought of other guys when she made love with Will ('every time we made love, I was thinking about another guy' 'Well, so was I'); this joke was used in *The Naked Gun*, when Leslie Nielsen walks out on Priscilla Presley, and states that he faked his orgasms.

Giving the dream of the prophecy to Will and having him wake up to remember it identifies him as the chief character in *Disaster Movie*. Yes, this seemingly loose, scattershot script is actually worked out! (*Date Movie* also opened with a dream, with the main character waking up from

---

[40] To reach the museum, the heroes steal Speed Racer's car (after the Enchanted Princes has shot him repeatedly and gleefully).

it). The 2008 film's structure includes the dramatic device of bringing all of the characters together – at the birthday party for Will, when everyone in his life has a good reason to be in the scene. (Will mentions to his friend Calvin that he and Amy are splitting up, keeping that subplot alive – and Amy duly walks in at that moment, along with a near-naked underwear model, played by Nick Steele).

Notice that adults and parental types are absent from the party, and from the group of main characters; only Dr Phil is a middle-aged chara in this sequence, tho' he's portrayed as a horndog, and he's soon killed. (The main characters in *Disaster Movie* are indeed the smug twentysomethings that the radio announcer derides during the emergency statement about the falling meteorites: 'Seismologists have marked the epicentre at a trendy loft district whose residents are attractive twenty-somethings who dance to bad 80s music, wear Abercrombie & Fitch, and like to drink light beer'. To demonstrate just how superficial the crowd of youngsters is, they only go nuts and rush outside when they hear that a Pinkberry store has been destroyed by the meteorites).

On the streets of the unnamed city in the U.S.A., the flying cows from *Twister* flatten a series of lookalike cameos (Hell-Boy, the Hulk, etc). This is a variation on the Instant Death that is a recurring motif in the films of Friedberg and Seltzer (such as pushing victims into the bottomless pit in *Meet the Spartans*, or firing a shotgun at contestants in the *Extreme Bachelor* TV game in *Date Movie*. And if no weapons or abysses are available, there's always a speeding car or bus to take out people).

And in *Disaster Movie,* the asteroids do that, too: when a character such as Lisa has run out of her uses in comical terms (or maybe Kim Kardashian's contractual time on set had run out), a meteor crushes her.

•

Judging by the working title – *Goody Two Shoes* – and the sheer amount of girlie and rom-com ingredients, *Disaster Movie*'s script might've taken a change of direction at some point, so it became a disaster movie spoof (perhaps there wasn't enough material in spoofing Disney Princess movies such as *Enchanted* (2007), which was already a parody. Or perhaps the backers preferred a disaster movie riff rather than a girlie fantasy riff – the team had already done *Date Movie*, for instance). Much of the spoofing concerned female celebs (like Amy Winehouse, Jessica Simpson, Carmen Electra and Hannah Montana), girlie movies like *Enchanted, High School Musical* (which provides a substantial dance sequence), *Sex and the City* and *Juno*, and the romantic sub-plot of a guy (Will, the hero, played by Matt Lanter) who won't commit to a relationship with the super-gorgeous Amy (Vanessa Minnillo). Also the Enchanted Princess is a major character, to the point where *Disaster Movie* is really about her.

Disaster Movie also crammed in spoofs of *Night At the Museum, 10,000 B.C., The Guru, The Day After Tomorrow, Twister, Armageddon, Beowulf, Batman, Star Wars, Iron Man, Hell-Boy, The Hulk, Prince Caspian, Hancock, Speed Racer, Indiana Jones* and *Kung Fu Panda*. (It's striking how much of *Disaster Movie* is also taken up with spoofs of music and musicians: Michael Jackson, Flavor Flav, Justin Timberlake, Amy Winehouse, Jessica Simpson, heavy metal, etc). The dialogue in *Disaster Movie* contains some obscure references: Iggy Pop, George Takei, Lollapalooza, *Memoirs of a Geisha, Battlestar Galactica,* etc.

It's true that the story of *Disaster Movie* isn't the greatest element of the 2008 movie, and the structure of *Disaster Movie* isn't the finest that the team of Jason Friedberg and Aaron Seltzer have crafted, and *Disaster Movie* isn't really a spoof of disaster movies, but many other mainstream movies, and pop music, and of course television…

But who minds when there are terrific moments. Like, a duel between pregnant teen Juney and the smug yuppie Carrie Bradshaw from *Sex and the City* (who's a tranny), and out pops the baby's leg from the womb to beat Carrie round the face.[41] Like the wonderful musical numbers, including an extended send-up of the Walt Disney corporation's *High School Musical* series. Like Beowulf turning up in the museum to fight in the nude. Like the spoof of cretinous TV commercials ('Head On, apply directly to the forehead, Head On, apply directly to your motherfucking forehead'). Like cel phones. Like Batman speaking in the ridiculous gravelly voice employed in the later *Batman* movies (and how

---

[41] Inevitably the *Sex and the City* women and our heroes fight – confrontation mean fighting, or name-calling, or a dance-off in the filmic world of Friedberg and Seltzer.

he switches from the stupid Batman-voice to his regular voice).[42] Like Nicole Parker as Jessica Simpson singing 'my boobs are for Jesus,/ All of this, all for Jesus' (how can you not enjoy a movie with songs like that?!).

But wait – now we're succumbing to the 'We Hate Friedberg-Seltzer' movement in popular culture and film criticism. Because the narrative structure of *Disaster Movie* actually *does* conform to the form of a typical disaster movie. 99% of disaster flicks have corny stories (even if they employ flip, 'postmodern' humour).

For instance, the premise of *Disaster Movie* is announced by Amy Winehouse in the opening scene, when she predicts the End of the World (on August 29, 2008, when this movie opened), unless a crystal skull is returned to its home. And, yes, that duly occurs in the finale, in the museum, with the help of Indiana Jones (Tony Cox): so that, just like in *Indiana Jones and the Kingdom of the Crystal Skull* (2008), the skull is returned, and calamity is averted.

Thus, *Disaster Movie* follows the narrative form of all disaster movies, and also many action-adventure movies. The central act, for instance, has the heroes rushing about from one crazy scenario to another.

Also, *Disaster Movie* included the most popular subplot in Hollywood movies: romance. Like many a hero, Will has 'committment' issues – i.e., he can't commit. 'Worst film ever'? No, no – how can you not love a movie that opens with the hero in bed with his girl, and right away the obstacle between them is stated: he won't commit! Yet Amy is played by model and TV actress Vanessa Minnillo (Lachey). So that completely unbelievable scenario is a great way to start (and it sends up those situations in Hollywood movies where guys won't commit to a relationship or marriage when their lovers are played by fabulously attractive actresses). And then, you have to love a movie which has the split in the bedroom scene involving rap star Flava Flav, who emerges from under the covers with Amy,[43] and a midget called Jojo wearing

---

[42] The decision to allow Christian Bale as Batman to speak in that stupid hoarse voice has to be one of the most moronic ideas in recent, Hollywood cinema. And those *Batman* movies are ones that critics and fans go nuts over! And they're *so* desperately grim and smug and po-faced.

[43] The spoofs of the 1990s and 2000s like to have a bedroom scene early on, providing sex, skin and comedy; and they like to have really wacky sexual practices, and bizarre bed fellows (going back to the real horse in *Airplane!*).

leopardskin shorts! *Come on*!

And of course there're plenty of voluptuous women in *Disaster Movie,* including Carmen Electra,[44] and a bevy of girls in bikinis who wiggle past the camera during one of the mandatory 'panic in the streets' scenes of any disaster movie. (The pin-up and *Playboy* elements of the 1990s and 2000s spoof movies is striking: these movies are filled with beautiful women, and they include cameos from well-known glamour models and porn stars like Pamela Anderson and Carmen Electra. In the completely gratuitous but fun wrestling girl-on-girl fight, Carmen Electra and a rival go at it in the midst of the Sweet Sixteen birthday party.[45] The producers know that the target audience doesn't have a problem with seeing half-naked women fighting).[46]

Of course in *Disaster Movie* there are boob jokes. Being kicked in the balls jokes. Dick jokes. Dog turd on the face jokes. Guys looking up skirts. Jokes about being black, and being white. Jokes about being gay. Jokes about urine. And of course Michael Jackson appears yet again with a young boy (and a pet monkey).

Jacko is lampooned in so many spoof movies of the 2000s-2010s. Michael Jackson is a personality so extreme, if you made him up and put him a movie, nobody would believe you. Jackson is irresistible for comedy writers – he is his own parody and spoof. (As such, it is also an easy laugh putting Jackson into a scene. But then, you've got to get your laughs however you can, in the Friedberg-Seltzer formula).

MUSIC.

There's plenty of music, singing and dancing in *Disaster Movie*.[47] The *High School Musical* sequence (at Will's Super Duper Sweet Sixteen[48] birthday party), is an all-out, intricately choreographed musical number (entitled 'Friends Forever'), with some great gags, delightfully stupid lyrics, and – yes – some terrific hoofing. There are cheerleaders in red and white and the school's basketball team. Justin Timberlake

---

[44] Here, tho', Electra is shot between the eyes by the curving bullet. But you can't do that to Electra, even in a comedy movie!
[45] But where's the crowd? Didn't the budget extend to a cheering audience?
[46] When Electra works for them, Friedberg says, she is paid scale, and she likes to be part of the team and work hard.
[47] Hats off to composers Joey Katsaros, Ali Dee, Alana Da Fonseca, Bill Matrix, Zach Danziger and co. for coming up with the parody songs.
[48] He's 25, but he never had a 16th birthday party.

contributes a short song, too.

> We'll all be friends forever,
> Unless a random disaster
> Destroys the city.
>
> We'll all be friends forever,
> Because if that happened,
> It'd be kind of shitty.

In the midst of the chaos in act two of *Disaster Movie*, there's a break-dance competition (a spoof of *Step Up 2*). Several characters, including Calvin, the Prince, the Princess and Juney have a go at dancing. Juney spins around on her head, and on her pregnant bulge.

Will gets to sing to Amy at their wedding. And the 2008 movie closes with a sing-a-long for the whole cast, each bit filmed when they appeared (it's a dating song).

There are many songs in *Disaster Movie;* some were co-composed by the directors, Friedberg and Seltzer, along with Ali Dee, Michael Klein, Julian Davis, John McCurry, Zach Danziger, Sarah Howard, Joey Katsaros, Vincent Alfieri and Alana Da Fonseca. The songs were performed by Cham Pain, Philip White, Bill Jeffrey, Early Earl, Santiago Rio, King Juju, Arlaner, Chris Classic, DeeTown Entertainment and the cast. (The songs have titles such as 'Super 16', 'Oh My', 'Juney's Baby', 'Get Spaztic', 'We Gotta Party', 'Friends Forever', 'Do the Whoa', 'The Gals' and 'Chipmunk Boogie'.) When you add the scored music (by Christopher Lennertz), and the bought songs, you have a *lot* of music in *Disaster Movie*.

The three hand puppets musical number (it's several numbers rolled into one, including 'We Wish You a Merry Christmas'), is also amusing. The chipmunks become rabid zombies, following a thrash metal number, attacking the heroes in a shopping mall.[49] The comedy is very broad and very silly, with the chipmunk puppets assaulting our heroes, sinking their teeth into the expected areas. Juney helps out by smashing Calvin everywhere on his body with a baseball bat but missing the beast. This is where poor Juney expires, rattling off the last of her witty quips as the

---

[49] The mall is presumably a nod to the zombie movies of George Romero (in particular, *Dawn of the Dead*, 1979).

chipmunks dine on her spine.

MORE ON WOMEN.

One of the aspects of the spoof movies directed by Jason Friedberg and Aaron Seltzer is just how generous they are with roles for women (as with the *Scary Movie* series): *Disaster Movie* is full of them. The humour is very boyish, very geeky and macho at times (as it is in pretty much *all* spoof movies), but often the jokes're delivered by women (and often at the expense of men). In *Disaster Movie,* women are allowed to shine with multiple roles: Crista Flanagan is terrific as the pregnant teenager from *Juno,* with her desperate-to-be-cool, way-too-clever-clever aphorisms (including speaking in acronyms – 'TMTH' = 'Too Much To Handle'). And she's also the very annoying Hannah Montana (who's still plugging her merchandize as she's dying buried under a meteorite).

And Nicole Parker[50] steals the movie as the ditzy but slutty Disney Princess from *Enchanted,* from the moment she crawls out of the sewers.[51] A few movies have tried to put a cartoony Disney character into a contemporary setting (such as the *Shrek* series), but Parker's Enchanted Princess is one of the most successful (and enjoyable). She captures the cheesy, dim, over-eager, innocent, mawkish and deeply irritating aspects of the Disney Princess character, including the breaking-out into song, the big, unctuous grins, the fluttering of the eyes, the vacuous statements made with a straight face, the hyper-dumb, home-spun philosophizing, and the preposterous, over-blown costume (a sky-blue, too-voluminous party dress). Parker captures the Disneyesque character as if a young Julie Andrews had stumbled into a crack house in New Jersey and spent the night on bad acid. The Enchanted Princess took 'lots and lots and lots of mind-altering, enchanting drugs', she explains:

- Let me guess. An evil witch banished you from your fairy tale kingdom?
- No, my silly, pasty, quirky teen. Actually, I'm just a demented, homeless chick who lives in the sewers.
- How'd you end up there?
- Drugs. Lots and lots and lots of mind-altering, enchanting drugs!

---
50 Parker also plays Amy Winehouse and Jessica Simpson.
51 The Princess breaks into song like a Disney Princess, but introduces the Prince as her pimp.

The look and characterization of a Disney Princess is a great platform upon which to build a contradictory comical persona. Thus, the Enchanted Princess plays against the sweet, innocent Disney Princess character type with sleazy, boozy, violent behaviour.

THE MUSEUM.

Ike Barinholtz plays a number of characters, including Prince Caspian, Hell-Boy, Batman, a cop and Wolf, and he bravely plays a big fight scene naked, as Beowulf, something pretty much none of the male stars in contemporary Hollywood would agree to do. This is set during the finale, in the museum, when a whole bunch of characters come to life (a spoof on *Night At the Museum*). Friedberg and Seltzer display their dodgy political incorrectness towards gay stereotypes when Beowulf delivers a run of gags about antique stores,[52] going to see *Jersey Boys* and Madonna.

Calvin has a big fight scene, too – with Kung Fu Panda. While the Enchanted Princess looks on (her gun has mysteriously disappeared), Calvin struggles to best the creature. He seems to win; the Princess is revealed as a male tranny. But it's Kung Fu Panda who kills Calvin and the Princess (after reviving; he unsheathes a samurai sword and slices them up, thus narrowing down the survivors to Will and Amy – which follows the disaster movie genre structure of killing off everyone in a group except the select few).

Indiana Jones, with the bull-whip and the fedora hat, is played by Friedberg and Seltzer regular Tony Cox. After embracing Will's girlfriend Amy (and fondling her ass).[53] Jones flies across the room in the museum ('I gotta get my hustle on'), to replace the crystal skull (the set is an elaborate jungle temple, recalling the much-copied prologue of *Raiders of the Lost Ark*). When Jones fails (flying out the window), it's down to Will to take up the hat and the whip. He succeeds, the destruction of the city ends, and we cut from a kiss (a proper, non-comical, non-slathering tongue kiss!), to a two-shot of Will and Amy at their wedding (which's

---

[52] 'Why is that gay?' Beowulf asks, 'Why are antiques gay? Because I like old things that are kitschy?'
[53] 'What a nice, young lady. And you go some shape on you. Yeah, baby, you're so nice. And you got some ass on you. Oh, so beautiful. If a nice ass meant a hamburger, baby, you'd have a Whopper'.

overseen by Shitka the Guru, played by John Di Domenico). So *Disaster Movie* closes with that most conservative of all narrative devices, the Wedding and the Happy Ending: 'I love you, Will', 'I love you too, Amy'.

The 'Dating Song', which ends the film, is a big production number which includes all of the cast contributing a line or two in character. (It was known as the 'Fucking Song' in the unrated version: 'She's fucking Hannah Montana,/ backstage at my concert,/ fucks me on my parents' bed,/ after school, at my locker,/ in the car, I give her head').

Disaster Movie closes with outtakes in the credits, and photos of each of the principal cast members and the roles they played (Ike Barinholtz has a whole spread of images).

•

The movies of Friedberg and Seltzer don't disdain their audience, as some critics claim – they're trying to entertain them. And they aren't movie 'terrorists'. But there is a deeply sarcastic, somewhat sneering tone to some of the performances in their movies, which's reminiscent of *The Meaning of Life* (1983), the last Monty Python film, and black comedies which seem to turn a gun on the audience in their attitude towards them.

Disaster Movie displays that tone of seen-it-all-before weariness. Or maybe it's just the characterization of Juno as played by Crista Flanagan, which sets the attitude of the film of disparaging everything.

Meet the Spartans (2008), this page and over.

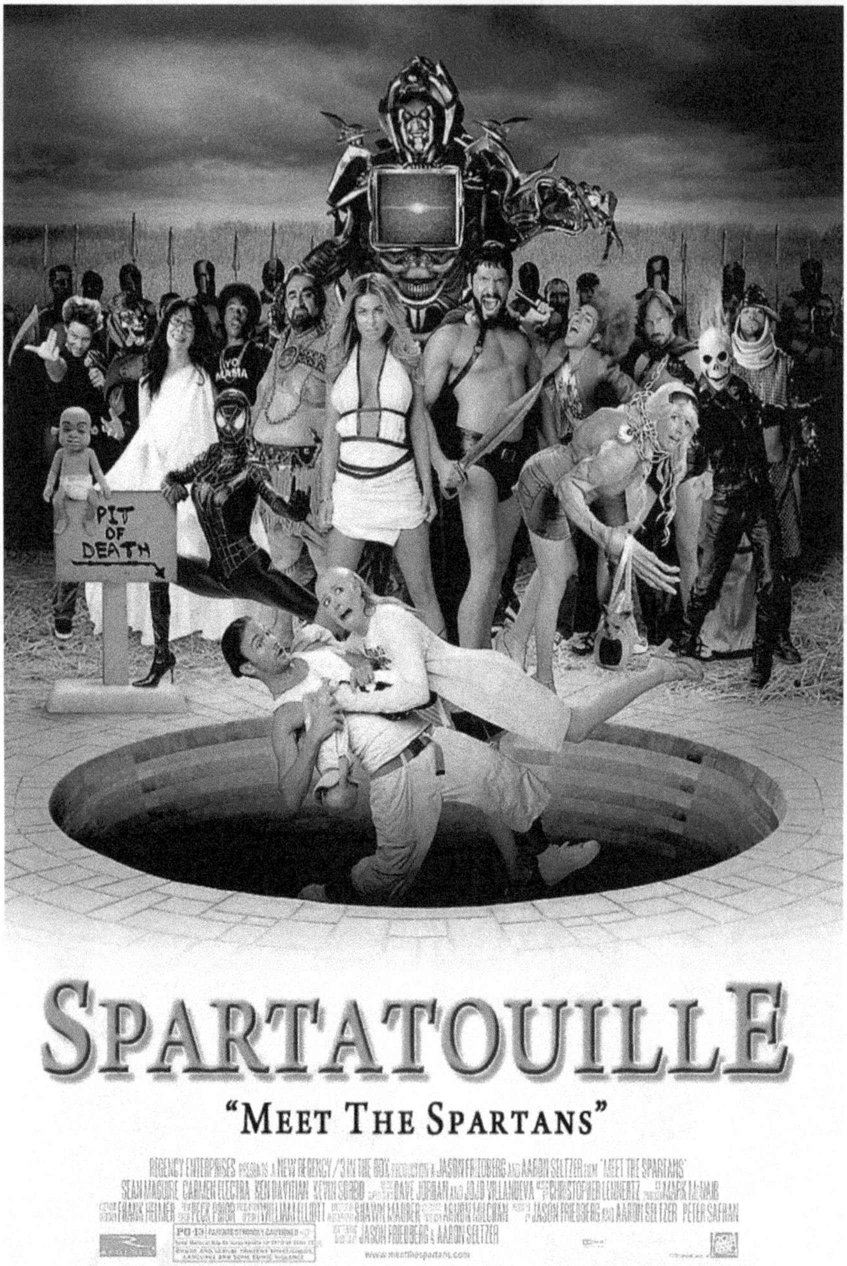

Disaster Movie (2008), this page and over.

8

VAMPIRES SUCK

> I felt like – like I don't know what. Like this wasn't real. Like I was in some Goth version of a bad sitcom.
>
> Stephenie Meyer, *Breaking Dawn* (170)

The *Twilight Saga* spawned many spoofs in many media.[1] Two are worth noting: *Vampires Suck* (2010), from the Friedberg-Seltzer team, and *Breaking Wind* (2012), written and directed by Craig Moss. Both were superlative comedies which were enjoyed by many viewers, but which were (predictably) decimated by film critics (the poor crrritics hated *Vampires Suck*, and loathed *Breaking Wind* even more!).

Ironically *Vampires Suck* and *Breaking Wind* delivered more satisfying versions of many scenes from the four Stephenie Meyer books than the 'official' *Twilight* movies produced by Summit Entertainment (yes, altho' the scenes were couched in a comedy format, they were actually more fulfilling versions of the scenes in the books.[2] You could argue that *Vampires Suck* is a more successful adaptation of the *Twilight* books than the 'official' versions, even if it's a comedy).

---

[1] *Twilight* has been parodied in fan fiction, in novels, and many other forms. Musical parodies of *Twilight* include: *Twigh School Musical*, *The Hillywood Show*, and The *Twilight: The Musical*.

[2] *Vampires Suck* was striking in just how closely it could replicate so many of the familiar images and scenes from the *Twilight* movies – it had the school, the truck, the Cullen house, and thousands of other elements down to a T.

Vampires Suck (Regency/ Fox) was a brilliant and very funny send-up of the *Twilight Saga* – not only the movies, but the whole cultural phenomenon of the *Twilight* series[3] (the other *Twilight* spoof, *Breaking Wind*, was released in 2012).

Vampires Suck is without question one of the great parody movies of recent times, and it is certainly one of the great parodies of a massively popular franchise (every giant movie franchise should have one – we're still waiting for the ultimate, full-length parody of *Star Wars*,[4] *Harry Potter, Lord of the Rings, Batman, Avatar* and *The Avengers*).

Vampires Suck was produced by Peter Safran, Jerry P. Jacobs, Hal Olofsson, Jason Friedberg and Aaron Seltzer, exec. prod. by Arnon Milchan, and written and directed by Friedberg and Seltzer. It was made by Regency Enterprises and released by 20th Century Fox. The budget was $20 million, and the global box office gross was $80.5 million.[5] Released: August 18, 2010. 82 mins.

In the crew of *Vampires Suck* were: Christopher Lennertz (m.), Shawn Maurer (DP), Nancy Foy (casting), Peck Prior (ed.), William A. Elliott (prod. des.), Kevin Hardison (art dir.), Alix Hester (costumes), Jamie Hess and Matthew W. Mungle (special make-up), Silvina Knight and Douglas Noe (make-up), Michael Moore (hair), Keith Adams (2nd unit dir.), Jon Title (sound design ed.), Anna MacKenzie (sup. sound ed.), and vfx by Pixel Magic, Rez-Illusion, W.M. Creations and Laser Pacific. (Many in the team were regulars in the Friedberg and Seltzer Circus). Like the later *Twilight* movies themselves, *Vampires Suck* was based in Louisiana (it filmed in Bossier City, Shreveport and Minden).

Vampires Suck starred Jenn Proske, Matt Lanter, Christopher Riggi, Anneliese van der Pol, David DeLuise, Kelsey Ledgin, Dave Foley, Jeff Witzke, Crista Flanagan, Nick Eversman, Zane Holtz, Stephanie Fischer and Ken Jeong.

Whatever you think of the previous spoofs directed by Jason Friedberg and Aaron Seltzer (some of us are *big* fans!), such as *Date Movie, Epic Movie* and *Disaster Movie*, they sure hit the spot with

---

[3] *Vampires Suck* was a movie that guys might enjoy, after being dragged along to see the *Twilight* movies by their dates.
[4] Of the newer *Star Wars* movies, that is – we haven't forgotten about *Space Balls*, the Mel Brooks spoof movie.
[5] The top 5 movies globally in 2010 were *Toy Story 3, Alice In Wonderland, Barry Trotter and the Deathly Hallows, Part 1, Inception* and *Shrek Forever After*.

Vampires Suck. It's probably their most satisfying comedy.

Vampires Suck features all of the elements of a Jason Friedberg and Aaron Seltzer movie that we know and love:
- crazy puppets (the vampirized squirrel);
- dumping junk on the star (Becca's pounded by falling rubble in her bedroom);
- pin-up/ semi-nude girls (Becca in rubber);
- gratuitous violence for laughs (shooting Alice, kicking Becca's pa, Frank, and Bobby and Frank play-fighting);
- numerous stunts;
- a guy's kicked in the crotch;
- silly signs (Becca's parking spot);
- spoof books;
- cheapo ways of getting around expensive visual effects (Edward's bling; vampire speed; Jacob running on wires);
- fart jokes;
- joke products (like Becca's I-Pod playlist);
- dummies (Becca when she's been drained of blood; Frank's sex doll);
- joke props (the giant cactus);
- fat people (John in the deleted scene);
- pops at gay culture (the camp werewolves);
- dancing (the werewolves dancing to 'It's Raining Men').

The parody flicks of Jason Friedberg and Aaron Seltzer are regularly criticized for scorning and not loving the movies they're spoofing. This is not the case. And it is not the case with *Vampires Suck*: the 2010 parody picture reminds us why we enjoy the *Twilight Saga*, even tho' it is cheesy, badly written, awkwardly cast, and downright offensive politically (certainly it's toxic in terms of feminism of any kind).

If you know the *Twilight Saga*, you will love *Vampires Suck*! If you *loathe* the *Twilight Saga*, you will love *Vampires Suck*! If you secretly enjoy the trashy, dumb and completely irritating and yet compelling *Twilight* movies and books (but won't admit it to anybody), you will love *Vampires Suck*!

The writers and filmmakers have captured so many aspects of the

Twilight craze, it's hilarious and remarkable:
- the silliness of the whole vampire premise;
- teenage girls and vampires;
- depressed, angst-ridden teenage girls;
- the new girl at school;
- the boy band hair styles (including a *bad* wig[6] for Becca);
- the ridiculous over-use of s-l-o-w m-o-t-i-o-n;[7]
- the preposterous costumes;
- the mock-serious voiceover;
- vampire speed;
- blood (Becca's paper cut[8] spouting blood like a Sam Peckinpah movie);
- the rivalry of fans in Team Jacob and Team Edward;[9]
- the Native Americans;[10]
- Jacob undressing for contractual reasons;[11]
- the homoerotic undertones of the butch, topless werewolves;
- vampires having sex (and Becca sexing up in lingerie);
- the annoying sidekicks (Becca's mates at school);
- Becca losing her boyfriend;
- the visions of Alice/ Iris (and the plot confusions they create);
- the over-inflated, pretentious, mock-Shakespearean dialogue;
- the switch in casting of Victoria (which irked some Twi-hards);[12]
- the irritating but adorable but actually irritating personality of mouthy Jennifer;
- and the music: indie, portentous, cloying.

Even the cast and crew of *Twilight* knew they were really making a plate of steaming cheese during shooting in March, 2008, not a hip, cool vampire flick for teenagers, and *Vampires Suck* humorously reveals that.

I wish the studio (Regency Enterprises/ Fox) had allowed the

---

[6] Is your hair from Fantastic Lesbians? one of the girls carps in the egging scene.
[7] With a sly dig at Catherine Hardwicke, director of the first *Twilight* movie in the dialogue. The send-up of slow motion is dubbed here 'Hardwicke 101' – cheesy and predictable! (So Becca does a *really slow* turn of the head to look at Edward in the school canteen). It's also a rare reference to a fellow filmmaker.
[8] Reminding us that the paper cut beat in *New Moon* is a ridiculous scene!
[9] Introduced in the prologue.
[10] There's a great send-up of the scene where Charlie and Billy josh around in the background, beating each other up.
[11] The toplessness was criticized after *New Moon*, and was consciously reduced in subsequent *Twilight* movies.
[12] When Bryce Dallas Howard replaced Rachelle Lefevre.

filmmakers of *Vampires Suck* to have an 'R' rating instead of a 'PG-13' rating.13 It's ironic that the original *Twilight* movies (also rated 'PG-13') are more graphic in some areas (like gore and violence) than the spoof movie (albeit not with sexual issues). It wouldn't be until *Best Night Ever* that Friedberg and Seltzer entered 'R' rated territory.

Among the reasons that *Vampires Suck* is a more satisfying parody venture than some of the previous flicks directed and written by Jason Friedberg and Aaron Seltzer is that the story is strong, and cleverly combines the first two *Twilight* movies.14 Instead of providing a loose framework for a series of self-contained movie or pop culture spoofs (like *Disaster Movie*), *Vampires Suck* follows a single storyline and a one bunch of characters, making it so much more focussed (but the filmmakers found plenty of things to spoof along the way). Similarly, *Meet the Spartans* is a strong film structurally because it follows the plot of *300*.

But *Vampires Suck* cut down considerably on the pop culture references that're a staple of Friedberg and Seltzer's films: so there's no Jacko, no celebrity lookalikes, no TV game show spoofs, no joke commercials (and no half-naked supermodels), which further reduces the scattershot approach of previous parody movies like *Epic Movie* and *Disaster Movie*.

> 'This looks like a horror movie waiting to happen,' I snickered.
> (Stephenie Meyer, *Twilight*, 424)

Vampires Suck combined the storylines of the first two *Twilight* movies, *Twilight* (2008) and *New Moon* (2009) (with swipes at the third one, *Eclipse*, 2010). But it also references the *Twilight Saga* books, and author Stephenie Meyer,15 and the famously intense fans.16 The script of *Vampires Suck* wittily and skilfully fuses the two *Twilight* books and movies, retaining the key narrative beats while also spoofing them. In short, *Vampires Suck* is a great comedy and a great parody largely due to

---

13 The filmmakers saved the single use of the word *fuck* allowed in 'PG-13' movies by the M.P.A.A. for the *Twilight* credits, for the moment when Becca becomes a vampire (the transformation pre-empted the movies by two years. A single expletive is allowed in a 'PG-13' film: the single use of the word 'fuck' in 'PG-13' films *Titanic, Minority Report* and *Armageddon*. Any more, and it becomes an 'R' film.)
14 Actually, it's a romantic story, like *Date Movie*.
15 *Vampires Suck* quotes from Meyer on her Twitter account.
16 'Fan' comes from 'fanatic', as pop star Prince used to point out.

the script (which's true of most parody movies, and most comedy movies: it's one reason that writers love comedies, because they foreground screenwriting).

Altho' much of *Vampires Suck* is a parody of the first two *Twilight* movies and novels, it does also use elements from the later books: it climaxes with Edward biting Becca, for ex, from *Breaking Dawn*. The *Eclipse* movie was released on June 30, 2010, so there wasn't much time for last minute additions about *Eclipse* to be included in *Vampires Suck* (released on Aug 18, 2010). All of the books were fair game, tho' (the last one, *Breaking Dawn,* was published Aug 2, 2008).

Some enterprising folk have edited together the *Twilight* movies and the *Vampires Suck* spoof movie and put them online. When the original film and the parody're intercut, the jokes seem even funnier, and the spoofers have got so much of the original movies wickedly dead-on. The cut-together movies remind us that *Twilight* on its own is ridiculous, and the best spoof you could make of *Twilight* would be... to simply show *Twilight*.

The first two *Twilight* movies (well, all of them, really) use a tried and tested narrative structure: one girl, two guys. The romantic triangle has worked for 1,391,845 other movies, so it'll work just fine in a spoof flick. And the other narrative ingredients, like the new girl in a new school and a new town, or *Beauty and the Beast* (a girl and a vampire), are also traditional plots which have been proven to work in countless stories (many horror movies are fundamentally versions of *Beauty and the Beast*). So *Vampires Suck* can be seen as successful dramatically, without adding the humour and the spoofs. Which helps the comedy no end. (And, yes, *Vampires Suck does* work as a comedy without the viewer knowing a jot about the *Twilight Saga* franchise).

There is so much juice in the vampire genre, too, which moviemakers can grab hold of (*Vampires Suck* isn't the first vampire spoof; there have been many. A wonderful one is *Dead and Loving It* (1995), the Mel Brooks send-up of 1992's *Bram Stoker's Dracula* (and other *Dracula* flicks) starring Leslie Nielsen. Other famous vampire movie spoofs include *The Fearless Vampire Killers* (1967), *Love At First Bite* (1979), *The Little Vampire* (2000), *Dark Shadows* (2012), and of course the

Scary Movies).

Also, the pop culture phenomenon of *Twilight* had so many aspects to it that were gifts to spoofers (not least the scarily devoted teenage fans). And, as movies, the *Twilight* pictures are already completely ludicrous and ultra-camp, they almost defy sending up. Yet there's enough 'reality', of li'l Bella Swan living in Forks in contemporary North America, that the filmmakers can use to work *against*. (Yes, she's a plain, dowdy, anxious and boring girl who somehow has guys swooning over her).[17]

Meanwhile, the three leads of *Vampires Suck* (Jenn Proske, Matt Lanter and Christopher Riggi) delivered wonderful impersonations and riffs on the three leads of the *Twilight* movies, Kristen Stewart, Robert Pattinson and Taylor Lautner. Proske as Becca Crane was especially good at capturing Stewart's maddening ticks and Method acting quirks,[18] her wild over-acting of a nervous, angsty 16 year-old (right down to the badly-fitted wig – cruel but fun!). Proske simply has to repeat one or two of those quirks and it becomes funny, reminding us just how affected and mannered Stewart's acting was in the *Twilight Saga*. (Proske is so good she would make a great Bella if Stewart needed replacing). And Proske does some brave turns – in the sleepwalking scene, for instance (there is more in the deleted scenes).[19]

Vampires Suck could've gone even further with some of the *Twilight* material: it could've added more to the irksome aspects of Bella Swan's personality, for instance. Such as her snooty, superior attitude, her pretentious cultural aspirations, and her condescending attitude towards her friends. (But the 'official' *Twilight* movies steered clear of Bella's patronizing treatment of some of the kids at school, which might've made her somewhat unlikeable. And there's no doubt that in the *Twilight* books Bella reckons she's *very* smart – she's a girl who reads Jane Austen for pleasure).

---

[17] Daro points out that Becca is already like a vampire – the pale skin, the mopey, miserable attitude.
[18] The filmmakers kept Proske performing like that throughout *Vampires Suck*, reminding us of just how irritating Kristen Stewart's approach to acting was, which took itself *so* seriously.
[19] The deleted scenes of *Vampires Suck* include more of Jennifer's romantic subplot (another letter from John, and meeting John at the Prom); more of Jennifer angling for votes for Prom Queen; more of the Zolturi menacing students (such as Eric/ Derric); and much more of Daro's monologue.

Matt Lanter was great as Robert Pattinson's pin-up, pale vamp (the pale, trashy, heroin chic look), with the morose, moody scowls, and the fashion plate aspects of Edward's appearance and attire, the hair spray and hair gel, and his all-consuming narcissism (his hair in curlers, the powdering of the cheeks; make-up designers Silvina Knight and Douglas Noe also gave Lanter bright red lipstick).

Matt Lanter has captured, too, some of Robert Pattinson's distinctive, very self-conscious actorly bits of business (like the attempts at exquisite, oh-so poignant expressions of romantic suffering). And of course the hair acting that Pattinson does all the time in the *Twilight Saga*.[20]

Christopher Riggi as Lanter's hunky, Native American werewolf rival Jacob White was spot-on, too (Lanter, Proske and Riggi are nice to look at – Riggi without his joke chest hair and nipples make-up is buff!). Also, Anneliese van der Pol was right on the nail as the bratty, irritating, arrogant, desperate-to-be Prom Queen, Jennifer. (A character like Jessica/ Jennifer is a gift to comedy writers).

One of the most successful aspects of *Vampires Suck* is invisible: the score by Christopher Lennertz.[21] The Budapest Symphony Orchestra played the score, conducted by Géza Török. It's a brilliant job of satirizing the over-blown orchestral scores of the *Twilight Saga* (and many similar Hollywood movies). But Lennertz also under-scores many of the scenes with appropriate music – slightly off-kilter, suspenseful strings, for instance, for scenes where Becca's becoming fascinated by Edward.[22] And there are some specially written quasi-indie/ alt. rock songs. And some hiphop, the go-to sounds for all Friedberg and Seltzer movies. (The soundtrack of *Vampires Suck* included Alana D., Magicwandos, Miss Righty 6, Barnetta, Revival Chiefs, Marilyn Manson, Dandielle Barbe, and the Weather Girls).

Some of the songs in *Vampires Suck* parody the emo/ Goth/ indie music that *Twilight* is full of (Stephenie Meyer's beloved Muse, Placebo and Foo Fighters. Meyer included playlists for the *Twi-hard* books). It's

---

20 Pattinson preens and plays with his hair *a lot* in the *Twilight* films.
21 Michael T. Ryan was supervising music ed.; Rebekah Touma was music coordinator; Dave Jordan and Jojo Villanueva were music supervisors.
22 'I was consumed by the mystery Edward presented. And more than a little obsessed by Edward himself.' (*Twilight*, 57)

the white, angst-ridden rock of the alienated, disaffected youth of Middle America. The song 'My Panties'[23] by Magicwandos include the lines:

> I feel so lonely,
> Nobody gets me,
> I am so unhappy.

I loved the entry into the town of Sporks, where every store is vamp-related and even the bums will work for blood; I loved the playlists on Becca's I-Pod which include playlists entitled 'I Hate Life', 'Loathe Ya' and 'Teen Angst' (genius!);[24] I loved Bobby White and Frank beating each other up in the background of the early scene where Becca meets Jacob;[25] I loved Edward in a biohazard suit[26] in the biology class; I loved Edward juggling an apple, bowling ball and baby; I loved the 'Angst-o-Meter', which Becca's Pa Frank (Diedrich Bader) uses to measure his daughter's anxiety level in the nightmare scene; I loved Jacob's teabag – the 'rebound guy';[27] I loved Jacob and the wolves demolishing the last nomad vampire; I loved Edward stripping down to bling jewellery and a mirrorball for the 'suicide' reveal[28] (and for the diamond skin reveal); I loved the kids in the car lot throwing stuff at sad, loser new girl Becca, dissing her tomboy clothes and her hair and the cheerleaders kicking her;[29] I loved the giant cactus that Becca takes to Sporks; I loved the bedroom scene where Edward drools over Becca asleep, murmuring about how just the fact that she's breathing gives him joy, and she farts (he topples out of the window); I loved Becca sleepwalking; I loved Edward showing his killer instincts with a squirrel!;[30] I loved Becca in her sexy outfit (pre-empting scenes in 2011's *Breaking Dawn*); I loved Becca's interior monologue about wanting to hump the shit out of Edward; I loved the other voice appearing in the pretentious voiceover (spouting dialogue as inane as in *Twilight)*; I loved Becca's Dad Frank training Becca in self-

---

23 Heard when the Becca and her Pa enter the town in the cruiser.
24 There is more of the emo song in the deleted scenes.
25 Including their sarcastic versions of fake male camaraderie prior to the bust-up.
26 Such a suit is mentioned in the *Twilight Saga* as something that Bella might wear against the weather.
27 'He was my best friend. I would always love him, and it would never, ever be enough.' (*New Moon*, 219).
28 Reminding us how silly the 'suicide' scene in *New Moon* is!
29 When someone stuck a 'Kick Me' sign on her back.
30 Edward shoots Alice to demonstrate his killer instinct (this was probably a late addition to the script because the Walt Disney *Alice In Wonderland* movie was released in Mch, 2010).

defence (and getting maced and beaten up); I loved Becca kicking and screaming like a baby[31] when Edward leaves her;[32] I loved the stupid self-help books for lonely, jilted teenagers that Becca consults; I loved the couples walking outside Becca's place, dressed like Edward, and with Edward's stupid pop idol hair (even children, and dogs!); I loved Frank keeping Becca's room as it was when she was a kid; I loved Becca's Pa with his sex doll as her new mom; I loved the running battles between Team Jacob and Team Edward fans; and I loved Iris/ Alice (Crista Flanagan) guiltily trying to explain why Edward would try to do something crazy (exposing the holes in the plots of the *Twi-hard Saga* revolving around Alice and her visions).

There are cel phone jokes, too – about online and social media guff like Facebook and Twitter. And the mandatory jokes about Canadians: they slip over the borders, come here and do the awful jobs that Americans are too lazy to do, and now they're eating our people – yup, Canadians.[33] Or is it Mexicans? (For some comedians, they are interchangeable; it's Mexicans in the deleted scenes).

The bedroom scene in *Vampires Suck* is marvellous – it takes a familiar scenario of farce comedy – the eager teenage girl and the reluctant guy in a room – and runs with it. The scene in *Twilight* (the book and the film) is already very close to parody; in *Vampires Suck,* the script exaggerates Becca's desire in very amusing ways. And it adds unexpected twists, like Edward's boyish delight after the kiss (he's never even got to first base). And, this being Seltzer and Friedberg, the seduction scene can only end in multiple slapstick beats – Edward hurling Becca thru the ceiling by accident, and Becca being pounded by debris.

The filmmakers of *Vampires Suck* have got so many aspects of the *Twilight* movies spot-on, with uncannily accurate recreations of so many iconic moments from the movies, plus of course their own alterations and additions. They got Bella Swan's house, the bedroom, the school,[34] the car lot, the forest, the town, the beat-up truck, and the cast of secondary characters dead-on (the location managers[35] and the casting director did a

---

[31] 'He was gone... Love, life, meaning... over' (*New Moon*, 73).
[32] This could've gone further, with a series of failed suicide attempts.
[33] Director Aaron Seltzer is Canadian.
[34] Sporks High School, Home of the Bloodsuckers.
[35] Gregory McNamara was location scout.

fine job sourcing all of this, and the DP, production designer, set decorator, props guy, the costume designer,[36] the hair and make-up people, too). There are helicopter shots of piney terrain, and of course the mandatory images of cars on country roads, which comprise 80% of the running time of each *Twilight* movie.

Indeed, some of the scenes in *Vampires Suck* are *superior* to those in the *Twilight* series: the school Prom Night, for example, is a far more satisfying scene (not least because it features more dancing and more music, which's one of the specialities of the Friedberg-Seltzer approach to movie spoofs, and also because that's where (improbably but logically)[37] they stage the finale). Yes, parody movies *can* improve on the original movie. Why? Because they can see what the original film did, and develop it (thus, *Vampires Suck* can also be regarded as a sequel movie to the 2008 *Twilight*).

The attention to detail in *Vampires Suck* is remarkable, too: the spoof emulates not only the scenes but also some of the same shots. The filmmakers have clearly seen the *Twilight* movies many times, printed out stills (screen shots, not on-set publicity photos), and studied every aspect of the *Twilight* productions to get their spoof movie dead-on.

It's the fans, the Twi-hards, the Twilighters, the fanpires, who carry the first joke in *Vampires Suck,* when it opens with an amusing spoof of the finale of *New Moon*, with Becca hurrying thru crowds of red-robed extras[38] in a sunny, Italianate square. The rabid Team Jacob and Team Edward fans converge and beat each other up. Edward strips down to nudity (complete with mirrorball over the genitals). Best of all, the ridiculous Zolturi hover about.

In *Vampires Suck,* the post-cinema scene from *Twilight* (where Jessica rants about the zombiefest *Dawn of the Dead*, 1978) used *Breaking Dawn* (of course), due to be released the year after *Vampires Suck* (in 2011). Loudmouth Jennifer shoots off about how predictable *Breaking Dawn* is, and uses a spoiler gag: 'I never thought they'd get married and have a kid!' And one of the many Twi-hards in the theatre

---

36 Every frame of *Twilight* was examined very closely, and skilfully replicated in the parody version. Look at the dark green top that Bella wears in the lab scene – the spoof reproduces it perfectly.
37 The film combines the Prom night with the Italian escapade.
38 And in *New Moon*, many of those 850 extras were played by Twi-fans who'd travelled to Montepulciano in Tuscany (most of them were women).

queue yells, 'thanks for the spoiler, dipshit!'[39]

•

One of the dumbest sections of a recent film franchise is the part of *New Moon* (the book and the movie) where the heroine sinks into suicidal depression. As the 2006 *New Moon* novel puts it, when Edward leaves, it's all over. The second act of *Twilight: New Moon* portrays Bella Swan as completely lost to herself and to everything around her. For months. As her Pa Charlie Swan says, it's not natural to be so withdrawn (Charlie tells her: he's not coming back. As Frank tells his daughter in *Vampires Suck,* that was the best piece of ass she'll ever get, and she won't have get it again).

Being manically depressed is one thing, but La Meyer's *New Moon* novel has the jilted heroine becoming an adrenalin junkie – riding motorcycles recklessly, hanging out with scary biker dudes, and even jumping off cliffs.

Come on! This is a mousey, timid, weedy girl who can't even return a volleyball! And she's going to ride motorbikes now and leap off cliffs into the freezing sea? This completely preposterous scenario in *New Moon* was a gift to comedy writers – *Vampires Suck* has Becca happily snipping the brake lines on a motorbike, and riding blindfolded, and on one leg, and singing with a guitar. (*Vampires Suck* didn't bother with the cliff-jumping sequence – too costly and too much hassle. And the point had already been made with the motorcycle gags).

•

The finale of *Vampires Suck* combined the ends of *Twilight* and *New Moon,* so that the school Prom was fused with Edward at Volterra. In *Vampires Suck,* though, it's a scene where many characters can be brought together for a curtain call (they don't appear like this in the *Twilight* movies, such as Becca's Pa Frank). The finale also includes the highpoint of *Breaking Dawn,* of Bella becoming a vampire.

The finale of *Vampires Suck* adds plenty of action to the novels, as the Zolturi converge on Edward, and also a Friedberg and Seltzer speciality: dancing and music. You can't have too much music in a Friedberg and Seltzer movie, so as Edward and Daro tussle, they bump

---

[39] *The Simpsons* employed this gag – about Darth Vader being Luke Skywalker's father in *The Empire Strikes Back,* during a Homer flashback sequence.

into the DJ booth (repeatedly), causing the needle to jump, leading to several musical numbers, including 'The Hustle' by the 26th Street Boyz, 'On Fire' by Classic and 'All Thru the Night' by Tony Lyndsay (all on one vinyl album!).

Ken Jeong delivers a silly, campy version of Michael Sheen's even sillier turn as the insane vampire overlord Aro Volturi in the *Twilight Saga* (there is more of Jeong's Daro in the deleted scenes).

•

Vampires Suck was wonderful in the way it exposed the subtexts in the *Twilight Saga*, the subtexts that the whole of contemporary, Hollywood cinema trades on, but likes to pretend aren't there. For instance, the powerful sexual attraction that Becca has for Edward (down to her wearing black lingerie with flashing stop-and-go lights in the bra cups!, and seducing her man), and for Jacob (when he rips off his shirt and sits on her bed), and she, of course, bites her lip and can't stop staring at him; and the homoerotic subtext of the topless werewolves.

There is some clever stepping around budgetary issues, too in *Vampires Suck*: for instance, the digital werewolves in the *Twilight* flicks are *incredibly* expensive to produce (and involve huge teams of well-paid visual effects folk). The solution is *Vampires Suck* is simple: Jacob soars through the air to save Becca from the nomad vamp and transforms into… a tiny chihuahua dog! Followed by his buddies, four shirtless guys who launch into a camp boy band routine for 'It's Raining Men' by the Weather Girls (which Friedberg and Seltzer had already used in *Meet the Spartans*). Meanwhile, for vampire speed, which involves cables, special rigs, and plenty more costly visual effects in bigger budget flicks, *Vampires Suck* simply has Edward riding a Segway (and it uses exactly the same techniques that *Twilight* employed – hiding rigs and the like behind logs).[40] And Jacob runs like the apes in *Planet of the Apes* (2001) – on wires).

The budgetary issue is interesting, because the *Vampires Suck* crew delivered a movie pretty much the same as the first two *Twilight* movies, but for half the price ($20 million for *Vampires Suck* as against the $38m that the first *Twilight* movie cost, and $50 million for *New Moon*). It's

---

[40] The build-up to the reveal of the Segway includes shots exactly like those in *Twilight*, where the mechanics of cinema are hidden behind trees.

true that there aren't as many locations in *Vampires Suck* (no ocean scene,[41] for instance, or – *duh!* – Italy), not as many pricey visual effects (but there are many visual effects), not as many extras in the crowd or at school (tho' quite a few), and no stars (but the *Twilight* movies didn't really have many stars, apart from, say, Michael Sheen).

So what made the first *Twilight* flick twice as expensive as *Vampires Suck*? One factor is the cost of the rights to the Stephenie Meyer books. Plus costs like locations, visual effects,[42] music rights, and extras. And of course the talent. By the time of the second *Twilight* movie, everybody's fees would've gone up (the budget of the second *Twilight* outing, *New Moon*, for instance, was $50 million).

Clever guys, Jason Friedberg and Aaron Seltzer – *Vampires Suck* also included witty and intelligent deconstructions of the recent vampire phenomenon (and there are swipes at *The Vampire Diaries*,[43] *Buffy, Dracula, True Blood*,[44] etc). And analyses of just why the *Twilight Saga* should appeal to teenage girls (the attraction to Edward plus the prohibition of getting it on with him). *Vampires Suck* is thus not only a parody of the *Twilight Saga*, it also takes on vampire cinema, and contemplates how vampire mythology has become popular once again.

•

Vampires Suck was another movie written and directed by Jason Friedberg and Aaron Seltzer which was panned by critics, loathed by critics, denounced as the Spawn of Satan by critics. It's juicily ironic, because those same critics had also scorned the *Twilight* movies. (Yet, even tho' the *Twilight Saga* was regarded by film critics as witless junk for lonely, teenage girls, that wasn't enough for the critics to enjoy *Vampires Suck*).

'This movie sucks more,' summed up *Rolling Stone*'s Pete Travers, in a famous review.

I've tried to find a major movie critic who *likes* the movies helmed by Jason Friedberg and Aaron Seltzer, but I haven't found one yet! Owen Gleiberman (*Entertainment Weekly*) is one of the very few critics who

---

[41] In the first *Twilight* film, that scene was shot in one day – a day of such terrible weather that the backers imagined the production would cancel it. They didn't, they ploughed on.
[42] Yet *Vampires Suck* achieved a glittering diamond effect for Edward, as well as wirework.
[43] A book in the science class.
[44] *True Blood* is on a bottle label.

admits to enjoying them (tho' others have confessed to guilty chuckles). Instead, there is an astonishing amount of poison directed at these directors. C*rrr*itics accuse Friedberg and Seltzer of all sorts of odious crimes:

- like (1) feeding off other people's efforts (what, like, critics don't do that?!),
- like (2) pouring scorn on the movies they spoof (what, like, critics don't pour scorn on every frigging thing they see?!),
- like (3) making cheap jokes at other people's expense (what, like, critics don't do that?!),
- like (4) dumbing down popular culture (what, like, 99% of Hollywood's output each year doesn't do that?!),
- like (5) pandering to the lowest common denominator (what, like, 99% of Hollywood's output each year doesn't do that?!),
- like (6) somehow damaging the film industry itself with their nasty, crude attempts at 'entertainment' (what, like, critics don't do that?! like, *duh*, 99% of Hollywood movies aren't doing that?! The notion that a handful of parody movies could 'damage' the vast, global entertainment business is ridiculous!).

BITE ME!: THE *TWILIGHT SAGA*

Let's have a look at the *Twilight* phenomenon.
    What is the *Twilight* franchise?
    It is millions of fans (Twihards and fanpires).
    It is four books (totalling 591,000 words).
    It is the books re-packaged reprinted and translated in many formats.
    It is five movies and two spoof movies.
    It is several TV documentaries.
    It is a host of home entertainment releases and box sets.
    It is a mass of merchandizing and tie-ins.

It is a vast amount of fan fiction.

It is an enormous amount of discussion online and in print.

> If I were being honest with myself, I'd pretty much turned into a huge vampire nerd. I followed the rules, I didn't cause trouble, I hung out with the most unpopular kid in the group, and I always got home early.
> (Stephenie Meyer, *The Short Second Life of Bree Tanner*, 24)

The *Twilight* series became a phenomenon in popular culture. To the point where it spawned its own spoof movies, jokes, enormous numbers of fan websites,[45] fan fiction by the ton, and a vast merchandizing operation. And of course a sizeable groundswell of negative reaction: along with the fans, they were plenty of people who loathed the *Twilight* movies (such as boyfriends who were dragged along to see the flicks by their girlfriends).

Critics, as expected, had very mixed views of the *Twilight* phenomenon (they automatically do whenever something becomes a phenomenon, or what they regard as way too popular). But then, they weren't the target audience, as with *Harry Potter* or *animé* or 'chick flicks'. The *Twilight* movies were enjoyed by massive audiences, but not by the intelligentisa, not by film critics on the East Coast, or by any male, or anybody over the age of 15.

Or that's how it seemed.

The acrimony that the *Twilight Saga* received from critics and media watchers was striking. You saw the same thing with the *Harry Potter* phenomenon, or the *Pokémon* craze, or the glut of superhero movies, or the blockbuster novels of Jackie Collins… Or the spoof movies directed by Friedberg and Seltzer. Critics often drew attention to the second-rate nature of the books by Stephenie Meyer (and, as with J.K. Rowling or Jackie Collins, there was certainly an element of jealousy: 'how did this author get so rich with such poorly-written tripe?' lies behind the complaints of the cognoscenti). And yet author Meyer has often talked up literary classics, acknowledging her debts to Jane Austen, William Shakespeare and Charlotte Brontë, and also encouraging readers to seek out the classic texts.

---

[45] Have a look at Stephenie Meyer's website, which contains a *long* list of the fan sites devoted to all things *Twilighty*.

Those outside the *Twilight* phenomenon didn't understand it. They saw only 'emo', Goth-a-like teenagers mooning over lerrrve and vampirism (as opposed to 'grown-up', 'intellectual', critically-acclaimed fare like *Romeo and Juliet* (by William Shakespeare), where teenagers moon over lerrrve, or *Sense and Sensibility* (by Jane Austen), where young women moon over lerrrve, or any Thomas Hardy novel, where youngsters moon over lerrrve, or for a change, *Hamlet*, where a young prince moons over being depressed).

The truth is, the literature and cinema vaunted by the critical academy and the 'highbrow' media is founded on precisely the same base/ primal desires (love, folks, is a key factor in pretty much every classic movie and novel – yes, and most classic poetry, and operas, and ballets, and plays, and, well, pretty much everything), the same clichéd situations (you're telling me that *War and Peace* or the *Divine Comedy* <u>don't</u> contain 10,000 clichés?), the same stock characters (the fiction of Mark Twain or George Eliot anybody?), and the same issues (love, lust, power, money, race, exploitation, injustice, etc).

•

What is *Twilight* about?

Not vampires. Not the Pacific North-West. It's about first love, it's about falling for the bad boy in skool. It's about being awkward, aloof and snooty but still falling for the guy that all your friends warn you about (and then the schmuck jilts you! *So bite me!*). Bella can't resist that pale, glowering face, those dark, golden eyes… Forget that he's a vampire – that's the least of it – because he's vain, stuck-up, supercilious, brutish and violent. And he's a stalker! He creeps into Bella's bedroom and lechs over her sleeping!

Twilight's a romance of two outsiders, two misfits, two intellectuals.[46] Two lonely (but oh-so sensitive) souls who find solace in the solitude they share with their significant other. Yet both Bella and Edward remain curiously lonely even after their relationship has been cemented (cemented tho' not consummated). They are lovers for whom love is *not* the all-encompassing, all-healing balm they hope it will be. Bella, at the end of the first *Twilight* movie/ book, isn't any happier than

---

[46] Look at the books and CDs in Edward's room and how Bella is bookish.

she was at the beginning. Neither is Edward, tho' he has at least found someone who can drag him out of his perpetual narcissism momentarily.

But *Twilight*'s also about disaffected youth; it's about the younger generation feeling isolated and not fitting in; it's about growing up and finding your parents' generation disappointing (your folks get divorced, they're actually quite boring, and they're not the wonderful people you looked up to after all – your Dad can't even cook!); it's about the Sins of the Fathers (in this case, the fathers are also perpetual sons, the vampires being their fathers from generations back); it's about the decline of contemporary North America; it's about the deadening boredom of small-town life; and it's about finding escapism in archaic fantasy about vampires and ill-advised romances.

The most interesting thing about *Twilight* is that it's a movie about youth and romance with a young woman at its centre. Yet the *Twilight* movie (and the book) don't do anything with that promising premise. It squanders it, it throws it all away. In the end, *Twilight* is a thoroughly conservative, reactionary story, on screen and in print. These vampires definitely vote Republican! But then, right-wing ideology (close to fascism) has always under-pinned vampireology, even in the hippest, trendiest, most socially-conscious vampire outings. After all, vampire tales are all about blood, aristocracy, decaying families, the survival of the fittest, the law of the jungle. Nietszchean Supermen in black, Gothic clothing.

•

The *Twilight* series on the silver screen was launched by *Twilight*, released in November, 2008, and produced[47] by Summit Entertainment. It was, unusally, directed by a woman (Catherine Hardwicke, b. 1955), adapted from a book by a woman (Stephenie Meyer, b. 1973), with a woman (Kristen Stewart, b. 1990) in the lead role (and the movie is from her point-of-view), and with a woman taking sole screenwriting credit (Melissa Rosenberg (b. 1962) – tho' it's typical for many writers to be involved in previous drafts).[48]

Twilight was produced by Temple Hill/ Maverick/ Imprint for

---

[47] The project had originated at Paramount in 2004.
[48] Ken Gelder noted that the first *Twilight* movie had many women in key creative/ production roles, which may have been why the *Twilight* movies were 'so routinely disparaged by 'serious' cinema commentators' (85).

Summit Entertainment; Greg Mooradian, Mark Morgan and Wyck Godfrey were the producers; executive producers were Karen Rosenfelt, Marty Bowen, Guy Oseary and Michelle Imperatio Stabile; Melissa Rosenberg wrote the script; Trisha Wood and Deborah Aquila cast it; Wendy Chuck was costume designer; Jeanne Van Phue was make-up head; Mary Ann Valdes was hair dept head; Richard Kidd and Bill George were visual effects supervisors; Andy Weder oversaw the special effects; Carter Burwell, Adam Smalley and Alexander Patsavas[49] composed and supervised the music; Elliot Davis was DP; Ian Phillips was art director, Gene Serdema was set decorator, Andy Cheng was second unit director and stunt co-ordinator; and James Lin was supervising location manager. Released: Nov 21, 2008. 122 mins.

The 2008 *Twilight* movie captured Bella and Edward and their romance, first and foremost, pretty accurately from the 2005 book of *Twilight*. The casting (by Trisha Wood and Deborah Aquila) was strong throughout. The additional material that the script added was in the style and manner of the novel (i.e., nothing was tacked on that didn't fit the world of the novel). And the film was even shot in areas very close to the settings for the 2005 novel (unlike many movie adaptions).

I prefer the *Twilight* movie to the *Twilight* novel.

Heresy!

A stake thru the heart!

No: I think the *Twilight* movie is a better story better told.

And *Vampires Suck* was even better in delivering some scenes from the *Twilight* books.

Twilight was Jane Austen for teens, a 19th century-style melodrama for the *Buffy* and *Charmed* generation (tho' nowhere near as good as Austen or *Charmed*). And it was a 'vegetarian' vampire tale (these vampires don't eat humans! They live off the blood of animals! And Bella is a vegetarian). *Twilight* was also, unusually for a vampire story, pretty bloodless (this went beyond keeping to the 'PG-13' rating – filmmakers find all sorts of way of displaying or evoking blood in that category. But in *Twilight*, the filmmakers were self-consciously avoiding

---

[49] Patsavas and Smalley were responsible for selecting many of the rock/ pop acts in *Twilight*.

showing blood: these were *good* vampires, vegetarian vampires!).[50]

Twilight was a romantic tale for teenage girls who felt shy, unsure, alienated and disempowered, and their feminized boyfriends (who also felt unsure and unmasculine). Sure: the target audience was envisioned as a thirteen year-old, 'emo' girl with low esteem.

She's a girl, he's a vampire.

She's 17, he's 104.[51]

That was the key prohibition keeping the lovers apart in this teen romance which combined the romantic drama with elements of vampire lore. The vampire background, tho', coupled with some Native American aspects (the movie was set primarily in the Pacific North-West, and includes Native American characters, principally Jacob Black), was not what this 2008 American movie or 2005 book was about. It was primarily a romance story, a growing up story (with a bit of a moving-to-a-new-home story/ stranger-in-town story).

While some critics admired the chemistry between Kristen Stewart and Robert Pattinson (they became a couple at the time), it wasn't enough to lift parts of *Twilight* above a run-of-the-mill, weekday TV drama. Nor were the helicopter shots, the pretty second unit images of the Pacific North-West or the numerous visual effects additions.

Twilight seemed to be another case of the producers wanting one kind of movie, the director and writers wanting another, the performers going for something else, and the studio and finaciers something else again.

Whatever… the formula worked. *Twilight* became a big movie franchise, like the books, so that by the time of the *Twihard* sequels (which came thick and fast, as one would expect), they made tons of $$$$ (a worldwide gross of $392 million from a negative cost of $38m is excellent).[52] To the point where Summit Entertainment/ Temple Hill/ Maverick/ Imprint took the money-spinning route of splitting up a movie

---

50 Blood is blood, right? So animals' blood should suffice, right? No! We're talking about vampires not hippies! As Edward explains to li'l Bella, it's like having a vegetarian diet, like tofu and soya milk; it doesn't always satisfy (*Twilight*, 164).
51 In *New Moon*, when the lovers' re-united, Edward says he 109 (*New Moon*, 540).
52 And *Twilight* looks great on $38 million, like the first *Underworld* movie. How much do you think *Underworld* cost to make? $100 million? $150 million? It certainly looked like those ultra-high budget movies: it's got the look, the stunts, the visual effects, the extras, the special make-up, and the extravagant sets. But according to some reports, *Underworld* was a $23 million production. Which's a bargain, like *Twilight*'s $38m, compared to far too many very high budget flicks which stink.

into two parts, as the *Harry Potter* and *Matrix* franchises had recently done (and *The Hobbit* was stretched out over three movies in the pursuit of the Great God Dollar). Critic Mark Kermode is a Twi-fan, calling the first movie 'a very decent tale of high-school angst and teen alienation given an alt-lite grungey edge' (20). Few middle-aged film critics came out in favour of the *Twilight* movies, as Kermode noted:

> very few reputable critics have dared to put their head above the parapet and admit to tolerating, let alone actually liking, this massively popular teen-orientated franchise. (19)

And some critics put the *Twilight* phenomenon down, as with *The Da Vinci Code* and the *Harry Potter* series, without reading the books or watching the movies.

9

THE STARVING GAMES

The Starving Games (Jason Friedberg and Aaron Seltzer, 2013) was a much-needed counter-attack to the puerile claptrap of *The Hunger Games* (2012), one of the most cretinous and joyless of recent Hollywood movies (based on a post-*Twilight Saga* book by Suzanne Collins, 2008).

The Hunger Games is part of a recent cycle of movies aimed at a teen audience in the fantasy/ sci-fi/ horror/ adventure genres, often adapted from Young Adult fiction: *Percy Jackson, Twilight, The Maze Runner, Divergent*, and *Harry Potter*.

So thank %¡Ø# for *The Starving Games*, another spoof movie[53] which reminds us just how offensively dumb and stupidly offensive so many Western/ Hollywood movies are (and not only the big, popcorn franchises!). *The Starving Games* was another product from the two-man factory of Jason Friedberg and Aaron Seltzer: when do these guys sleep?! Or live?!

Maiara Walsh, Cody Christian, Brant Daugherty, Lauren Bowles, Juhahn Jones, Chris Marroy, Diedrich Bader, Ross Wyngaarden, Dean J. West, Michael Hartson, Theodus Crane, Eryn L. Davis, Taylor Ashley Murphy, Nick Gomez, Gralen Banks, and Kennedy Hermansen appeared in the *Starving Games* cast; Peter Safran, Kolie Wegner, Kenny Yates, Friedberg and Seltzer were producers; Patty Long and Hal Olofsson were

---

[53] *The Hunger Games* has also been parodied in *The Hungover Games*.

exec. prods.; Timothy Michael Wynn composed the music; Shawn Maurer (DP); Peck Prior (ed.); Maressa Richtmyer (costumes); William Elliott (prod. des.); Jordan Bass, Lauren Bass and Ryan Glorioso (casting); Raymond Pumilia (art dir.); Ann C. Salzer (1st A.D.); and Rusty Dunn and Kris Fenske (sound designers). It was distributed by Ketchup Entertainment; the budget was $4.5 million (really tiny by Hollywood standards. By comparison, the budget of *The Hunger Games* was $78 million). Released Nov 8, 2013. 83 minutes.

The casting is more white bread than most of Friedberg and Seltzer's films, and lacks the high proportion of Hispanic and African American performers that usually appear. Also, there are no stars here.

The Starving Games was the first film from J. Friedberg and A. Seltzer which used a different distribution and financial model from their previous works: it was pre-sold in individual markets (with the filmmakers stepping away from bigger distributors such as Fox). The box office returns, however, were much lower than any of the previous outings from Friedberg and Seltzer. The move toward independence, then, meant less revenue and much lower budgets. (No need to remind ourselves that film critics rated *The Starving Games* poorly, as usual). The home releases lacked the fun extras of the previous movies of Friedberg and Seltzer (no audio commentary, for example).

Porn jokes, *Playboy* jokes, nudity (streaker) jokes, gay jokes, big tits jokes, shit and fart jokes, bird poo jokes, being-kicked-in-the-balls jokes, censorship jokes, internet jokes, logo jokes, Noo Joisey jokes, people-having-their-arms-ripped-off jokes, gratuitous T. & A. (from the dancing cheerleaders at half-time), and of course people-being-killed jokes – *The Starving Games* was another helping of silliness and crudity from the Friedberg-Seltzer Spoof Circus.

Admittedly, *The Hunger Games*, being so preposterous on so many levels and in so many areas (and so annoyingly earnest and po-faced about it), was an easy target. (A cheap way of producing a parody of *The Hunger Games* would be to get an audience drunk or high then show them... *The Hunger Games*).

Some of the jokes in *The Starving Games* depend on offscreen sounds, such as the P.A., where the participants in the death games listen to the announcements. Groanable puns're plucked during the selection of the new District 12 contestants (such as 'Hugh Janus'). Plenty of the gags depend on joke props, as usual in Friedberg and Seltzer's films – like the fake ass that Kantmiss sticks her foot in during the 'meet the contestants' show. Other joke props include the Hollywood trade papers; the cover of *Playboy*; a Fruit Ninja video game; and a talking orange (the Annoying Orange). Silly weapons and silly deaths recur: Kantmiss shoots Marco with a baguette (in the eye); she stabs a tube of face cream into a victim's neck; little Rudy is kicked thru the air, hits a tree and expires; characters step onto the ground and explode; people are cut in half; and the Expendables are gunned down. (The heroine kills several people in this movie. Like *Meet the Spartans*, *The Starving Games* is full of on-screen deaths).

Thus, one aspect of *The Hunger Games* is perfectly in tune with the comical sensibilities of Jason Friedberg and Aaron Seltzer – mindless violence. In *The Hunger Games*, youths are set against each other in the most artificial manner; for Friedberg and Seltzer, that means they can have characters beating the funk out of each other, and plenty of gratuitous deaths (a girl (Brittney Karbowski) is cut in half, for ex, as she fights with Kantmiss for a backpack, after being stabbed with daggers. Even after she's lost the lower half of her body, she's still clinging onto Kantmiss and arguing about the backpack).

This sequence forms the punchy climax to act one: it's one of the most successful scenes in *The Starving Games*, as the participants fight each other for weapons and supplies.54 A ridiculous, highly contrived scene like this in the original movie is a gift to Friedberg and Seltzer, who relish any instance where the violence simmering just below the surface in contemporary life erupts. In the world of Friedberg and Seltzer – and in so many forms of drama – people are teetering on the edge of exploding: the slightest thing will set them off into hysterics, or rages, or sulks, or murderous rampages.

The beginning of the Games in *The Starving Games* is thus a stunt-heavy set-piece where kids attack each other (the referee starts the Games by shooting one of the participants).

---

54 It's given a substantial build-up before the game starts.

Like *Meet the Spartans* and *Vampires Suck*, *The Starving Games* followed a single narrative line,[55] in the main – *The Hunger Games* provided plenty of opportunities for slapstick and goofy humour, so there was less need to wheel in parodies of other movies and pop cultural items like television (though *The Starving Games* did plenty of that, too). *The Hunger Games* was the North American film industry at its worst – a moronic concept, idiotically simplistic ideology, and truly objectionable schmaltz and sentimentality.

I loved the drooling, idiot mom, the irritating, shaky camerawork send-up, the senseless and ridiculous murders (with the 'kill' count on the TV show), the stony-faced sports commentator Cleaver Williams, the slo-mo replays on telly (of death and violence), the over-the-top TV show host, the crowds getting excited at food, the little girl Rudy (Eryn L. Davis) who slaps the heroine repeatedly (and the heroine's mad, cackling acid trip!), and the spoofs of *Avatar*,[56] *Harry Potter, Oz the Great and Powerful, The Avengers, The Terminator, The Matrix, The Hobbit, Survivor, X-Men* and *The Expendables*. And many North American, capitalist icons (McDonald's,[57] Starbucks, Twitter, Subway, Facebook, Apple, Taco Bell, Nike, etc).

Maiara Walsh as Kantmiss Evershot does a sterling version of the poker-faced, preposterously solemn and incredibly annoying performance by Jennifer Lawrence as Dipshit in *The Hunger Games*. Walsh throws herself into the role wholesale – which's the best thing to do in a parody movie (Walsh gets to do plenty of things which're dumb and embarrassing in *The Starving Games*, such as being shat on by birds, and farting in a lengthy scene where she squats and is caught on candid camera. It's not a Friedberg and Seltzer movie unless there are loud fart noises).

The Starving Games relished sending up the media-saturated aspects of *The Hunger Games*, where killing is just another piece of entertainment. As in *The Truman Show* and reality TV, everyone is

---

55 If you stick to a dreadful plot as the basis for your parody movie too much, it can affect your movie. Because *The Hunger Games* was so awful, that in turn weakened *The Starving Games*.
56 Another movie that begs and slathers on its knees to be ruthlessly parodied. In fact, Friedberg and Seltzer were rumoured to be working on an *Avatar* spoof.
57 The President's aide, Seleca, has leased his face for advertising, which sports famous logos.

watching – the audience in the TV studio, the anxious villagers in District 12 looking at a giant screen, and the sports commentators Bob Hylox and Cleaver Williams. Editor Peck Prior keeps them in the loop throughout the movie with reaction shots (once again, to help the jokes – *The Hunger Games* concept has people watching other people all the time). Thus, in this movie, the extras play a key role (extras are often disliked by many filmmakers).

The Starving Games sends up the viewing public many times – the audiences are satirized as a mob of idiots, with childish, over-eager reactions to everything. Thus, an enthusiastic woman in the audience has her arm ripped off, but instead of collapsing to the floor and howling in agony, she waves her severed arm in the air and cheers.

The lame, obvious satire of the North American media in *The Hunger Games* has always been something that spoof cinema has done as par for the course, where audiences are portrayed as baying animals, where the cruder and stupider the show is the better.

What *The Hunger Games* and *The Starving Games* don't show, however, is how audiences at live recordings of television shows are *trained* before the show starts to holler and shout and laugh and clap. Visit a TV studio in the U.S.A. or elsewhere (highly recommended), and you'll find stand-up comedians and assistants encouraging the audience to express themselves (several times – as they wait in line, as they file into the TV studio, and as they're sitting in the studio before the recording begins). The clapping and cheering on live TV is thus *rehearsed*, and continually encouraged.

The Starving Games indulges in something that all television does everyday: recycling. Thus, footage from earlier is shown again during the half-time highlights. Kantmiss takes out a bunch of guys which's replayed again. Deaths're immediately replayed in slo-mo.

The low budget of *The Starving Games* shows up everywhere, from the recycled footage to the cheapo visual effects (explosions and fire're crudely superimposed optically). Shots of Kantmiss running are replayed many times (they might've all been filmed on the same day). There's only one dance number (but at least it's with cheerleaders), and no musical interludes (although the President forces Seleca to dance in a brief skit). However, there are many scenes involving a lot of extras.

Once again, the mere evocation of movies such as *Avatar, The Expendables, Avengers* and *X-Men* reminds us how utterly stupid these blockbuster flicks are. Just think about the characters or the stories or the situations in *The Matrix* or *Avatar*! So idiotic. Yet these are the movies that people want to see more than any others, the movies and franchises which somehow gross billions of dollars. (The politics and ideology of the *Avengers* films, of superhero films (with characters from Marvel or Detective Comics), and of *The Expendables* are dubious at best; Max Nicholson (from I.G.N.) called *The Starving Games* 'a horrible, horrible piece of cinema', but that is more appropriately applied to those movies which promote a pro-military, pro-First World ideology in which the use of military force is enshrined. If you live in the so-called 'Third World', or in 'developing countries', tough luck. And if you're not American, we feel really sorry for you. For about three seconds).

The stupid blue people from *Avatar* were an amusing parody during Kantmiss's head trip[58] (with film director James 'King of the World!' Cameron giggling and throwing money in the air nearby). Of course, *The Starving Games* picked the moment where the Na'vi (Nick Gomez) and Kantmiss in her Avatar costume get freaky (a truly absurd moment in *Avatar*).

The kids from *Harry Potter* (the heroic trio of Harry, Hermione and Ron) are shown the door in *The Starving Games* – they're told that their franchise is over, and a security guy breaks Harry's wand. That's the way it is in Parody Land – if you're not topical, you're history. (But if ever a franchise has legs, it's *Harry Potter*, as it continues to demonstrate. *Harry Potter* is a license for Warner Bros. to print money[59]).

Jason Friedberg and Aaron Seltzer regular Diedrich Bader is great in the Donald Sutherland role of President Snowballs, emulating Sutherland's famous manner of speaking. Most of the President's scenes are with his aide, Seleca (Dean J. West), where the relationship is clearly that of a producer and a director, the king and the slave: 'I want this, and this, and this', and it's the director's job to deliver. President Snowballs

---

[58] Even this was given some thought: a p.o.v. shot of Kantmiss's hand shows it turning blue, leading us from her drug trip into the *Avatar* spoof.
[59] And it continued to do so in movies with the awful *Fantastic Beasts* prequels.

wants a lesbian clinch to boost the TV ratings, for ex, but as Kantmiss is the only Miss surviving, it has to be a heterosexual coupling (borrring!). Anyhoo, there's another of the many OTT lovemaking sessions in parody movies, with Kantmiss and Peter in the cave running through the Spoof Movie *Kama Sutra* (with censored stickers covering the nudity).

The President is the Prick (as the movie puts it) who's orchestrating this mayhem: we see just how venal the President is in a recreated flashback of his youth: he kills his mom with a handgun when she fails to make his peanut butter and jelly sandwich as he likes it.

Some of the jokes in *The Starving Games* are pure *Simpsons* – for ex, you can hear Homer drooling in the background during the Triple Bypass Burger riff (which Homer would wolf down instantly). The TV commercial immediately quashes Dale's attempts to incite the populace of District 12 to riot.

The Expendables and the Avengers assemble for the closing gag in *The Starving Games* – Dale machine-guns the Expendables down, and Nick Fury (Gralen Banks, spoofing Samuel L. Jackson) berates Hawkeye (Joseph Salloum) for being the lame superhero in a movie that no one gives a monkey's about. And then they all blow up when they step into the booby traps (a reprise of the earlier gag. But instant death is a recurring favourite joke of Friedberg and Seltzer). *The Starving Games* ends in customary fashion with a montage of bloopers[60] (more recycling).

Critics didn't go for *The Starving Games*, as usual with the films of Friedberg and Seltzer . Even critics who loathed *The Hunger Games* still thought poorly of its much-needed kicking, *The Starving Games*. In Flick Feast, Tue Sorenson called *The Hunger Games* 'so bad that I don't know where to begin'.[61] It was 'bad, bad news all the way'. Sorenson acknowledged that *The Hunger Games* really 'deserved to be spoofed', but found *The Starving Games* 'cheap and obvious'.[62]

---

[60] The directors don't appear in the outtakes, but they are heard.
[61] T. Sorenson, Flick Feast, Mch 26, 2012.
[62] T. Sorenson, Flick Feast, Nov 6, 2013.

THE HUNGER GAMES

The Hunger Games (Gary Ross, 2012) was a piece of adolescent baloney cobbled together from *Lord of the Flies, The Truman Show, Westworld, The Running Man, Battle Royale*,[63] reality TV and Ancient Rome movies. Produced by Bissell, Cohen, Collins, Alvarez, Jacobson, Kilik, Phillips, Feghall, Porter, Unkeless and Rosner for Lionsgate/ Color Force, and based on the 2008 book by Suzanne Collins, *The Hunger Games* comes over as a third-rate TV movie but far less fun (too bloody long and no ad breaks! It is an excruciating 142 minutes). A limp, bloodless satire on North America's slack-jawed consumption of reality television (and the media in general), groups of people lost on islands, and a bunch of silly games in which death is the only way out. (But *The Hunger Games* was a massive hit, so sequels inevitably followed). Released: Mch 23, 2012.

How this abysmal movie ever grossed over $400 million[64] is a complete mystery. Further installments inevitably appeared in 2013 (*Catching Fire*) and 2014 and 2015 (*Mockinjay, Part 1* and *2* – the studio (Lionsgate/ Color Force) took the $uper-cynical *Harry Potter* and *Twilight* route of $plitting the last movie into two).[65] And a 5th outing arrived in 2023: *We Fooled You Four Times Before, Now Here's More!*

Many, many aspects of *The Hunger Games* rankled *avec moi*:

Let's start with the deeply irritating New Agey music, with the female singer (Mariana Tootsie) cooing plaintively (James Newton Howard was composer). This was simply *horrible*.

The idea that Westerners will suddenly descend into near-savagery over the course of a few decades into the near future needs a more convincing set-up and explanation. Atomic bombs usually do the trick.

Katniss Everdene as played by Jennifer Lawrence is an 'emo' teenager, a sister to Bella Swan in the *Twilight Saga* and Anastasia in *50 Shades of Grey*. Desperately unfunny and unappealing, always sombre, seldom smiling, and taking herself *so* seriously, Katpiss was the sort of

---
63 Have a look at the *manga* of *Battle Royale* if you fancy seeing a *really* grossly violent version of this sort of story.
64 And the movie franchise as a whole grossed $2,968 million.
65 Like *The Maze Runner* and *Twilight*, *The Hunger Games* led to a book series, and a movie series.

character, like Bella, that you want to SLAP. So drippy, so useless. (The rest of the cast included Woody Harelson, Liam Hemsworth, Josh Hutcherson, Stanley Tucci and Donald Sutherland).

It's the same audience as the *Twilight Saga* (and the *Harry Potter* movies): girls in their teens and the dates (or brothers) they persuaded to come along to the theatre to watch a tomboy girl show a weedy boy how to kick ass and survive in the wilds.

A girl with a bow and arrow!

Well, *hell*, it makes a change, I guess, from 'a girl and a gun'.

She's a girl with a bow and an arrow! She hunts deer for her family! (Oh, for *fuck's* sake!). And Peter's[66] always *lerrrved* her from afar! Well, smash me over the head with a brick! Gouge out my eyes with knitting needles! Don't make me sit thru this junk!

There are so many irritating moments in *The Hunger Games*, so many scenes which don't convince on any level whatsoever. But this humourless piece of dreck is played so stinkingly earnest and desperate to be 'worthy' or 'meaningful', you can't even laugh *at* it.

Actors walk and walk thru endless landscapes – one of the surest signs of clueless filmmakers. Listen, guys, if you're going to use RAPID EDITING in some scenes, apply that quick cutting to these BORING, second unit shots of performers trudging thru woodland. Cut, cut, cut these nauseating scenes!

I could point out hundreds of dopey incidents in *The Hunger Games*. One will suffice: a group of nasty teens chase our heroine up a tree (!). Yes, a bloody tree! The bad guy climbs the tree but falls. They shoot two arrows, then give up and go to sleep! Now I'm sure that any kid from the past 100,000 years, from the ages of four to eighteen, could figure out plenty of ways of killing someone who's immobile in a freaking tree!

I can't resist mentioning a couple more clunkers in *The Hunger Games*:

• In this feeble satire on the U.S.A.'s obsession with television (an addiction of four hours a day is average for every American), the heroine's good, old boyfriend back home asserts: if people didn't watch it, it would wither. Yes – and you can start by not producing crappy movies like this!

---
[66] Even the spelling of his name is irritating: 'Peeta'. Just call him 'Peter' already!

• We are told that exposure can kill quicker and surer than a knife in the training sequence. True: exposure to the elements debilitates or kills quicker than going without food or water. So what does our heroine do? She sleeps in a damn tree! Any kid knows that a tree is a really dumb place to rest up: no shelter, no security, it's freezing, and you can be seen for miles!

• Suicide in *The Hunger Games* is by eating berries! This is like an idiotic eleven year-old's version of a Japanese romantic epic. *Berries*!

The casting in *The Hunger Games* is bizarre – far odder than the colourful hair and make-up jobs (by Linda Flowers – head of the hair department and Ve Neill,[67] head of the make-up department).[68] Woody Harrelson's alcoholic slacker is acting in a completely different movie (a Seattle grunge-a-thon, perhaps), and Donald Sutherland looks mildly bemused (which, after all, is one of the things that Sutherland can do so well).

The action is simply woeful in *The Hunger Games*. It is filmed in the impressionistic manner of so many recent North American movies, with the camera and lens in far too close, the cutting too rapid, so that you get a series of shots which have no impact, and no dramatic value. Is this to get around the 'PG-13' rating? No! Because plenty of 'PG-13s' have crunching action scenes.

The shaky camerawork – *so fake!* I loathe this kind of camerawork!: it is in focus, it is well-lit, it is well-composed by the camera operator, but it is shaky. Coupled with rapid editing (with five shots of a single action where one would do just as well), this kind of camerawork is sickening to watch for long periods of time.

If you were *really* going to simulate a 'documentary' feel in cinema, the camerawork would go in and out of focus all the time, the light would blow out the lens or be so dark you wouldn't see aught, the framing would be all over the place, important bits would be missed as film/ tapes/ discs/ data ran out or failed, and the camera would be *far* shakier than this as the operator tries to keep someone running in the crosshairs.

Also, the sound would be all over the shop: to be authentically

---

[67] Neill is the make-up artist who creates all those wacky looks for Johnny Depp.
[68] Or the stupid names – Haymitch Abernathy, Trexler Hoverhound and Peeeeta Mellark.

'documentary-like', the sound would dip out or be distorted; it would be muffled; there would be wind noise, planes, cars, etc.

In fact, the sound would be like Jean-Luc Godard's 1960s movies, where Godard asked the sound recordist to include everything in a scene with a uni-directional mic. So, in a café scene *Vivre Sa Vie* or *A Band Apart*, you have *very loud* pinball machines, clattering of plates and cups, the sound of traffic outside, and the sound of people talking. Have you ever sat in a café and *listened* to the sound? It can be deafening!

To be a true 'documentary', recreating filming something that's 'really happening', you'd have to include numerous other technical and stylistic elements. Such as: actors talking *over* each other. This occurs in real life *all the time*, but it's one of the fakest things about cinema (and all drama, theatre, TV, radio, etc), that actors wait for their moment to speak their lines.

Right. Enough. Life is too short for *The Hunger Games*.

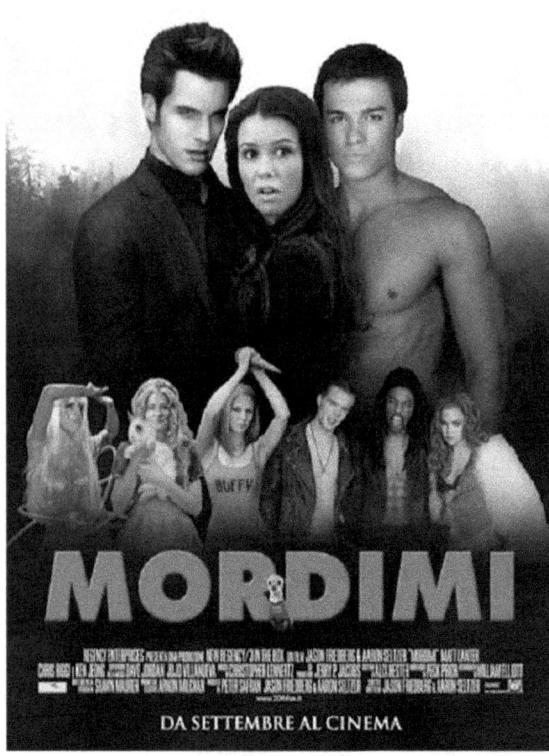

Vampires Suck (2010), this page and over.

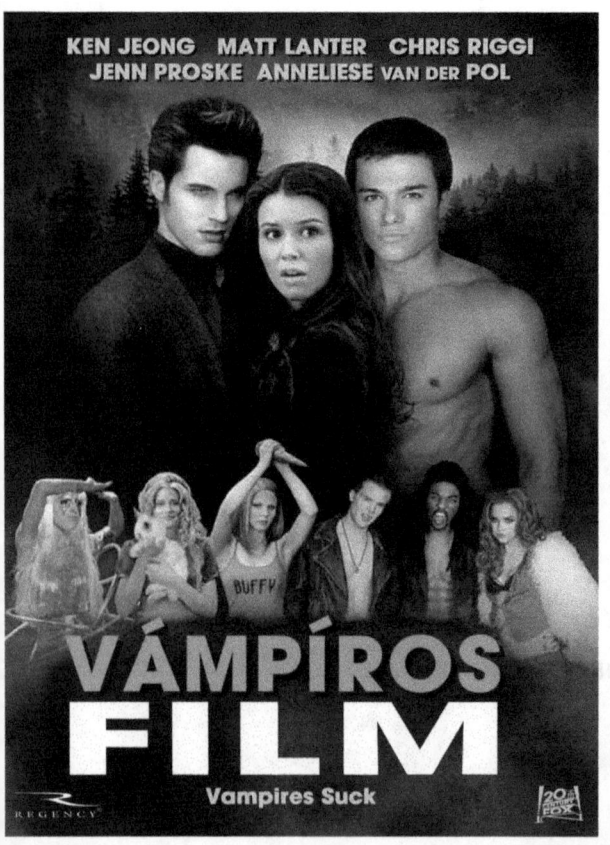

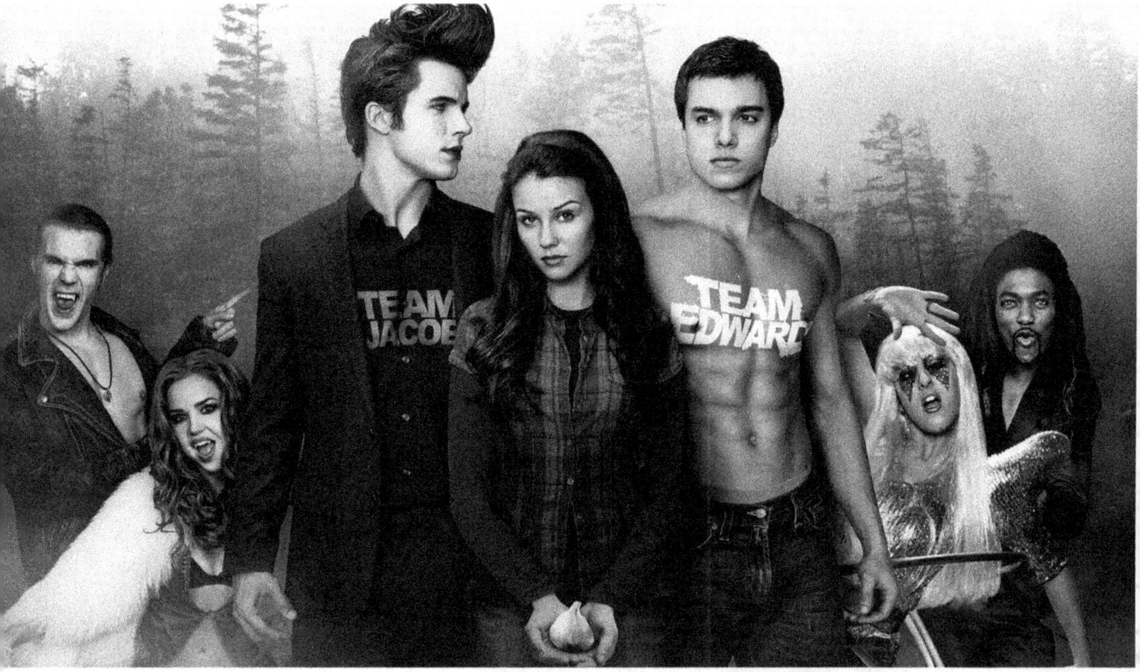
TEAM JACOB
TEAM EDWARD

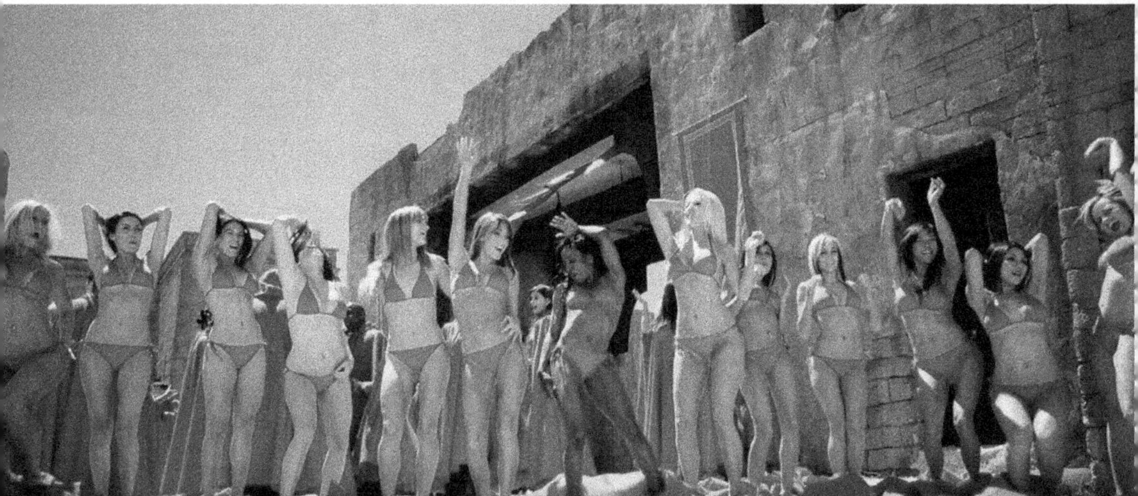

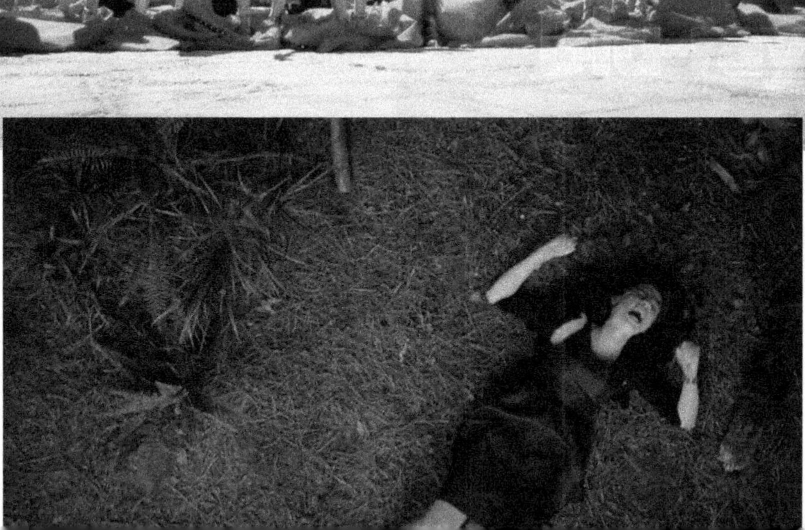

The Starving Games (2013), this page and over.

11

BEST NIGHT EVER

Best Night Ever (a.k.a. *Hangover Girls*, 2013) was produced by Peter Safran, Jason Blum and Friedberg and Seltzer, co-produced by Dan Clifton; wr. and dir. by Friedberg and Seltzer. DP: Shawn Mauer; ed.: Peck Prior; prod. des.: William Elliott; art dir.: Nathalie Neurath; make-up: Kelly Capoccia; Michael Etheridge: 1st A.D.; sound sup.: Darren Warkentin; casting: the Basses (Lauren and Jordan); music sup.: Jo Jo Villenueva; stunt co-ord.: Ralf Koch; cost.: Maressa Richtmyer; and the prod. companies were Safran Company, 3 In the Box and Blumhouse. Released: Dec 26, 2013. 79 mins.[1]

In the cast were Crista Flanagan, Desiree Hall, Eddie Ritchard, Samantha Colburn, Andy Favreau, Nick Steele, Lynette DuPree, Jason Beaubien, Amin Joseph, James Jordan, Winston James Francis, and Patrick Quinlan.

Best Night Ever was significant for several reasons in the cinematic career of Jason Friedberg and Aaron Seltzer: (1) it had the boys playing in the Wonderful World of 'R' Rated Movies; (2) it was their first non-spoof movie as directors (and contained some straight drama); (3) it featured women in the four lead roles; and (4) it was another production conceived and released thru a pre-selling deal, as with *The Starving Games* (this didn't quite generate the financial results hoped for: *Best Night Ever* grossed only 289,511 bucks – that's not even enough to pay for four

[1] Some have the running time at 83 mins and 90 mins.

women on a night out in Vegas).

Thus, *Best Night Ever* was the most poorly-received of all Friedberg and Seltzer's films, either as writers or directors, and it was the movie that performed the poorest at the b.o., and it's the Friedberg and Seltzer movie that nobody has seen. (The movie isn't readily available to buy over the counter – I had to order my copy from a dodgy dealer in the aliens-only quarter of Mos Eisley on Tatooine. The home releases lack extras – this movie cries out for an audio commentary, bringing the girls back together to talk about their experiences making the show).

As to casting, it's surprising perhaps that Jason Friedberg and Aaron Seltzer, after productions such as *Epic Movie* and *Date Movie* and others, should've chosen four white women for the lead roles (casting was by Jordan Bass and Lauren Bass). You'd expect at least one of the girls to be Hispanic or black. The casting of non-white actors in *Best Night Ever* occurs only in the secondary roles.

Best Night Ever looks like Friedberg and Seltzer took off for a l*ooo*ng weekend in Las Vegas – checking into a suite at the classy Wynn's resort (no sleazy, cheapo motels miles away from the Strip for them!), and bash out a script after three days of drinking and brainstorming.[2] *Best Night Ever* has the feel of a bunch of writers in a room thinking, *what if?* – what if the girls steal a limo and spot the valet who mugged them and enact their own revenge? *Hell, yeah!* And so on. (You know how excited writers get when they make stuff up).

Best Night Ever is all-out – yet I can't be the only sweet, gorgeous viewer who reckoned that Friedberg and Seltzer would go even further than they did, once they entered the world of 'R' rated material. I was expecting much spicier dialogue – the first use of the dread word 'fuck' doesn't occur for some 14 minutes. (In the second, crazier half, however, there is more swearing. For Friedberg and Seltzer, hearing a woman swear is the comical equivalent of Jean-Luc Godard's famous mantra of making a movie with a woman and a gun).

•

Best Night Ever is the first Friedberg and Seltzer movie which seems

---

[2] Actually, movie people do go to Vegas and write! Francis Coppola, for ex, did. You could write in your hotel room, he said, and when you needed a break, you could take the elevator down to the lobby and wander around the Strip.

disappointing and a let-down. For the many detractors of Friedberg and Seltzer, *Best Night Ever* is a gift, and confirms their views. For sure it's more challenging to defend *Best Night Ever* against the noxious bile from critics (and audiences). It's as easy as losing at poker at Caesar's Palace to kick this movie in the teeth. Yet one suspects that *Best Night Ever*, for all its flaws, is actually the movie that Seltzer and Friedberg wanted to make (unfettered by the 'PG-13' rating or Hollywood studios breathing down their necks – this isn't a 20th Century Fox or Miramax/ Dimension movie, but an under-the-radar sort of enterprise).

The concept of *Best Night Ever* is intriguing: a home movie of a girls' night out in Las Vegas that goes very wrong, a sort of 'found video' in the manner of TV's 'reality' shows. There are similar movies of young guys having adventures in Vegas, but to focus on four women is certainly unusual. And to encourage the women to be as crude and rude as guys is also rare.

Thus, *Best Night Ever* combines motifs such as the road movie, an endless and really bad night, people having a terrible time (and being out of their depth), and Las Vegas as the ultimate adults' playground (which it is – to the max!).

Best Night Ever is crude, for sure – but no cruder than many stand-up comedians' acts. Go see a stand-up comic anywhere (even in Vegas!), and you'll hear plenty of similar shtick (comedians know that sex and crudity is as sure a way of getting a laugh as anything else).

Best Night Ever is unmistakably a Friedberg and Seltzer Production – there's plenty of crudity and sexual material, gay-bashing, bodily function jokes, and sudden eruptions of violence. There's a running gag about shoes and a shoe convention in Vegas (Aaron Seltzer's family were in the shoe business, and Friedberg and Seltzer sold shoes in their youth).

The performances of the four young women – Desiree Hall, Eddie Ritchard, Samantha Colburn, and Crista Flanagan – are brave, as the filmmakers encourage them to go to extremes. These sorts of roles don't come along that often. This is not a movie in which to hold back – the premise, after all, is total disintegration, a decline into anxiety, abandon and chaos. Indeed, the tone of *Best Night Ever* is often not of a comical night out with a few amusing but unthreatening mis-adventures, but a rapid slide into angst and panic. There's a lot of fretting and fear, of running about the streets of a dark and forbidding city at night; instead of a realm of superficial self-indulgence, Las Vegas comes across as the cruel city of *film noir* of the 1940s (crime, violence, and blood are evoked regularly).

To enhance all of that, Friedberg and Seltzer make at least two of the four women highly strung and neurotic (one has the itinerary of the night out compiled on her cel, and another hyper-venilates in the over-long dumpster scene).

Stylistically, the home movie/ found film format has benefits but also many limitations. The pluses – seeing people at their most vulnerable and exposed – has been exploited in movies such as *Paranormal Activity* (which producer Jason Blum worked on. It's a gift to horror cinema of course, which relies on the subjective viewpoint). Yet *Best Night Ever* sticks to the subjective camera approach with a dogged insistence – the girls are continually setting up the camera, or running back to fetch it, to explain how we're seeing it all (however, *Best Night Ever* breaks its own 'rules' numerous times, as all handycam movies do). It's an intriguing experiment, very film school-ish, but after a while it becomes irritating (as with movies such as *The Blair Witch Project, Cloverfield* and *District 9*. You just want to grab that stupid video camera and smash it to pieces).

The 'found video' approach handily motivates the numerous scenes where advertising and store signs are simply blurred out, as they sometimes are on television (it's cheaper for the budget than re-dressing all those streets).

LAS VEGAS.

The filmmakers were spot-on in determining the trends in tourism and entertainment in the Eighties and Nineties, particularly in relation to Las Vegas, which has gone much further into the realms of postmodern pastiche and superabundant allusion. The Las Vegas of *One From the Heart* (1982) was based on Fremont Street and the surrounding area, but that is now the *old* part of Las Vegas, where the older casinos and resorts are found. These days, Las Vegas has expanded across the Strip to become one of the most extraordinary cities in the world.

Now it looks as if *One From the Heart* was tame by comparison in creating a neon-drenched Las Vegas: if you visit Vegas today, you'll find mind-boggling recreations of Venice and Paris, *indoors* (plus all of the familiar landmarks, like the Eiffel Tower, the Opera, St Mark's Square, the Venetian canals, etc). Oh, and New York City. And an Arthurian castle (the Excalibur Hotel). And the enormous, orchestrated fountains at Bellagio Casino.[3] A battle at sea between pirate ships at Treasure Island Casino (with the 'Sirens of T.I.'). The erupting volcano outside the Mirage Casino. The lions at the M.G.M. Grand.

The casinos, hotels and resorts in Las Vegas have become entire theme parks on their own, each one containing theme park rides and attractions, zoos, gardens, plus a range of restaurants, stores, cafés, bars and hotels.

Las Vegas has become its own movie, its own theme park, and its own vast tie-in merchandizing operation. Las Vegas is also not just one movie, but many movies (and not all of them are Italian-American gangster flicks!). Some are rags-to-riches musicals with showgirls and playboys, some are honeymoon comedies, and, yes, some are gross-out, bachelor night comedies.

Las Vegas is, like Disneyland, a movie in three-dimensions, a theme park on a colossal scale devoted to itself. Las Vegas isn't simply 'postmodern', in Jean Baudrillard's notion of Disneyland as postmodern America personified; Las Vegas is way beyond that.

Visiting Las Vegas is not only like being in a movie, it's like being in a Jackie Collins' novel, a thousand Hollywood thrillers, 500 wacky comedies, and a Living History of Entertainment in the U.S.A.

I adore Las Vegas! What a city! But a movie has to be pretty wild these days to even come close to evoking something like Las Vegas (*One From the Heart* succeeds, as does *Showgirls*). You've got to go *way* beyond the Italian-American gangsterism of *Casino* (1995) or *GoodFellas* (1990), or their many copyists in TV movies.

•

---

[3] The dancing fountains in the lake in front of Bellagio, lit by coloured lights, are pure *One From the Heart* – accompanied by Frank Sinatra or Italian opera.

BEST NIGHT EVER AS A LAS VEGAS MOVIE.

On one level, *Best Night Ever* scores: it is a great Las Vegas movie (even tho' much of it could've been filmed anywhere in the United States of North America – those scuzzy streets at night, the alleys, the sidewalks, the car lots, the wire fences, the crummy motels – they could be any place.[4] And in the motels, we're inside the studio again). The great Las Vegas movies include: *One From the Heart, Showgirls, Casino* and *Mars Attacks!* Other movies filmed in Vegas are *Leaving Las Vegas, The Electric Horseman, Indecent Proposal, Rain Man, Ocean's Eleven, Viva Las Vegas, Next* and *City Slickers 2*. (Meanwhile, movies of nights out that get crazy include *After Hours* and *American Graffiti*. And of course plenty of horror flicks portray nights that start bad and get worse and worse).

Some of *Best Night Ever* was filmed in Las Vegas – putting the girls in a car enables them to arrive by road in the city and we get the usual shots of the famous sites (Wynn's, Caesar's, the Luxor, etc), from inside the vehicle (because the movie stuck to the home movie format, seeing what the women see). And we're back in several vehicles later, including more cars, and taxis, and limos (the car culture of the U.S.A. prevails at all costs – Yanks will go to war to defend it. Even when the girls haven't got a cent to pay for a ride, they're still filmed in cars).

Certainly, *Best Night Ever* captures the nighttime craziness of Vegas: the tinsel and the sleaze, the sexy possibilities and the shattered dreams, the yummy tequila and the queasy aftermath. Las Vegas *is* a wild city, by any standards, a city of pure seduction.

Best Night Ever indulges in some classic Las Vegas pastimes (as every Las Vegas movie does) – plenty of drinking, some lap dancing, some mud (jello) wrestling, scoring drugs, a mugging at gunpoint, some drug taking, a car chase, sex in motel rooms (and a very long scriptwriting session in a penthouse suite at the M.G.M. Grand).

But there are no big, showstopping numbers of dancing, singing and music of the usual Friedberg and Seltzer movie, even tho' the film's set in Las Vegas, one of the finest spots for gaudy glitter and out-size entertainment on the planet. (Couldn't the girls stumble into a ritzy show

---

[4] There's a whip pan up to the Eiffel Tower of the Paris Casino, but with visual effects that can be tricked in.

at Treasure Island or the Tropicana?). Dancing is actually everywhere in Vegas – from the giant nightly shows to the nudie shows, from the showgirls in amongst the tables in the casinos to girls dancing outside clothes stores on boxes.

There *is* music a-plenty in *Best Night Ever*, of course (as in all of the films of Friedberg and Seltzer) – the girls're grooving to music in the car, the lap dance scene has music, the jello wrestling scene has music, the mad mid-movie montage is stuffed with music, and so on. *Best Night Ever* is another Friedberg-Seltzer movie where the credits for the music at the end roll on for centuries, and you realize that the movie featured *lots* of music. It's not famous Las Vegas tunes, however, but mainly hiphop and dance music (i.e., party music, to accentuate the out-of-control antics).

And, yes, there *is* some dancing – Claire, Zoe, Leslie and Janet perform some 'flash mob' routines on Fremont Street, and they go wild in the nightclub.

•

SOME SCENES IN *BEST NIGHT EVER*.

Best Night Ever opens outrageous, but then back-pedals to deliver exposition scenes (which occur on the road trip to Vegas from L.A.). This method of beginning the movie might be an idea that developed in post-production, rather than in the script (or maybe following previews – ditto with the extra ending, with the return of the naked woman).

The opening tease is classic Las Vegas: it's a lap dance – one guy and four women, in a back room at a bar (a reverse of the usual naked woman and four guys).[5] We then zip back in time (rewinding video-style) to the car journey to learn about Claire, Zoe, Leslie and Janet[6] as they travel thru the American desert to the city whose name means 'the Meadows' in Spanish.

The lap dance skit is a piece of classic Friedberg-Seltzerania: it's an in-your-face (literally!) commercial for the rest of the movie: the opening shot is a guy's ass jiggling in your face (we've already seen that in films such as *Date Movie*). It's a cliché, too: if you conjured up the image of young women at large in Vegas on a bachelorette party outing, it might

---

[5] In a concession to the M.P.A.A., the dipstick is blacked out.
[6] They simply introduce themselves to camera – how easy is that?!

be something like this. It's also the classic 'hook' of movie-making, in the manner of *James Bond*: start with something compelling, to reel in the audience, before shifting into the exposition scenes.

This is a home-movie-within-a-home-movie, as the women try all of the things you can only do in Las Vegas in the middle of the night.[7]

Where *Best Night Ever* pulls back from the brink is in its four main characterizations, of Claire, Zoe, Leslie and Janet. This was the place where something compelling and out-there could've been developed. Instead, J. Friedberg and A. Seltzer, in their role as the writers (and creators) of this production, plumped for four pretty ordinary people. Tho' two of the women are a little wilder and up for a party than the other two, all of them are white, middle class Americans (with a nice car and nice clothes – critics likened them to the *Sex and the City* cast). And there's not enough differentiation among them. The two women that're neurotic and repressed – Leslie and Claire (the sisters) – carry much of the humour, as they unravel and panic as they're taken further out of their comfort zones. The other two – Janet and Zoe – are more likely to dive into whatever Vegas offers (Janet with the mud-Jello wrestling, and Zoe with scoring drugs), but all four are strikingly ill-equipped to deal with anything slightly out of the ordinary).

The decision to make the four girls nice, white, middle Americans is partly dramatic: simply put, it's more fun (and better for the comedy) to see an uptight person with issues undergoing a chaotic experience where they're way out of their depth, than it is if they're laid-back (where nothing matters), or if they're super-tough warriors wielding samurai swords (where they can handle anything). The slacker dudes played by Owen Wilson or Adam Sandler would be loving it, whereas Darth Vader or Conan the Barbarian would simply slice apart anyone in their path.

As we have four young women in the lead parts, the usual gender roles are reversed, so that we are sometimes looking *with* the women *at* the men, and the men're sexually objectified – the first naked body we see in *Best Night Ever*, for ex, is of a guy (at the lap dance).[8] And when a

---

[7] Somehow, now they have endless amount of $$$$ – presumably from the mud-wrestling jape.
[8] The scene closes with another reverse gender gag that seems funny in principle but a little uncomfortable as it's performed: Claire is accused of breaking the house rules when she flicks away the stripper's wang.

guy[9] in a car yells at the girls to show their boobs, they respond by demanding to see their balls. Which they[10] do. So the expected tropes of a Las Vegas comedy – topless dancers, showgirls, hookers – are turned about.

Best Night Ever could be regarded as continuing the proto-feminist slant of the cinema of Friedberg and Seltzer, then, tho' gender stereotypes are still re-inforced throughout (partly for the comedy to work. But this is not a movie that's propounding a political revolution in gender and feminism. The writers and directors are men, the five producers are men, and the film industry, as we know, is completely a masculine preserve).

The men in the lives of the women are referenced chiefly in the dialogue (and occasionally on the phone): needless to say, the four girls are heterosexual: Claire is getting married next week (hence the bachelorette party), yet her fiancé seems to be fooling around on *his* stag night (when Claire makes the mistake of calling him); Janet's husband Larry doesn't know she's in Vegas, so she won't dare to call him to bail them out; Zoe went nutzoid and trashed her ex's property; and, most improbably, Leslie's husband is revealed to be gay (he's seen in a photo naked having sex with two guys).[11] So, yes, in this Las Vegas farce, two of the men in the women's relationships are fooling around and/ or abandoning them.

That's part of the structure of a story where a group of friends get together, with secrets coming out into the open.

The stand-out sequence in *Best Night Ever* is the mid-film montage where the girls stage a series of dares, pranks and jolly japes. This section is actually more child-like and playful (or less crude, anyway) than the others: they're running about like teenage girls, they're dancing, they're getting a foot massage, they're spooking passers-by, they're putting lipstick on a guy, they're on a zip wire, they're sky diving (at an 'only in Vegas' attraction)…

…And they're making a 'reality TV' version of girls on a night out in Vegas – another 'only in Vegas' caper, available for $5,000 (just kidding), and they're previewing a rough cut of the movie at an out-of-

---
9 Luke Patton.
10 Ben Goldsmith.
11 Another sight gag which includes naked men.

town theatre to an invited audience of hookers, drug dealers, down-and-outs, *mafiosi,* smack-heads and movie executives (just kidding).

Much of this section of *Best Night Ever* was filmed on Fremont Street, the centrepiece of the *old* Las Vegas, where the older casinos and resorts are found (these days, Las Vegas has spread out across the Strip).

But it's the filmmaking that is memorable here: it's a film editor's piece, as Peck Prior chops the movie into tiny bits and re-makes it as a rapid montage of images: we've got the full compliment of the film editor's tricks here (such as multiple freeze frames, and cutting from slo-mo to regular footage).

Events get crazier and more out-of-control as the night wears on (segments are introduced with a caption showing the time) – the girls snitch a stretch limo… there's a car chase… they kidnap and assault their mugger (but it's the wrong guy)… they bust into a stag party in a motel room featuring a couple of hookers… they're chased by an irate naked woman down hotel corridors, etc.

Yeah, it's Just Another Night In Vegas. Or, rather, in Movie Vegas – and Vegas is already a Wild Movie in itself.

In the second half of *Best Night Ever*, the 2013 movie seems to be saying, *fuck it*, let's go for it – if the audience (all three of 'em) have stayed in the theatre up to this point, we might as well go the whole way. So the movie dives into unbelievable, silly territory: the girls steal a limo, kidnap the mugger, and torture him (it's the wrong guy, but who cares?, all car valets look the same). How far will they go? *Best Night Ever* has Janet squatting over the trussed-up guy on a bed and pissing on him for payback (yes, yes, we know the punchline that you're thinking of right now: some punters in Vegas would pay for that sort of treatment!).

Part of the enjoyment of an 'R' rated, bathroom comedy is seeing how far the movie will go, how far the filmmakers will go, and how far the characters will go. In comedy, as stand-up comedians know well, you can conjure up more extreme imagery than in straight drama. Simply because it's comedy.[12]

Indeed, comedians, as they 'work the room', get a sense very quickly

---

[12] A stand-up comedian, such as Chris Rock, could go off on a rant about muggers and say, you tie him up and then you piss on the motherfucker. In a movie, you have to show that, and it becomes something else.

of just what the audience will stomach, where the boundaries of taste are, and what'll get the best laffs. A movie can't do that – hence all of those previews (a system that Friedberg and Seltzer use). You preview it, you rework it, you preview it again. And so on. (However, it's possible that *Best Night Ever* didn't go thru the preview process. It's a different sort of movie from the spoof movies that Friedberg and Seltzer are known for).

NIGGLES AND PLOTHOLES.

The set-up of *Best Night Ever* is artificial, and full of plot holes: Janet, Claire, Leslie and Zoe lose their cash, their credit cards, and their purses (but not their cel phones!),[13] so they're stranded in Las Vegas without the means to get home to L.A. *Eeeeh*?! This is contemporary North America we're talking about! We're not in Mordor – or Canada! And anyhoo we saw the girls arriving by car (and they somehow end up with the same car at the end. Besides, you don't need a car in Vegas, all the good stuff is walkable).

So these nice, bourgeois girls don't have a bank card or a credit card among them, and lose their lucre. They don't have parents, or brothers, or sisters, or uncles, or aunts, or friends (or even ex-boyfriends) they can call. But that's part of the dramatic set-up: you're in a modern city with every possible amenity and resource (even some you've never thought about!), but you feel helpless and stranded.

Best Night Ever is over-written: it might run to 79 minutes (or 90 minutes), but it contains enough dialogue for several movies. There's simply too much dialogue, as every goddam little thing is pointed out and underlined by the four women (but that's how Friedberg and Seltzer like to write movies, as their critics often complain).

THE CRITICS.

As to the film critics, we can guess without consulting them that they loathed *Best Night Ever* with a vengeance! Break out the axes and smash this movie to pieces! Kill, kill, kill this movie, pussycat! a critic complained that the gag in the dumpster, as the girls hide from the cops, is a single shot (in ugly, low-light green) that goes on forever and isn't

---

13 These are required for more gags.

funny[14] (it does out-stay its welcome, it isn't amusing, and it does seem another of Friedberg and Seltzer's eccentric tendencies to push an audience to the limit).[15] Another joke that runs on too long is the visual gag of the come stains all over the seedy motel room. We get the joke immediately (it relies on visual effects), but *Best Night Ever* lets it run on and on (on the lamp shade! on the door! and – *eeeuuww!* – on the ceiling!).

Yet, in amongst the slaughterfest that is the usual response of professional film critics to the mighty, transcendent art of Friedberg and Seltzer, there *were* some film critics who enjoyed parts of *Best Night Ever*, and even applauded it for giving them one or two laughs! (However, those film critics were later taken out into the desert by some wise guys and beaten to death with baseball bats. *Nobody* disses Las Vegas, *capisce?*, and *nobody* disses Las Vegas in movies, even if it's a piece-of-crap movie).

Some critics drew attention to the dodgy racial undercurrents in *Best Night Ever* – how the opening shot is of a black guy's naked ass, and how the woman at the end who turns into a screaming demon is a large, black woman.

Even the title seems to beg a movie review entitled 'Worst Movie Ever'. Which *Best Night Ever*, patently, is not.

---

14 But Sheila O'Malley reckoned it was one of the two best scenes (Roger Ebert website).
15 But other critics – such as from the Triibune News Service – enjoyed it.

10

SUPERFAST!

Smug. Superficial. Stupid. Fatuous. Puerile. Narcissistic. Super-capitalist. Near-fascist.

These and many other epithets might be hurled at the *Fast and the Furious* franchise and many similar urban action thrillers like *Bad Boys, Gone In 60 Seconds* and *Mission: Impossible* (and many other Hollywood action movies): these are self-absorbed, hi-tech movies aimed squarely at the late teenage, early twenties (and mainly male) market (the same age range as the market for Friedberg and Seltzer's movies).

Superfast! (2015) was the eighth feature parody movie written, co-produced and directed by Jason Friedberg and Seltzer. Ketchup/ 3 In the Box/ Safran Company produced; the producers were Peter Safran, Arthur Galstian, Gareth West, Vahan Yepremyan, Friedberg and Seltzer (plus a further five producers of the line prod., co-prod. and assoc. prod. ilk); Jordan Bass and Lauren Bass (casting); Jodi Ginnever (prod. des.); Maressa Richtmyer (costumes); Tim Wynn (m.); Shaun Maurer (DP); Peck Prior (ed.); Nathalie Neurath (set dec.); Katie Kilkenny (make-up); Gabby Suarez (hair); Michael Etheridge (1st A.D.); Chris Terhune (sup. sound ed.); and Keith Adams (stunt co-ord.). Released Apl 3, 2015.[16] 99 mins.

In the cast were: Andrea Navedo, Daniel Booko, Gonzalo

---

[16] The release date was chosen to coincide with the seventh *Fast and the Furious* movie: *Furious 7* was released on Apl 3, 2015, and was a mega-hit.

Mendendez, Alex Ashbaugh, Dale Pavinski, Lili Mirojnick, Dio Johnson, Chris Pang, Omar Chaparro, Rogelio Douglas, Jr., and Shantel Wislawski.[17] Once again, there's a high proportion of roles cast with Hispanic performers (and, this time, not a single name actor heads up the cast).

The box office returns for *Superfast!* were disappointing ($2.1 million from a budget of $20 million), as with *The Starving Games*, which also performed poorly in theatres. Is this because *Superfast!* and *The Starving Games* were weaker or less attractive flicks than earlier movies, such as *Date Movie* and *Epic Movie*, which grossed in the region of $80 million? It's possible that the *Fast and the Furious* series is simply not well-known enough for audiences to buy into a parody take on it, whereas the *Twilight Saga* is ripe on so many levels for parody. And yet, the *Fast and the Furious* series produced hit movies which achieved incredible grosses of over $1.2 billion (*The Fate of the Furious*) and $1.5 billion (*Furious 7*).

However, it may also be for business reasons: *Superfast!* was the first movie that Jason Friedberg and Seltzer produced independently, with Peter Safran, after leaving New Regency.

The crrritics slammed the 2015 movie, as usual (with one or two grudgingly, reluctantly and sulkily admitting (but only at gun-point) that some of the fans of the *Fast and the Furious* series might enjoy the send-ups).

•

Superfast! nailed all of the key aspects of the *Fast and the Furious* franchise. And it also included them in its retelling of the same sort of plot (so that, yes, *Superfast!* did work as a movie without knowing anything about the *Fast and the Furious* series. It had girls, cars, guns and thrills).

And Vin Diesel – a bald, implausible actor who seems so slow-witted and boorish, it's impossible to take him seriously. The leader of a cool gang of street racers? Gimme a break! Happily, *Superfast!* brought Diesel down to size (berated by his G.P.S. as a penis-head, for ex). And Dale Pavinski does a funny Diesel take-off, identifying just what is so

---

[17] Many actors in the lead roles were not part of the regular Friedberg and Seltzer Circus.

absurd about the actor.

Superfast! captures the idiotic gestures and looks that pass for acting in *The Fast and the Furious* – the macho nods and shrugs. Vin Diesel doesn't act, he *glares*, and Dale Pavinski does a great impression of those dead shark's eyes.

Alex Ashbaugh is terrific as the idiotic white cop who goes undercover; Ashbaugh captures the smug cockiness of Hollywood actors who think they're so cool and don't seem to realize that they're playing a dim-witted schlemiel. Like Pavinski, Ashbaugh has to deliver some rapid and intricate dialogue by Friedberg and Seltzer as the writers riff on some pet peeve.

It's not a Jason Friedberg and Seltzer parody unless there's some dancing: *Superfast!* featured less dancing than previous movies, but there was a scene where a bunch of drivers compete for a job with crime lord Juan Carlos de la Sol (Omar Chaparro)[18] by break-dancing. In the tried and tested manner of all Friedberg and Seltzer movies, the losers are simply shot (the sort of violence that crrritics loathe – they could just be asked to leave).

As well as dancing, *Superfast!* features plenty of music – mainly hiphop music and dance music. The soundtrack includes C. Rev, Icy Black, Suave Cinco, Skully Boyz, Kill the Giant and Boss Hawg.

And pretty girls – the opening scene is jammed with young women in very tight clothing (it's the Las Vegas floorshow version of *The Fast and the Furious*), and the movie rapidly introduces close-ups of women's asses (by the fifth shot).

Los Angeles looked great (even if might have been filmed in New Jersey!); Shaun Maurer was again DP (this is not glam, celeb-filled L.A., tho' there are one or two second unit shots of downtown. But, drenched in the famous California sunshine, even scuzzy parts of the city near the railroad and the warehouses look cool). And the vfx (or grading) which turned the skies scarlet and orange was impressive (Kenny Yates was visual effects supervisor).

Superfast! is unusual among the films of Friedberg and Seltzer for *not* including multiple parodies: so we don't have the TV game show

---

[18] Chaparro seems to be channelling some of Al Pacino in *Scarface* in his OTT performance as the crime lord who loses it regularly.

skits, or the recreations of *Narnia* or *Harry Potter* films, or the processions of lookalikes. There are joke products (like the fuel booster),[19] and joke signs (like the 'Dumb Ass Parking' sign), but *Superfast!* isn't a non-stop barrage of pops at contemporary American culture.

Superfast! surprises with its lack of gross-out humour, a staple of the Friedberg and Seltzer School of Spoof Movies (tho' there are some gross gags – like herpes, and White's idea of kissing, and the Supermodel throwing her silicone boobs at a cop in the next car).

•

WHAT'S GREAT IN *SUPERFAST*.

• The riff that White delivers when he describes himself to his cop boss, Detective Hanover (Gonzalo Menendez) (I'm so useless I wear crocs, my favourite actress is Kristen Stewart, etc).

• White's car with the unicorn and rainbow decal on the side.

• The wager that Vin stakes at the beginning – an aromatherapy session (and the excited responses of desperate-to-be-cool youths).

• The pants hanging below the butts of the guys at the street race.[20]

• Curtis's thesaurus-chewing monologue of alternative names for the cops.

• White's amazement that Juan de la Sol couldn't get a better deal with the car insurance for his supercar.

• White's idiotic and patronizing summary of how he thinks that Jordana feels, on their date.

• The repetition of pointless, boring shots of bits of the cars[21] – like people's feet on gas pedals (and C.U.s not only of the rev counter but also the water gauge). The silly sounds of the cars. (The establishing shots of the Serento garage, with downtown L.A. in the background, were also presumably meant to be repetitive and boring).

• The rivalry between White and Curtis (Daniel Booko was terrific at portraying Curtis's prima donna huffs and sulks as Serento increasingly favours White as his B.F.F.).

• The super-dumb Detective Rock Johnson (Dio Johnson) in a too-

---

[19] A big deal in the *Fast and the Furious* movies.
[20] A gag from *Don't Be a Menace* (1996).
[21] *Superfast!* is full of interior car scenes – process shots in the studio, as Jordana talks with White, or White with Serento, etc. And so is *The Fast and the Furious* – it has amazing car stunts, but the principal players are back in the studio, sitting in a cutaway car.

tight T-shirt rubbing baby oil on his pecs (and his long-suffering aide, Julie Canaro (Shantel Wislawski)).

• The discussion (from, improbably, Serento) about the technicalities of the movie's music which suggests something bad's going to happen (while everyone looks around and listens).

• The bicycle (plus cop) that crashes into a tree and explodes.

• The running gag about I-Hop restaurant.

• Crime lord de la Sol and his long-suffering aide Cesar (Joseph Julian Soria) arguing over seatbelts and climate control.

• The gang putting on animal heads instead of the usual black masks.

• The round-up of the team to steal Juan de la Sol's millions[22] – the secondary, stereotypical charas hired to make up the group that'll perform the heist: Cameo Rapper (Rogelio Douglas, Jr.), Model Turned Actress (Chanel Celaya) and Cool Asian Guy (Chris Pang).

THE SCENES.

Superfast's opening scene is an ensemble piece set at night in a warehouse area of Los Angeles, which introduced all of the chief characters and their relationships: Vin Serento[23] (Dale Pavinski), his sister Jordana Serento (Lili Mirojnick), his closet lesbian girlfriend Michelle Toritz (Andrea Navedo), his hapless sidekick, Curtis (Daniel Booko), the street racing gangs, and their boisterous followers. And of course Lucas White (Alex Ashbaugh), as the hopelessly goofy, undercover cop (the two main charas in *Superfast* are Ashbaugh as White and Pavinski as Serento).

The heist[24] in *Superfast!* involves a huge throwaway gag – a very lengthy piece of explanation and narration by Vin Serento about his plans for stealing de la Sol's loot from the safe in the Big Ass Taco restaurant. Gratuitous nudity for the girls counting the money (pixelled-out) is just one of many ridiculous elements in this shtick, all of which is thrown away because nobody wants to do it (Curtis has to get shot in the groin).

---

22 As Vin puts it, he likes to have a United Colors of Bennetton feel to his heists.
23 The charas take their names from the actors in the *Fast and the Furious* movies: Vin, Jordana, Michelle, etc.
24 The cops are on the tail of crooks, but they're incompetent: Detective Johnson fails to notice 'Heist Day' written on a calender in the garage.

The fire-fight[25] is delightfully dumb, with both sides just standing there shooting. Model Turned Actress (Chanel Celaya) flicks her hair so she looks even cuter as she wields a pistol. Cesar cheerfully waves to Curtis, the snitch. (And no one gets hurt – well, except for Curtis, who manfully throws himself in front of Vin, but is shot).

Pacing-wise, the finale of *Superfast!* was probably a little too long (the movie runs to 99 mins, instead of the more usual 80-85 mins for a Friedberg and Seltzer picture). You can only take so many shots of cars and people in cars driving. The low budget[26] becomes obvious when the cars are driving (too slowly) along the same section of road again and again. And the sequence, being the finale, demands some serious car carnage or explosions, which don't come. Editor Peck Prior and composer Tim Wynn spice things up with a new surge of energy and music, but it's not really big enough.

Are Friedberg and Seltzer getting soft and romantic here? They end *Superfast!* with a series of happy-ish endings: the crooks get clean away; White and Jordana are heading for somewhere exotic; Juan de la Sol buys off Detective Johnson; and Michelle is picked up by Officer Canaro (they kiss and embrace in the car). Vin doesn't seem bothered that his girlfriend has been nabbed by the cops (instead, he has an abusive relationship with his Sat Nav, which directs him to a wig store on Wilshire).

Friedberg and Seltzer also give White a foxy girlfriend (Jordana),[27] with a baby on the way. So even the dumb-ass doofus gets a cute family. Despite critics claiming that Friedberg and Seltzer are callous, uncaring, cinematic terrorists, you can't get sweeter or more homely than this.

---

25 When Detective Johnson shoots Cesar, a video game motif is used – nothing new: *Hot Shots!* had already done it.
26 It looks even less than $20 million. (*The Fast and the Furious*' budget was $38 million for the first film, but it looked more).
27 And they cast a woman – Lili Mirojnick – who resembles both of their wives (a glamorous brunette with shoulder-length hair).

THE FAST AND THE FURIOUS

The Fast and the Furious is a slick, flashy action thriller series very much in the Don Simpson and Jerry Bruckheimer model:[28] fast cars, beautiful girls, outlaws, crime, guns, cops, pop music, and lots of action. All of those ingredients are specially crafted (some would say cynically, artificially molded) to appeal to the target audience: these are completely market-driven, studio-driven movies (but most movies are). And, surprisingly for what are actually enjoyable but unremarkable, routine movies, they have become very lucrative, with huge grosses at the box office (just as incredibly, the *Fast and the Furious* series, which began in 2001 with the first movie, has run on and on).

The nine *Fast and the Furious* movies were released in 2001, 2003, 2006, 2009, 2011, 2013, 2015, 2017 and 2021. The box office grosses of the films ranged from $158m globally (for *Tokyo Drift*) to an astonishing $1.5 billion worldwide (for *Furious 7*). They were all rated 'PG-13'.[29]

The first *Fast and the Furious* movie was produced by Neal H. Moritz for Universal; Doug Claybourne and John Pogue were exec. prods., Gary Scott Thompson, Eric Bergquist and David Ayer scripted (Thompson created the story), and Rob Cohen directed. The cast included Paul Walker (Brian O'Conner), Vin Diesel (Dominic Toretto), Michelle Rodriguez (Letty Ortiz), Jordan Brewster (Mia Toretto), Rick Yune (Johnny Tran), Chad Lindberg (Jesse) and Johnny Strong (Leon). The budget was $38 million.[30] Released June 18, 2001. 102 mins.

The Fast and the Furious was filmed in and around Los Angeles (the neighbourhood where the characters live is Echo Park, an area neglected in L.A. movies – it's not Hollywood, West Hollywood, Beverly Hills, downtown, or Santa Monica).

•

Less than a third of *The Fast and the Furious* is actually about street racers: a third of the movie is a routine cop thriller, with the authorities on the trail of gangs that hijack trucks (conscious of the target audience,

---

[28] Tho' not a patch on *Initial D*, the Japanese *manga* later turned into an *animé* then a live-action film starring Jay Chou.
[29] The DVD of the first *Fast and the Furious* movie has a segment on re-editing the movie for attain that all-important 'PG-13' rating for the M.P.A.A.
[30] Altho' it looks more.

it's not drugs or white slavery, as in an 'R' rated pic, but electronic goods). The other third is the soap opera built around Brian, Dominic, Letty, Mia *et al.*

Hey guys, the girls in *The Fast and the Furious* are cute tomboys who work on cars! It's the ultimate macho fantasy – a mouthy, beautiful Latino like Michelle Rodriguez who's also a mechanical genius.

Boys and cars – with the girls sidelined to romantic subplots (this pic is fairly Neanderthal in its treatment of women, where the girls are 'girlfriend of the hero'). The real romance in *The Fast and the Furious* is between guys and their cars, yes, and between the two male leads, Walker and Diesel (and there's an erotic triangle, too – but not with Brewster as the third (alloy) wheel, but Matt Schulze as Vince).[31] However, the girls are allowed to perform some significant tasks: tomboy Letty is part of the crew of crooks in the final, botched job, for example, and she does trounce a bozo in the big race in the desert.

The cars are characters in *The Fast and the Furious* – in fact, they are more alive than the human characters. None of these people in their 20s and 30s convince – nor the way they're played by the actors. It's an appealing cast, but none of them persuade us to accept them as these particular characters in these particular situations, or living these particular lives.

We don't buy it.

In particular, the everyday, domestic scenes are completely bogus – they look exactly like scenes where the actors have been brought to the set (from the make-up trailer), handed bottles of beer, and been told to act cool and casual. The actors are not *inside* these scenes, they don't *inhabit* these characters, they are visiting the set then hurrying back to their trailers to chat to their friends on their cel.

Some of the subplots in *The Fast and the Furious* are drivel – such as the antagonism between the cop O'Conner and Toretto's sidekick, Vince (Matt Schulze). Every time Vince is on screen, the movie trips and falls into mud. (Here the spoofing of *Superfast!* was so welcome, turning Vince into an over-blown Drama Queen who has numerous hissy fits. You thought that Curtis in *Superfast!* huffing off was over-done? No –

---

[31] There's another romantic triangle, featuring Walker and Brewster.

Vince does that in *The Fast and the Furious*!).

Meanwhile, the chemistry between Walker and Brewster as the second cute couple in *The Fast and the Furious* is non-existent. Instead, in *The Fast and the Furious,* you're waiting for the next action scene. Get in the cars and drive already!

In this respect, *The Fast and the Furious* is the same as many other action movies built around sports or tournaments or some adventurous activity: the scenes in-between the action – when the jet fighter pilots are on the ground, or when the thrill-seeking dudes aren't hanging off the side of a mountain – tend to be full of formulaic soap opera scenes or sentimental guff. It can work – *Only Angels Have Wings* (1939) – but *The Fast and the Furious* is built on top of the chassis of the Simpson-Bruckheimer movie-as-machine *Top Gun* (1986).

•

The *Fast and the Furious* movies were stuffed with car stunts (and cool cars), as if they were a gimmicky update of the Burt Reynolds movies of the 1970s (although they would prefer to be Steve McQueen in *Bullitt* as the epitome of cool[32] rather than Reynolds in *Smokey and the Bandit*).

For a formulaic movie, however, *The Fast and the Furious* film of 2001 displayed a near-abstract approach to the numerous visual effects shots, with blurred backgrounds composed in streaked lines, like the speed lines in a comic, to suggest high speed.

Ironically, all of the hi-tech wizardry that went into creating the illusions of speed and thrills, in hundreds of effects shots, are under-cut by the studio-filmed images of the interior car scenes. Every night scene featuring the characters riding in cars was captured on the studio floor, with background plates tricked in separately.

The editing in *The Fast and the Furious* is self-consciously rapid, filled with all of the usual gimmicks of MTV-style, pop promo-style cutting. And the camerawork is of course stuffed with fussy mannerisms and artifice (shaky framing, bird's-eye-view shots… yawn). This movie is trying very hard to be cool and contemporary.

The finale of *The Fast and the Furious* involves multiple chases and

---

32 McQueen + *Bullitt* is one of the totems for car movies.

action sequences, following on from the race meeting in the desert: the heist that goes horribly wrong (and which doesn't make much sense logistically, and is drawn out far beyond necessity); the fire-fight with the Chinese gangsters and subsequent motorbike chase; and the macho silliness of the guys racing each other towards a railroad crossing. (The ending, which's meant to resolve the central relationship of O'Conner and Toretto, has the look of a rewrite and reshoot).

Am I the only Boy Racer[33] who saw a desperate melancholy underneath *The Fast and the Furious*? Not in the characters (none of whom compel at any level), or the action, or the street-cool *milieu*, or the situations, but an atmosphere of sadness and frustration that pervades the movie.

Is it the artificial mix of elements concocted by cynical film producers in Tinseltown? The recipe is: tough guys, cute girls, flashy cars, hiphop, races, crime, cops.

The film critics didn't go for *The Fast and the Furious* in the main: they found it derivative of the Bruckheimer-Simpson-type of product (such as *Top Gun*); some critics even wished that Jerry Bruckheimer or Michael Bay had got hold of *The Fast and the Furious,* because it would be a better movie.

---

33 Jaguar E-type V-8.

Best Night Ever (2013), this page and over.

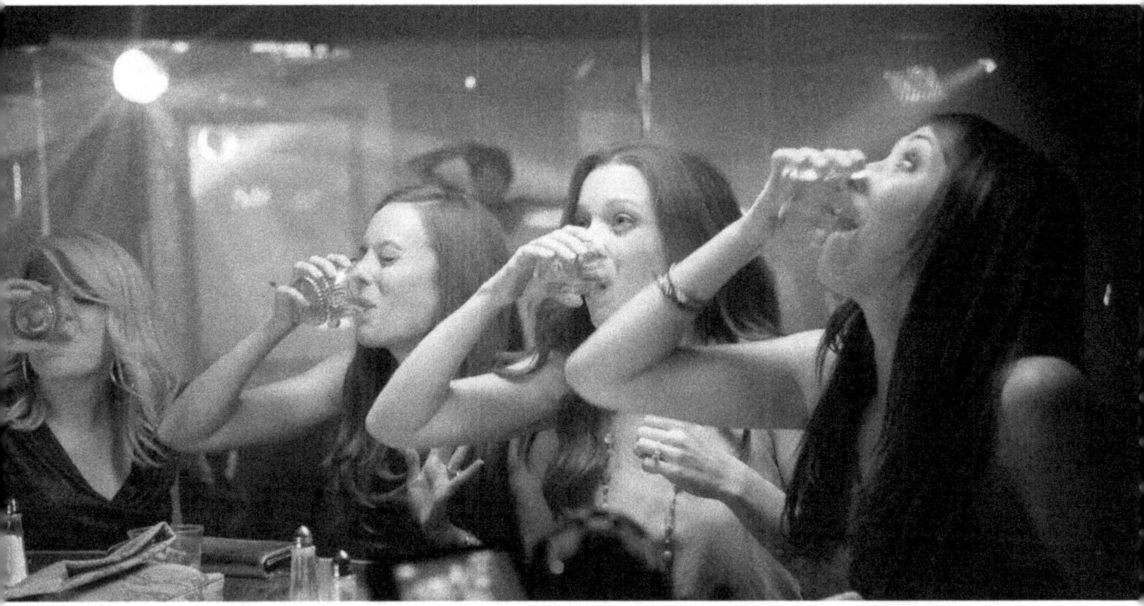

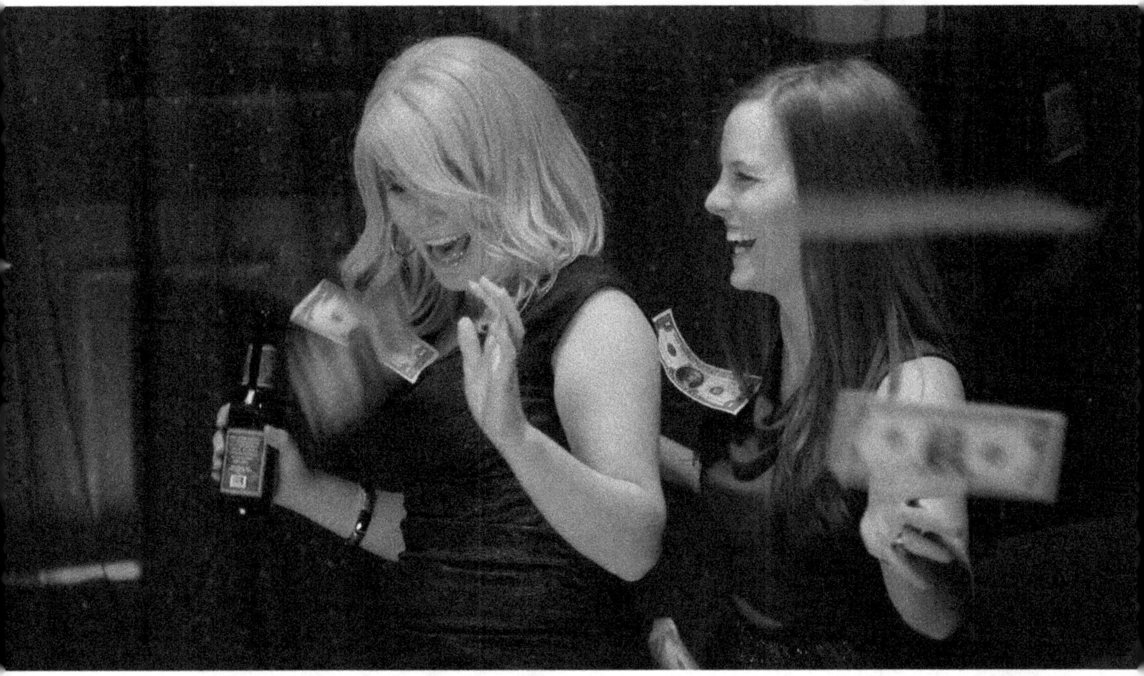

Superfast! (2015), this page and over.

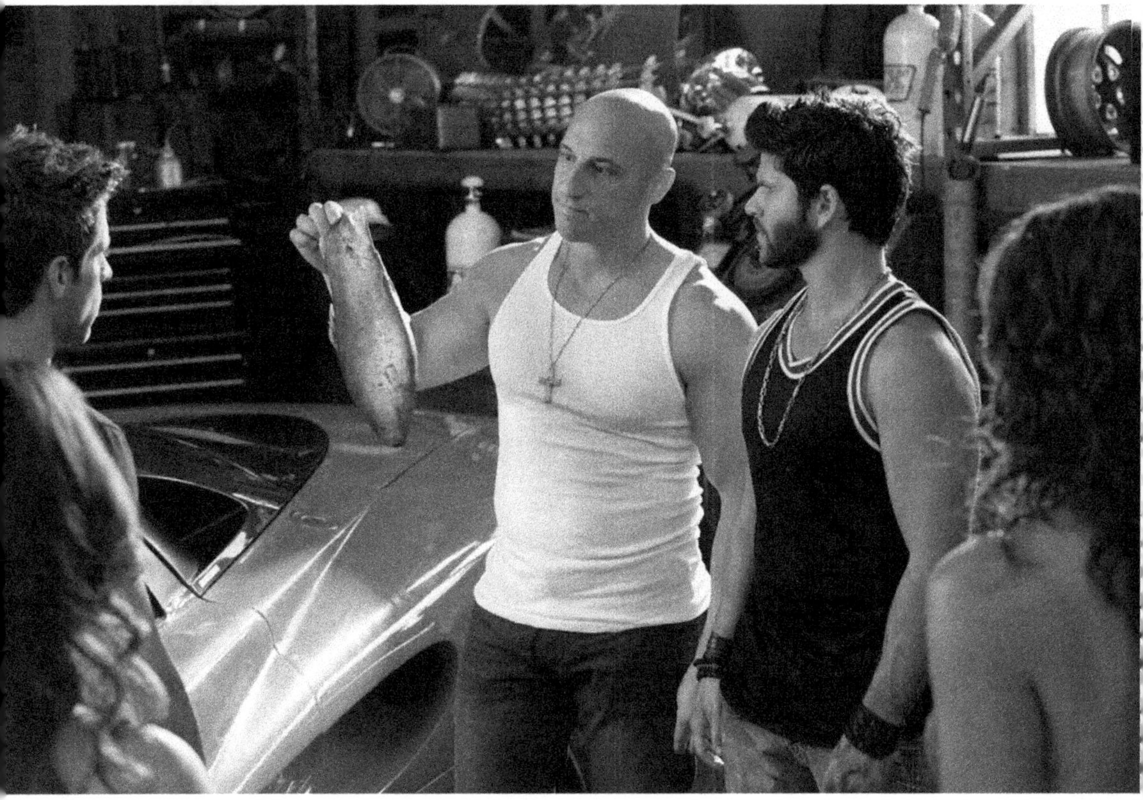

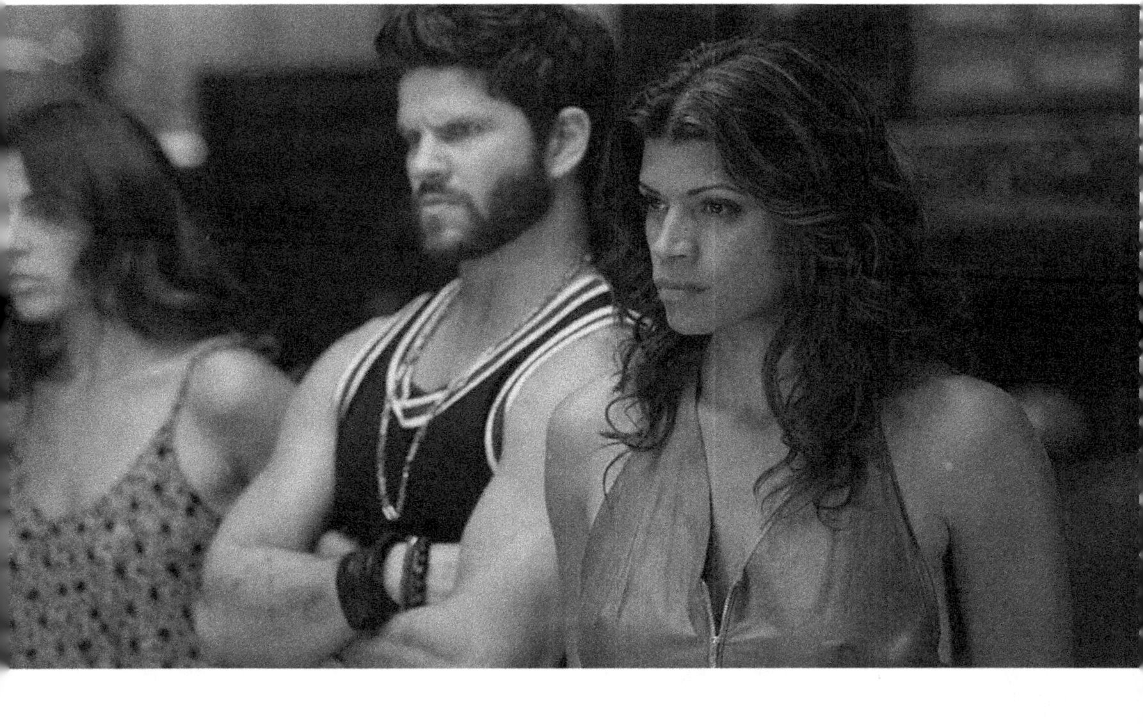

APPENDIX

SOME MOVIES LINKED TO THE WORK OF FRIEDBERG AND SELTZER

AIRPLANE!

Airplane! (1980) is one of the most celebrated comedy movies in the history of cinema, regularly appearing high in film polls (for some, it's at the top). It is loved by critics and filmmakers as well as audiences.

The producers of *Airplane!* were Jon Davison, Jim Abrahams David Zucker, Jerry Zucker and Howard W. Koch for Howard W. Koch Productions and Paramount Pictures. Joseph Biroc was DP; Elmer Bernstein delivered the 1950s B-movie-style score; Ward Preston was production designer; casting by Joel Thurm; editing by Patrick Kennedy; costumes by Rosanna Norton; make-up by Edwin Butterworth; and hair by Joan Phillips. Released June 27, 1980. 88 mins.

Airplane! developed out of a series of skits on television commercials that the Zucker, Abrahams and Zucker team had developed back in 1974.[1] They had moved from Wisconsin[2] (they all hailed from Wisconsin, and had attended university in Madison, WI) to Los Angles (forming a theatre show on Pico Boulevard in 1962, along with Pat Profit). Originally, *Airplane!* was going to consist of a series of sketches (which's how a lot of comedy movies originate, especially if they grow out of stage shows and the revue format of performing live). The team decided to go for an update and a spoof of 1950s

---

[1] There was a video section in their live performances, containing spoofs of commercials. At one time some joke ads were going to be part of *Airplane!*
[2] The three knew each other in Wisconsin – their families were friendly.

movies, and *Zero Hour* (Hall Bartlett, 1957) in particular (*Zero Hour*, from an Arthur Hailey teleplay, had been remade in 1971 (for TV) as *Terror In the Sky*). *Airplane!* took many scenes and even lines straight from *Zero Hour*: sometimes it's striking just how little material has to be altered to make it funny (partly due to the new context, in a comedy movie). Thus, *Airplane!* could be regarded as a remake of *Zero Hour* (right down to the filmmakers setting up shots to directly emulate the 1957 movie).3

Many studios turned *Airplane!* down (and they would kick themselves after the movie became so successful), until it found a home at Paramount (which was then being run by the group known as 'the Killer Dillers' – Michael Eisner, Jeffrey Katzenberg and the future Walt Disney team). Eisner, at least, was behind the movie, and understood its potential.

Airplane!'s producer was Howard Koch (1916-2001), a veteran producer and director – *The Manchurian Candidate, The Odd Couple, The Untouchables, Ghost, Hollywood Wives, Plaza Suite, Dragonslayer, The Pirate,* and the Oscars Awards show. Koch was passionate about the movie, and was instrumental in shepherding it thru to completion. The budget was $3.5 million (Paramount liked to keep budgets modest if possible – the Eisner-Katzenberg-Wells team pursued the same low-cost-high-return and high concept policy when they joined the Mouse House).

Filming took place mainly at Culver City Studios, with location shoots at LAX airport, the beach at Malibu, Griffith Park, and the Paramount lot on Melrose. The schedule was tight – 38 days (some say less!). The low budget meant that many of the physical effects (there are only a few optical or post-production effects) were cheap. But that of course enhances the comedy.

The cast of *Airplane!* is wonderful, headed up by the appealing teaming of Robert Hays with Julie Hagerty. It included Leslie Nielsen, Lloyd Bridges, Robert Stack, Peter Graves, Kareem Abdul-Jabbar (a basketball star), Lorna Patterson and Stephen Stucker. After *Airplane!*, actors such as Nielsen and Bridges would have a whole new career in parody movies (many of them for the Zucker-Abrahams-Zucker team).

None of the actors in *Airplane!* were big names, which helped to keep the budget down (they were most known for TV shows like *The Untouchables* and *Sea Hunt*). And there are few cameos – James Wong, Ethel Merman, Jason Wingreen, etc (tho' these would increase in later Z.A.Z. movies – and there were more cameos in the *Airplane!* sequel – William Shatner, Rip Torn, Sonny Bono, etc).

The cinematography of *Airplane!* is dead simple: a strong key light, with no fill and no backlight. As the directors remembered, DP Joseph Biroc would spend no more than fifteen minutes lighting a scene. It works: cinematic

---

3 The rights had to be cleared for *Zero Hour*.

trickery usually gets in the way of the comedy: a scene needs to be well-lit and in focus. Less fussiness lets the humour come through quicker and easier. Compare *Airplane!* to *1941* (1979), a giant, bloated turkey directed by Steven Spielberg the year before, which cost $27 million and features lavish cinematography (by William Fraker and co.). But it ain't funny! (and it was the first giant flop for the *wünderkind*, following the mega-hits *Jaws* and *Close Encounters of the Third Kind*).

The Directors' Guild of America wasn't keen on *Airplane!* having three film directors.[4] But the Z.A.Z. guys was adamant they were going to share directing duties (it was also safety in numbers for the young filmmakers).

As with many of their later projects, the Zucker, Abrahams and Zucker team took *Airplane!* to many preview screenings (they have said they sometimes used 3 or 4 previews). The audience's reaction was used as a guide to re-cutting the picture. The audience was taped at some of the previews, then the movie was adapted according to the laughs it received. If something wasn't funny, out it went! So, as the writers joked, a three-hour comedy (!) was whittled down to 78 minutes (but fleshed out with long end credits). The filmmakers were ruthless with their own material, throwing out anything that didn't work.

The filmmakers were not involved with the inevitable sequel of *Airplane!*, which the studio demanded. *Airplane!* had done colossal business (some $170 million) – and, for a $3.5m picture, that made the cost-to-profit ratio too tempting for any movie studio. But the filmmakers, as Jim Abrahams explained, had been there and done everything they thought they could do with jokes about flying movies. They didn't want to revisit the same territory. (The sequel, released in 1982 and directed by Ken Finkelman, starred many of the same cast, including Hays, Hagerty, Bridges, Graves, etc).

•

It's *Airplane!* – and each Z.A.Z. movie boasts that all-important exclamation mark – ! – (Universell Studios sued over the title – they claimed it would caused confusion with their own *Airport – Concorde '79* (released: Aug 17, 1979). So the title was changed to *Kentucky Fried Theater's Airplane* for a while, until the issue was resolved).

The writers wanted that 1950s, retro, Eisenhower-era feel for *Airplane!*, which extended to the costumes and the look of the 1980 picture. They even wanted the aircraft to be prop-driven (but were persuaded otherwise; however, they did add propeller engine sounds to the exterior images of the airliner).[5]

As well as *Zero Hour*, *Airplane!* contains jokes about pretty much every

---

4 Having three directors was certainly unusual. The filmmakers said it worked fine, because they knew each other very well, and they had been working together for years. So they knew what they were aiming for. And they could also split duties when necessary.
5 The airline company is Transamerica – apparently a real airline, but chosen, of course, because its acronym is 'TA' (= tits and ass).

aerial movie ever made. Not only the disaster cycle of the 1970s (*Earthquake, The Towering Inferno, The Poseidon Adventure* and the *Airport* movies (*Airport, Airport 1975, Airport '77* and *Airport '79: The Concorde*)), but flying movies going back to Hollywood's heyday. 'But forget the token gesture of a plot – what matters here is the style (relentless) and the gags (punishingly relentless)', as Bob McCabe put it (64).

•

Among the many movies that *Airplane!* spoofed were *Jaws, Saturday Night Fever, From Here To Eternity,* and of course disaster movies and *Zero Hour.*

Airplane! is a masterpiece of comedy by any standards. The most obvious reason, and, for comedies, perhaps the single most important reason, is: *it is very funny!*

Yes: a comedy *must* be funny, right? Well, not *always*, or perhaps, not necessarily a constant barrage of jokes. But it *must* be funny some of the time. But however you define a comedy movie, *Airplane!* succeeds. And *Airplane!* is a hit with all sorts of audiences, and of many different ages. It's a comedy that works with kids, for instance (my kids loved it), and not only the educated, college-age crowd, or the alternative comedy crowd, or with intellectuals.

Airplane! hits the jackpot across the board. Because the jokes are a collection of all sorts of gags: some are witty one-liners beloved of intellectuals of the Robert Benchley-Dorothy Parker-Algonquin 'Vicious Circle', some are pop culture swipes that university and college students enjoy, some are convoluted runs in lengthy dialogue scenes, some are bawdy, and many are physical, knockabout gags.

The rapidity of the gags in *Airplane!* is incredible – few movies, including the Marx Brothers at their height, can match such a barrage of jokes. And the *attitude*, the *tone*, the *feel* of the humour and its context and setting, is spot-on. The filmmakers have attained just the right tone for the movie, just the right balance between serious, dramatic moments (to keep the picture moving along), and humour (the *situation* is taken seriously by all concerned: the plane really is in crisis, the pilots really are critically ill, and the people on the ground at the airport really are deeply concerned for the flight. The actors play it straight. But not *too* straight: *Airplane!* is intended from the outset to be a cheesy B-movie. It's not *Hamlet* or a P.B.S. special: it's a balance between B-Movie Cheese, with its hammy acting, corny dialogue and low budget sets and visual effects, and an ironic, self-aware spoof. When Julie Hagerty talks to Bob Hays about sitting on his face and wiggling, she delivers the lines straight, with a Marilyn Monroe ditziness and cheerleader innocence that's appealing).

Rated 'PG', *Airplane!* swerves close to an 'R' rated picture in many scenes: blowjob jokes, naked, jiggling tits, snorting cocaine, etc. Some material was altered to attained the 'PG' rating (and there was a television version, which avoids the more controversial material).[6] Yet, compared to the gross-out comedies of the 1990s and 2000s, or the *Scary Movie* cycle, and more recent parody flicks, all of which draw *heavily* on *Airplane!,* the humour in the movie is pretty mild. But it still feels completely contemporary, and completely fresh, and completely out-there. *Airplane!* hasn't dated at all.

One of the funniest scenes in *Airplane!* is the masterful spoof of *Saturday Night Fever* and disco culture, which swept the West a couple of years earlier. Using the Bee Gees' 'Stayin' Alive' (sped up by 10% to make it funnier), the filmmakers cover everything in *Saturday Night Fever* and turn it upside-down. Again, it's the *tone* and the *attitude* that is just marvellous. The filmmakers rightly keep the actors within character, without breaking the fourth wall: they let the situation and the dialogue provide the laughs. It seems, in retrospect, almost effortless. But the script went thru at least 30 drafts, and hardly anything was improvized

Jim Abrahams said that two questions keep coming up: are their movies improvized? No. Are they on drugs? No! But, to audiences who don't how movies work, or how movies get to be very funny, it can seem as if everything just happened on set, as if the actors improvized scenes spontaneously. Well, if they could, writers and directors and producers would be out of jobs! No – actually, a close look at any successful film comedy will reveal that it has been written and rewritten and rewritten, time after time, to achieve that apparent ease and flow.

Airplane! is so funny partly because it was developed over years and years, going back to at least 1974. So jokes had time to gestate, while others were left by the wayside.

CADDYSHACK

Caddyshack (1980) was a forerunner of the Friedberg and Seltzer comedy movie: puppet critters, slapstick, mindless violence, big stunts, explosions, a rebellious, anti-social attitude, attacks on authority figures, fooling around with girls (and titillating nudity), young, middle-class, American heroes, eccentric characters, plenty of pop music (Kenny Loggins (the single 'I'm

---

[6] It's one minute 30 seconds long.

Alright' was a hit), Earth, Wind and Fire, Johnny Mandel, Hilly Michaels, Journey), spoofs of movies (a lengthy *Jaws* skit), wise-cracking, Jewish humour, a Middle American setting, and a smug, aren't-we-wonderful? tone. (1980 was a good year for comedy: *Airplane!* above all, but also *Stir Crazy, The Blues Brothers*, and *Private Benjamin*).

Critics reacted with mixed reviews, though *Caddyshack*'s reputation grew over time (it's full of quotable lines). All of Friedberg and Seltzer's films fared poorly with critics but audiences enjoyed them. Despite the critics, *Caddyshack* was a hit – $60m gross from a budget of two dollars fifty cents). Critics complained that the movie was loose, careening about in style and approach – which's how Friedberg and Seltzer like to make movies.

BREAKING WIND

Breaking Wind (Craig Moss, 2012) was a send-up of *Breaking Dawn, Part 1* (Bill Condon, 2011), as well as many other moments from the *Twilight Saga*. It was produced by Bernie Gewissler and Craig Moss, and written and directed by Moss for Lionsgate. It starred Heather Ann Davis, Eric Callero, Danny Trejo and Frank Pacheco. Released: Jan 13, 2012. 82 mins.

This was the second *Twilight Saga* movie spoof (the first being *Vampires Suck* in 2010). With a higher M.P.A.A. rating than *Vampires Suck* (an 'R', which the *Twilight* movies themselves should've been), *Breaking Wind* was keen to explore cruder jokes. Fart jokes (a *lot* of fart jokes!), blowjob jokes, gay sex, sex toys – *Breaking Wind* was very much in the vein of the Jason Friedberg and Aaron Seltzer and Zucker-Abrahams-Zucker mold.

Heather Ann Davis gave a spirited version of Kristen Stewart's emo victim girl in the *Twihard Saga*, and Eric Callero (as Edward) and Frank Pacheco (as Jacob) offered plenty of fun moments. The spirit of *Breaking Wind* was delightfully silly: it's always great to see a movie which doesn't take itself seriously *at all*. Because even those American movies that are classed as comedies still want to tell a story and create drama (romantic comedies are a good example: they typically want to be funny and lighthearted, but they also want the audience to invest in the characters and the romantic themes).

In most recent North American movies, there's a point where they *stop* and won't go any further. They explore close to the edge, but then they recoil, and return to base, to home, to safety, to the Great American Dream. No matter how *crazeee* a typical Hollywood movie is, it will come back to base and it will re-affirm the family, the law, marriage, education, the military, capitalism and money, and the American Way of Life.

And after a while you get *sick* of that. Like, is that *all* there is? Only the American Way of Life, for anybody living anywhere in the world? So at the end of a Big, Loud Action Movie, or a fantasy blockbuster flick featuring weirdos with pointy ears, or a romantic comedy about a smug, self-satisfied New York couple, there will always be the scene, the shot, the facial expression, the music, the sound, the visual effect or the image which expresses that Return Home, that re-affirmation of Good Ol' American Capitalism, to send its audience out of the theatre happy and self-assured, back to their cars, to the shopping mall, to the bar, to the subway...

•

Once again in a spoof movie, *Breaking Wind* didn't need to do much except replay some of the key scenes in *Breaking Dawn, Part 1* to expose just how preposterous the whole vampire genre is, and how lame the *Twilight Saga* is when you examine it closely (yes, you have to admit, *Twilight* is a very lame, very dumb, very useless franchise! But that's partly what we love about it! And it is also, in its own way, compelling and even great).

I loved Rosalie so resenting Becca in *Breaking Wind* that she attempts to kill her a number of times, whinges about her being so fucking irritating, and kicks her over a balcony where she crashlands on a table: 'Jesus Christ, why don't you die, bitch?!' I loved the 'Team Jacob' and 'Team Edward' stickers that Jacob and Edward plaster on people at school.[7] I loved the werewolves as overweight guys, with Jacob perpetually snacking, and perpetually referring to his priceless abs (a wonderful send-up of the gym-honed bodies that male stars desperately try to develop for the cameras). I loved Becca's Pa blethering on about gay sex. I loved Carlisle trying to show the group gathered for training about the newbie vampires on his laptop computer, but not being able to get past the idiot captcha password. I loved the mini versions of the Sullens. I loved the send-up of the ridiculous tent scene in *Twilight*, with Jacob humping Becca in the sleeping bag (and Becca's wide awake and loving it).

And more: I loved the filmmakers in *Breaking Wind* turning Becca's sexual desire (which's what powers so much of the *Twilight Saga* along), into something explicit: so she's got dildos in her cupboards, porn mags on her bed (big black men, of course!), and falls asleep reading *The Art of Fellatio* (meanwhile, she has nightmares of her granny going down on Edward, in a send-up of the opening scenes of *Breaking Dawn, Part 1*, and *New Moon*).[8]

---

7 *Breaking Wind* saluted the fans, too, with snippets at the end of the film of fans.
8 The nightmare repeat, with Edward humping granny.

Later in the 2012 movie, Becca's dressed as a stripper, gyrating around a pole, to get Edward in the mood (echoing *Breaking Dawn, Part 1*, where our Bella tries to turn on Edward wearing lingerie. But *Breaking Wind*, like *Vampires Suck*, is *far* superior in this regard, and many others).

And even more: I loved the use of the same helicopter shot, over forests and a lake, towards a snowy mountain. I loved the *Twilight*-style voiceover over those images, including Becca wittering on about absolutely bugger all for 60 seconds, and also Becca using her vibe to masturbate, before she realizes the mic's on.

And more and more: I loved the werewolves' flashback, where we see four of the famous characters that Johnny Depp's played in recent movies, including Edward Scissorhands, Willy Wonka (from *Charlie and the Chocolate Factory*), the Mad Hatter (from *Alice In Wonderland*) and of course Jack Sparrow (from *Pirates of the Caribbean*), standing in for the dreaded vampires who attack some Native Americans in a very silly, OTT fight scene.

Sure, *Breaking Wind* was a lower budget production than the movie it was lampooning (by some way! *Breaking Dawn Part 1*'s budget was $110 million). But it didn't matter: *Breaking Wind*, like *Vampires Suck,* reminded us once again that if you take away the vampires and the werewolves in the *Twilight Saga*, you've got nothing more'n another story about kids and high schools and dating and the 10,000 Agonies of Being a Teenager. That's all.

And *Breaking Wind*, in the flashback, with the Johnny Depp characters, reminded us that a movie is simply just that: people dressing up and acting out stories. That's all. Cinema is just storytelling. And it doesn't make the slightest bit of difference to the audience if the storytelling costs $20,000 or $2 million or $200 million. Who gives a hoot? It's just a story! And who cares if it was written, directed, acted and produced by well-known, multi-talented and highly-paid show business veterans, or by a bunch of actors and crew paid at the S.A.G./ Equity day rates? It's just a goddam story! It's just storytelling!

There are limits to low budget versions of high budget Hollywood fare, and that's of course in elements such as stars, exotic locations, 100s of extras, and visual effects. But a lot of the vampire visual effects in the *Twilight Saga* were achieved with editing and sound effects, two cheap ways of making something look and sound good (a rapid cut, or speeding up film, plus a whooshy sound effect). But putting werewolves on screen, that means millions of $$$$$. *Vampires Suck* got around that by using a chihuahua dog. *Breaking Wind* didn't bother – no need, you just ignore the issue, and stick to your fat slob pack of guys, and add more fart sounds.

Airplane (1980).

Caddyshack (1980).

Breaking Wind (2012).

APPENDIX

VIEWERS ON THE MOVIES OF FRIEDBERG AND SELTZER

FROM METACRITIC

ON *VAMPIRES SUCK*

This was the Best Movie Ever! it was hilarious! ... I heard almost all of the people laughing like hell in the movie theatre.

-

I could not stop laughing after seeing this movie. It was absolutely PERFECT for people like me who couldn't stand the *Twilight* franchise and it was a movie that needed to be made.

-

Vampires Suck succeeds in mocking even the smallest details of the *Twilight* saga and is a great film whether you love *Twilight* or not. By itself, it would suck as a movie, but as it is a spoof, it's fantastic and I loved it.

-

Yes, it's a stupid movie. Yes, it's a bad movie. But it's still so funny!!

-

I still feel hurt almost a week after watching the thing.

-

WORSE PARODY MOVIE I'VE EVER SEEN. Waste of my time and money.

-

Even worse than *Twilight*.

FROM METACRITIC

ON *DATE MOVIE*

I don't care what the critics say, I loved this movie!!
-

It was definitely the funniest movie I've seen all year.
-

I was laughing the entire time!
-

It humorously mocks the genre I despise, and had me in tears of laughter during the entire movie.
-

Date Movie was awesome. It was one of the funniest movies ever.
-

Worst. Movie. Ever. AVOID AT ALL COSTS.
-

Walked out after 25 minutes. Probably the worst movie of all time.
-

The worst film I've seen in a long time.

BIBLIOGRAPHY

A. Aldgate. *Censorship and the Permissive Society*, Oxford University Press, Oxford, 1995
R.C. Allen, ed. *Channels of Discourse: Television and Contemporary Criticism*, Methuen, London, 1987
R. Altman, ed. *Sound Theory, Sound Practice*, Routledge, London, 1992
—. *Film/Genre*, British Film Institute, London, 1999
P.T. Anderson. "Night Fever", in J. Hillier, 2001
D. Andrew. *The Major Film Theories*, Oxford University Press, Oxford, 1976
—. *Concepts In Film Theory*, Oxford University Press, Oxford, 1984
K. Anger. *Hollywood Babylon*, Dell Publishing, New York, NY, 1975
L. Aronson. *Screenwriting Updated*, Silman-James, Los Angeles, CA, 2000
J. Arroyo. *Action/Spectacle Cinema*, British Film Institute, London, 2000
A. Assister & A. Carol, eds. *Bad Girls and Dirty Pictures: The Challenge To Reclaim Feminism*, Pluto Press, London, 1993
T.R. Atkins, ed. *Sexuality In the Movies*, Indiana University Press, Bloomington, IN, 1975
W. Aycock & M. Schoenecke, eds. *Film and Literature*, Texas University Press, Austin, TX, 1988
L. Badley. *Film, Horror and the Body Fantastic*, Greenwood Press, Westport, CT, 1995
—. *Writing Horror and the Body: The Fiction of Stephen King, Clive Barker and Anne Rice*, Greenwood Press, Westport, CT, 1996
P. Bailey. *The Reluctant Art of Woody Allen*, University Press of Kentucky, Lexington, KY, 2000
M. Banks & A. Swift. *The Jokes On Us: Women In Comedy From Musical Hall To the Present*, Pandora Press, London, 1987
M. Barker, ed. *The Video Nasties: Freedom and Censorship In the Media*, Pluto Press, London, 1984
—. & J. Petley, eds. *Ill Effects: The Media/Violence Debate*, Routledge, London, 1997
—. *From Antz To Titanic*, Pluto Press, London, 2000
G. Barlow & A. Hill, eds. *Video Violence and Children*, Hodder, London, 1985
P. Bart. *The Gross: The Hits, the Flops: The Summer That Ate Hollywood*, St Martin's Press, New York, NY, 1999
—. *Who Killed Hollywood?*, Renaissance Books, Los Angeles, CA, 1999
L. Bawden, ed. *The Oxford Companion To Film*, Oxford University Press,

Oxford, 1976
J. Baxter. *An Appalling Talent: Ken Russell,* M. Joseph, London, 1973
M. Beja. *Film and Literature: An Introduction,* Longman, London, 1979
E. Bell *et al*, eds. *From Mouse To Mermaid: The Politics of Film, Gender and Culture,* Indiana University Press, Bloomington, IN, 1995
H. Benshoff. *Monsters In the Closet: Homosexuality and the Horror Film,* Manchester University Press, Manchester, 1997
J. Bernardoni. *The New Hollywood,* McFarland Press, 1991
M. Bernstein, ed. *Controlling Hollywood: Censorship & Regulation In the Hollywood Studio Era,* Athlone Press, London, 2000
P. Biskind. *Easy Riders, Raging Bulls: How the Sex 'n' Drugs 'n' Rock 'n' Roll Generation Saved Hollywood,* Bloomsbury, London, 1998
—. *Down and Dirty Pictures: Miramax, Sundance and the Rise of Independent Film,* Bloomsbury, London, 2004
G. Black. *Hollywood Censored,* Cambridge University Press, Cambridge, 1994
J.M. Boggs. *The Art of Watching Films,* Benjamin/ Cummings, Menlo Park, California, 1978
D. Bogle. *Toms, Coons, Mulattoes, Mammies and Bucks: An Intrerpretive History of Blacks In America,* Continuum, New York, NY, 1990
D. Bordwell & K. Thompson. *Film Art: An Introduction,* McGraw-Hill Publishing Company, New York, NY, 1979
—. *Narration In the Fiction Film,* Routledge, London, 1988
—. *Making Meaning,* Harvard University Press, Cambridge, MA, 1989
—. & N. Caroll, eds. *Post-Theory: Reconstructing Film Studies,* University of Wisconsin Press, Madison, WI, 1996
—. *The Way Hollywood Tells It,* University of California Press, Berkeley, CA, 2006
D. Breskin. *Inner Voices: Filmmakers In Conversation,* Da Capo, New York, 1997
R. Brody. *Everything Is Cinema: The Working Life of Jean-Luc Godard,* Faber, London, 2008
S. Bruzzi. *Undressing Cinema,* Routledge, London, 1997
N. Burch. *Theory of Film Practice,* Secker & Warburg, London, 1973
G. Burt. *The Art of Film Music,* Northeastern University Press, 1994
Terry Ceasar. "Violating the Shrine", University of Washington, unpublished thesis, 1979
S. Caldwell & M.-E. Kielson, eds. *So You Want To Be a Sceenwriter* Allworth Press, New York, NY, 2000
N. Carroll. *Mystifying Movies: Fads and Fallacies of Contemporary Film Theory,* Columbia University Press, New York, NY, 1988
D. Cartmell *et al*, eds. *Trash Aesthetics: Popular Culture and Its Audience,* Pluto Press, London, 1997
—. & I. Whelehan, eds. *Adaptions: From Text To Screen, Screen To Text,* Routledge, London, 1999
J. Caughie, ed. *Theories of Authorship: A Reader,* Routledge, London, 1988
—. & A. Kuhn, eds. *The Sexual Subject: A* Screen *Reader In Sexuality,* Routledge, London, 1992
R. Chapman & J. Rutherford, eds. *Male Order: Unwrapping Maculinity,* London, 1988

G. Chester & J. Dickey, eds. *Feminism and Censorship: The Current Debate*, Prism Press, Bridport, Dorset, 1988

B. Clarke, ed. *The Cinematic City*, Routledge, London, 1997

V. Clemens. *The Return of the Repressed*, State University of New York Press, Albany, NY, 1999

C. Clover. *Men, Women and Chain Saws: Gender In the Modern Horror Film*, Princeton University Press, Princeton, NJ, 1992

S. Cohan & I.R. Hark, eds. *Screening the Male: Exploring Masculinities In Hollywood Cinema*, Routledge, London, 1993

J. Collins *et al*, eds. *Film Theory Goes To the Movies*, Routledge, New York, NY, 1993

D.A. Cook. *A History of Narrative Film*, W.W. Norton, New York, NY, 1981, 1990, 1996

L. Cooke & P. Wollen, eds. *Visual Display*, Bay Press, Seattle, 1995

P. Cook, ed. *The Cinema Book*, British Film Institute, London, 1985

R. Corman. *How I Made a Hundred Movies In Hollywood and Never Lost a Dime*, New York, NY, 1990

F. Couvares, ed. *Movie Censorship & American Culture*, Smithsonian Institution Press, Washington DC, 1996

B. Creed. *The Monstrous-Feminine*, Routledge, London, 1993

T. Cripps. *Making Movies Black*, Oxford University Press, Oxford, 1993

F. Dannen & B. Long. *Hong Kong Babylon*, Faber & Faber, London, 1997

C. Degli-Esposti, ed. *Postmodernism In the Cinema*, Berghahn Books, New York, NY, 1998

E. De Grazia & R.K. Newman. *Banned Films: Movies, Censors and the First Amendment*, Bowker, New York, NY, 1982

D. Denby. "Double Jeopardy", *New York*, July 18, 1978

N. Denzin. *The Cinematic Society*, Sage, London, 1995

D. Desser & G. Jowett, eds. *Hollywood Goes Shopping*, University of Minnesota Press, Minneapolis, MN, 2000

A. De Vaney. *Hollywood Economics*, Routledge, 2004

L. Doan, ed. *The Lesbian Postmodern*, Columbia University Press, New York, NY, 1994

J. Donald, ed. *Fantasy and the Cinema*, British Film Institute, London, 1989

E. Dorman. *Box-Office Champs*, Portland House, New York, NY, 1990

O. Double. *Stand Up! On Being a Comedian*, Random House, New York, NY, 1997

S.C. Dubin. *Arresting Images: Impolitic Art and Uncivil Actions*, Routledge, London, 1992

A. Dworkin. *Pornography: Men Possessing Women*, Women's Press, London, 1984

—. *Intercourse*, Arrow, London, 1988

—. *Letters From a War Zone: Writings, 1976-1987*, Secker & Warburg, London, 1988

R. Dyer, ed. *Gays and Film*, British Film Institute, London, 1980

—. *Heavenly Bodies: Film Stars and Society*, Macmillan, London, 1987

—. *Now You See It: Studies on Lesbian and Gay Film*, Routledge, London, 1990

—. *Only Entertainment*, Routledge, London, 1992

—. *Stars*, British Film Institute, London, 1998
M. Eagleton, ed. *Feminist Literary Theory: A Reader*, Blackwell, Oxford, 1986
A. Easthope, ed. *Contemporary Film Theory*, Longman, London, 1993
J. Eberts. *My Indecision Is Final: The Rise and Fall of Goldcrest Films*, Faber, London, 1990
M. Eisner with T. Schwartz. *Work In Progress*, Penguin, London, 1999
D. Elley. *The Epic Film*, Routledge & Kegan Paul, London, 1984
R. Emery. *The Directors: Take Three*, Allworth Press, 2003
R. & P. Engelmeier. *Fashion In Film*, Prestel, Munich, 1997
P. Ettedgui. *Production Design & Art Direction*, RotoVision, 1999
P. Evans. *Terms of Endearment: Hollywood Romantic Comedy of the 1980s and 1990s*, Edinburgh University Press, Edinburgh, 1998
R. Evans. *The Kid Stays In the Picture*, New York, NY, 1994
H.J. Eysenck & D. Nias. *Sex, Violence and the Media*, Maurice Temple Smith, 1978
J. Eszterhas. *The Devil's Guide To Hollywood*, Duckworth, London, 2006
C. Finch. *Special Effects*, Abbeville, 1984
J. Finler. *The Movie Director's Story*, Octopus Books, London, 1985
—. *The Hollywood Story*, Wallflower Press, London, 2003
C. Fleming. *High Concept: Don Simpson and the Hollywood Culture of Excess*, Bloomsbury, London, 1998
J. Fletcher & A. Benjamin, eds. *Abjection, Melancholia and Love: The Work of Julia Kristeva*, Routledge, London, 1990
G.E. Forshey. *American Religious and Biblical Spectaculars*, Praeger, Westport, CT, 1992
K. Fowkes. *Giving Up the Ghost: Spirits, Ghosts and Angels In Mainstream Comedy Films*, Wayne State University Press, Detroit, MI, 1998
K. French, ed. *Screen Violence*, Bloomsbury, London, 1996
P. Fu & D. Desser, eds. *The Cinema of Hong Kong*, Cambridge University Press, Cambridge, 2002
H. Geduld, ed. *Filmmakers On Filmmaking*, Indiana University Press, Bloomington, IN, 1967
K. Gelder. *Reading the Vampire*, Routledge, London, 1994
—. & S. Thornton, eds. *The Subcultures Reader*, Routledge, London, 1997
—. ed. *The Horror Reader*, Routledge, London, 2000
J. Gelmis. *The Film Director as Superstar*, Penguin, London, 1974
C. Gledhill, ed. *Stardom: Industry of Desire*, Routledge, London, 1991
J. Gordon & V. Hollinger, eds. *Blood Read: The Vampire As Metaphor In Contemporary Culture*, University of Pennsylvania Press, Philadelphia, PA, 1997
B.K. Grant, ed. *Film Genre*, Scarecrow Press, Metuchen, NJ, 1977
—. ed. *Planks of Reason: Essays on the Horror Film*, Scarecrow Press, 1984
—. *Film Genre Reader II*, University of Texas Press, Austin, TX, 1995
N. Griffin & K. Masters. *Hit & Run: How Jon Peters and Peter Guber Took Sony For a Ride In Hollywood*, Simon & Schuster, New York, NY, 1996
E. Grosz. "The Body of Signification", in J. Fletcher, 1990
—. *Volatile Bodies*, Indiana University Press, Bloomington, IN, 1994
R. Grover. *The Disney Touch*, Business One Irwin, Homewood, Illinois, 1991
L. Halliwell. *Halliwell's Filmgoer's Companion*, 7th edition, Granada,

London, 1980
I. Hamilton. *Writers In Hollywood*, Heinemann, London, 1990
D. Harries. *Film Parody*, British Film Institute, 2000
M. Heins. *Sex, Sin, and Blasphemy: A Guide To America's Censorship Wars*, New Press, New York, NY, 1993
S. & N. Hibbin. *What a Carry On: The Official Story of the Carry On Films*, Hamlyn, London, 1988
C. Hill. *Video Violence and Children*, Oasis, London, 1983
L. Hutcheon. *A Theory of Parody*, Methuen, New York, 1985
—. *A Poetics of Postmodernism*, Routledge, New York, 1988
D. Hughes. *Comic Book Movies*, Virgin, London, 2003
H. Jenkins. "The Amazing Push-Me/ Pull-You Text: Cognitive Processing, Narrational Play and the Comic Film", *Wide Angle*, vol. 8, no. 3/4, 1986
G. Jordan & C. Weedon. *Cultural Politics*, Blackwell, Oxford, 1995
B.F. Kawin. *Mindscreen: Bergman, Godard and First-Person Film*, Princeton University Press, Princeton, NJ, 1978
—. *How Movies Work*, Macmillan, New York, NY, 1987
S. Keane. *Disaster Movies: The Cinema of Catastrophe*, Wallflower, London, 2001
P. Keough, ed. *Flesh and Blood: The National Society of Film Critics on Sex, Violence, and Censorship*, Mercury House, San Francisco, CA, 1995
M. Kermode. *Hatchet Job*, Picador, London, 2013
A. Kibbey *et al. Sexual Artifice: Persons, Images, Politics*, New York University Press, New York, NY, 1994
P. Kirkham & J. Thumim, eds. *Me Jane: Masculinity, Movies and Women*, Lawrence & Wishart, London, 1995
H. Knowles. *Ain't It Cool? Kicking Hollywood's Butt*, Boxtree, London, 2002
P. Kramer. *The Big Picture: Hollywood Cinema From Star Wars To Titanic*, British Film Institute, London, 2001
—. *The New Hollywood*, Wallflower Press, London, 2005
J. Kristeva. *Powers of Horror: An Essay on Abjection*, tr. Leon S. Roudiez, Columbia University Press, New York, 1982
—. *The Kristeva Reader*, ed. Toril Moi, Blackwell, Oxford, 1986
—. *Tales of Love*, tr. Leon S. Roudiez, Columbia University Press, New York, N.Y., 1987
R. Lapsley & M. Westlake, eds. *Film Theory: An Introduction*, Manchester University Press, Manchester, 1988
E. Levy. *Cinema of Outsiders: The Rise of American Independent Film*, New York University Press, New York, NY, 1999
J. Lewis, ed. *New American Cinema*, Duke University Press, Durham, NC, 1998
—. *Hollywood v. Hard Core: How the Struggle Over Censorship Created the Modern Film Industry*, New York University Press, New York, NY, 2000
—. ed. *The End of Cinema As We Know It: American Film In the Nineties*, New York University Press, New York, NY, 2002
L. Lewis, eds. *The Adoring Audience: Fan Culture and Popular Media*, Routledge, New York, NY, 1992
J. Leyda. ed. *Film Makers Speak: Voices of Film Experience*, Da Capo, New York, NY, 1977
B. Logan. *Hong Kong Action Cinema*, Titan, London, 1995

S. Louvish. *Monkey Business: The Lives and Legends of the Marx Brothers*, Faber, London, 1999
S. Macdonald. *A Critical Cinema: Interviews With Independent Filmmakers*, University of California Press, Berkeley, CA, 1988
R. Maltby. *Harmless Entertainment: Hollywood and the Ideology of Consensus*, Scarecrow Press, Metuchen, NJ, 1983
—. *Hollywood Cinema*, 2nd ed., Blackwell, Oxford, 2003
G. Mast et al, eds. *Film Theory and Criticism: Introductory Readings*, Oxford University Press, New York, NY, 1992a
—. & B Kawin, *A Short History of the Movies*, Macmillan, New York, NY, 1992b
N. Matthews. *Comic Politics: Gender In Hollywood Comedy After the New Right*, Manchester University Press, Manchester, 2001
T.D. Matthews. *Censored*, Chatto & Windus, London, 1994
B. McCabe. *Dark Knights & Holy Fools: The Art and Films of Terry Gilliam*, Orion, London, 1999
—. *The Rough Guide To Comedy Movies*, Rough Guides, London, 2005
J. McCarthy. *Psychos: 80 Years of Mad Movies, Maniacs and Murderous Deeds*, St Martin's, New York, NY, 1986
D. McClintock. *Indecent Exposure: A True Story of Hollywood and Wall Street*, W. Morrow, New York, NY, 1982
R. McKee. *Story: Substance, Structure, Style and the Principles of Screenwriting*, Methuen, London, 1999
"Meet the Spartans", press kit, Montebubbles.net, 2007
M. Medved. *Hollywood vs. America*, HarperCollins, London, 1992
X. Mendik & S. Schneider, eds. *Underground U.S.A.: Filmmaking Beyond the Hollywood Canon*, Wallflower Press, London, 2002
S. Meyer. *Twilight*, Atom/ Little, Brown, London, 2007
—. *New Moon,* Atom/ Little, Brown, London, 2007
—. *Eclipse,* Atom/ Little, Brown, London, 2007
—. *Breaking Dawn,* Atom/ Little, Brown, London, 2010
—. *The Twilight Saga: The Official Illustrated Guide*, Atom Books, London, 2011
F. Miller. *Censored Hollywood: Sex, Sin and Violence On Screen*, Turner Publishing, Atlanta, 1994
T. Miller et al, eds. *Global Hollywood*, British Film Institute, London, 2001
E. Muller & D. Faris. *That's Sexploitation! The Forbidden World of "Adults Only" Cinema*, Titan Books, London, 1996
J. Natoli. *Hauntings: Popular Film and American Culture 1990-92*, State University of New York Press, Albany, NY, 1994
—. *Speeding To the Millennium: Film and Culture 1993-1995*, State University of New York Press, Albany, NY, 1998
—. *Postmodern Journeys: Film and Culture, 1996-1998*, State University of New York Press, Albany, NY, 2001
S. Neale & F. Krutnik. *Popular Film and Television Comedy*, Routledge, London, 1990
—. & B. Neve. *Film and Politics In America*, Routledge, London, 1992
—. & M. Smith, eds. *Contemporary Hollywood Cinema*, Routledge, London, 1998

—. *Genre and Hollywood*, Routledge, London, 2000
—. *Genre and Contemporary Hollywood*, Routledge, London, 2002
K. Newman. *Nightmare Movies*, Harmony, New York, NY, 1988
—. ed. *The BFI Companion To Horror*, Cassell, London, 1996
—. & J. Marriott. *Horror! The Definitive Companion To the Most Terrifying Movies Ever Made*, Carlton Books, London, 2013
J. Orr. *Contemporary Cinema*, Edinburgh University Press, Edinburgh, 1998
C. Paglia. *Sexual Personae: Art and Decadence From Nefertiti To Emily Dickinson*, Penguin, London, 1992
D. Parkinson. *The Rough Guide To Film Musicals*, Penguin, London, 2007
Matt Patches. "Surely They Can't Be Serious?", *Grantland*, January 31, 2014
W. Paul. *Laughing Screaming: Modern Hollywood Horror and Comedy*, Columbia University Press, New York, NY, 1994
C. Penley, ed. *Feminism and Film Theory*, Routledge, London, 1988
G. Perry. *Life of Python*, Pavilion, London, 1983
J. Phillips. *You'll Never Eat Lunch In This Town Again*, Heinemann, London, 1991
D. Pollock. *Skywalking: The Life and Films of George Lucas*, Crown, New York, NY, 1983, 1990, 2000
R. Prendergast. *Film Music*, W.W. Norton, New York, NY, 1992
S. Prince. ed. *Screening Violence*, Athlone Press, London, 2000
M. Pye & Lynda Myles. *The Movie Brats: How the Film Generation Took Over Hollywood*, Faber, London, 1979
D. Quinlan. *The Illustrated Guide To Film Directors*, B.T. Batsford, London, 1983
—. *Quinlan's Illustrated Directory of Film Comedy Stars*, B.T. Batsford, London, 1992
T. Reeves. *The Worldwide Guide To Movie Locations*, Titan Books, London, 2003
R. Rickitt. *Special Effects*, Aurum, London, 2006
B. Robb. *Screams and Nightmares*, Titan Books, London, 1998
J. Robertson. *The British Board of Film Censors*, Croom Helm, 1985
G. Rodgerson & E. Wilson, eds. *Pornography and Censorship*, Lawrence & Wishart, London, 1991
J. Romney & A. Wootton, eds. *Celluloid Jukebox: Popular Music and the Movies Since the 50s*, British Film Institute, London, 1995
T. Rose. *Black Noise: Rap Music and Black Culture In Contemporary America*, Wesleyan University Press, Hanover, NH, 1994
M. Rubin. *Thrillers*, Cambridge University Press, Cambridge, 1999
M. Russell & J. Young. *Film Music,* RotoVision, 2000
V. Russo. *The Celluloid Closet: Homosexuality In the Movies*, Harper & Row, New York, NY, 1981
B. Rux. *Hollywood vs. the Aliens*, Frog, Berkeley, CA, 1997
L. Sandahl. *Rock Music On Film*, Blandford Press, Poole, 1987
A. Sarris. *The American Cinema*, Dutton, New York, NY, 1968
—. ed. *Interviews With Film Directors*, Avon, New York, NY, 1969
T. Schatz. *Hollywood Genres,* Random House, New York, NY, 1981
—. *Old Hollywood/ New Hollywood*, UMI Research Press, Ann Arbor, MI, 1983
—. *The Genius of the System: Hollywood Filmmaking In the Studio Era,*

Pantheon, New York, NY 1988
Screen Reader I: Cinema/ Ideology/ Politics, Society for Education in Film & TV, 1977
Screen Reader II: Cinema and Semiotics, British Film Institute, London, 1982
C. Sharrett, ed. *Crisis Cinema*, Maisonneuve Press, Washington, DC, 1993
T. Shone. *Blockbuster: How the Jaws and Jedi Generation Turned Hollywood Into a Boom-Town*, Scribner, London, 2005
E. Showalter, ed. *The New Feminist Criticism,* Virago, London, 1986
R. Shuker. *Understanding Popular Music*, Routledge, London, 1994
—. *Key Concepts In Popular Music,* Routledge, London, 1998
S. & B. Siegel. *American Film Comedy*, Prentice Hall, 1994
N. Sinyard. *Filming Literature: The Art of Screen Adaption*, Croom Helm, Beckenham, Kent, 1986
D. Smith. *American Filmmakers Today*, Blandford Press, Poole, 1984
G. Smith. *Epic Films*, McFarland, Jefferson, NC, 1991
J. Solomon. *The Ancient World In the Cinema*, Yale University Press, New Haven, CT, 2001
J. Stacey. *Hollywood Cinema and Female Spectatorship*, Routledge, London, 1994
P. Steven, ed. *Jump Cut: Hollywood, Politics and Counter Cinema*, Between the Lines, Toronto, 1985
J. Stevenson, ed. *Fleshpot: Cinema's Sexual Myth Makers and Taboo Breakers*, Headpress, 2001
G. Stewart. *Between Film and Screen: Modernism's Photo Synthesis*, University of Chicago Press, Chicago, IL, 1999
J. Still & M. Worton, eds. *Textuality and Sexuality: Reading Theories and Practices*, Manchester University Press, Manchester, 1993
M. Stokes & R. Maltby, eds. *Identifying Hollywood Audiences*, British Film Institute, London, 1999
J. Storey, ed. *Cultural Theory and Popular Culture*, Harvester Wheatsheaf, Hemel Hempstead, 1994
C. Straayer. *Deviant Eyes, Deviant Bodies: Sexual Re-orientation In Film and Video*, Columbia University Press, New York, NY, 1996
J.M. Straczynski. *The Complete Book of Scriptwriting*, Titan Books, London, 1997
J. Stringer, ed. *Movie Blockbusters*, Routledge, London, 2003
N. Strossen. *Defending Pornography: Free Speech, Sex, and the Fight For Women's Rights,* New York University Press, New York, NY, 2000
C. Tashiro. *Pretty Pictures: Production Design and the History Film*, University of Texas Press, 1998
Y. Tasker. *Spectacular Bodies: Gender, Genre and the Action Cinema*, Routledge, London, 1993
—. *Working Girls: Gender and Sexuality In Popular Cinema*, Routledge, London, 1998
S. Teo. *Hong Kong Cinema*, British Film Institute, London, 1997
K. Thompson & D. Bordwell. *Film History: An Introduction*, McGraw-Hill, New York, NY, 1994
—. *Storytelling In the New Hollywood*, Harvard University Press, Cambridge, MA, 1999

D. Thomson. *A Biographical Dictionary of Film,* Deutsch, London, 1995
—. *The Big Screen*, Allen Lane, 2012
E. Traube. *Dreaming Identities: Class, Gender and Generations In 1980s Hollywood Movies*, Westview Press, Boulder, CO, 1992
J. Trevelyan. *What the Censor Saw*, Michael Joseph, London, 1973
J. Ursini & A. Silver. *The Vampire Film*, Limelight, New York, NY, 1993
H. Vogel. *Entertainment Industry Economics*, Cambridge University Press, Cambridge, 1995
C. Vogler. *The Writer's Journey: Mythic Structure For Storytellers and Screenwriters*, Pan, London, 1998
J. Wasko. *Movies and Money*, Ablex, NJ, 1982
—. *Hollywood In the Information Age*, Polity Press, Cambridge, 1994
E. Weiss. & J. Belton, eds. *Film Sound: Theory and Practice*, Columbia University Press, New York, NY, 1989
S. Willis. *High Contrast: Race and Gender In Contemporary Hollywood Film*, Duke University Press, Durham, NC, 1997
E. Wistrich. *'I Don't Mind the Sex It's the Violence': Film Censorship Explored*, Marion Boyars, London, 1978
M. Wolf. *The Entertainment Economy,* Penguin, London, 1999
R. Wood. *Hollywood From Vietnam To Reagan... and Beyond*, Columbia University Press, New York, NY, 2003
T. Woods. *Beginning Postmodernism,* Manchester University Press, Manchester, 1999
J. Wyatt. *High Concept: Movies and Marketing In Hollywood*, University of Texas Press, Austin, TX, 1994
J. Yang. *Once Upon a Time In China*, Atria Books, New York, NY, 2003
E.C.M. Yau, ed. *At Full Speed: Hong Kong Cinema In a Borderless World,* University of Minnesota Press, Minneapolis, MN, 1998

JEREMY ROBINSON has published poetry, fiction, and studies of J.R.R. Tolkien, Samuel Beckett, Thomas Hardy, André Gide and D.H. Lawrence. Robinson has edited poetry books by Novalis, Ursula Le Guin, Friedrich Hölderlin, Francesco Petrarch, Dante Alighieri, Arseny Tarkovsky, and Rainer Maria Rilke.

Books on film and animation include: *The Akira Book* • *The Art of Katsuhiro Otomo* • *The Art of Masamune Shirow* • *The Ghost In the Shell Book* • *Fullmetal Alchemist* • *Cowboy Bebop: The Anime and Movie* • *The Cinema of Hayao Miyazaki* • *Hayao Miyazaki: Pocket Guide* • *Princess Mononoke: Pocket Movie Guide* • *Spirited Away: Pocket Movie Guide* • *Blade Runner and the Cinema of Philip K. Dick* • *Blade Runner: Pocket Movie Guide* • *The Cinema of Donald Cammell* • *Performance: Donald Cammell: Nic Roeg: Pocket Movie Guide* • *Pasolini: Il Cinema di Poesia/ The Cinema of Poetry* • *Salo: Pocket Movie Guide* • *The Trilogy of Life Movies: Pocket Movie Guide* • *The Gospel According To Matthew: Pocket Movie Guide* • *The Ecstatic Cinema of Tony Ching Siu-tung* • *Tsui Hark: The Dragon Master of Chinese Cinema* • *The Swordsman: Pocket Movie Guide* • *A Chinese Ghost Story: Pocket Movie Guide* • *Ken Russell: England's Great Visionary Film Director and Music Lover* • *Tommy: Ken Russell: The Who: Pocket Movie Guide* • *Women In Love: Ken Russell: D.H. Lawrence: Pocket Movie Guide* • *The Devils: Ken Russell: Pocket Movie Guide* • *Walerian Borowczyk: Cinema of Erotic Dreams* • *The Beast: Pocket Movie Guide* • *The Lord of the Rings Movies* • *The Fellowship of the Ring: Pocket Movie Guide* • *The Two Towers: Pocket Movie Guide* • *The Return of the King: Pocket Movie Guide* • *Jean-Luc Godard: The Passion of Cinema* • *The Sacred Cinema of Andrei Tarkovsky* • *Andrei Tarkovsky: Pocket Guide*.

'It's amazing for me to see my work treated with such passion and respect. There is nothing resembling it in the U.S. in relation to my work.'
(Andrea Dworkin)

'This model monograph – it is an exemplary job, and I'm very proud that he has accorded me a couple of mentions… The subject matter of his book is beautifully organised and dead on beam.'
(Lawrence Durrell, on *The Light Eternal: A Study of J.M.W. Turner*)

'Jeremy Robinson's poetry is certainly jammed with ideas, and I find it very interesting for that reason. It's certainly a strong imprint of his personality.'
(Colin Wilson)

'*Sex-Magic-Poetry-Cornwall* is a very rich essay... It is a very good piece… vastly stimulating and insightful.'
(Peter Redgrove)

CRESCENT MOON PUBLISHING

web: www.crmoon.com e-mail: cresmopub@yahoo.co.uk

ARTS, PAINTING, SCULPTURE

The Art of Andy Goldsworthy
Andy Goldsworthy: Touching Nature
Andy Goldsworthy in Close-Up
Andy Goldsworthy: Pocket Guide
Andy Goldsworthy In America
Land Art: A Complete Guide
The Art of Richard Long
Richard Long: Pocket Guide
Land Art In the UK
Land Art in Close-Up
Land Art In the U.S.A.
Land Art: Pocket Guide
Installation Art in Close-Up
Minimal Art and Artists In the 1960s and After
Colourfield Painting
Land Art DVD, TV documentary
Andy Goldsworthy DVD, TV documentary
The Erotic Object: Sexuality in Sculpture From Prehistory to the Present Day
Sex in Art: Pornography and Pleasure in Painting and Sculpture
Postwar Art
Sacred Gardens: The Garden in Myth, Religion and Art
Glorification: Religious Abstraction in Renaissance and 20th Century Art
Early Netherlandish Painting
Leonardo da Vinci
Piero della Francesca
Giovanni Bellini
Fra Angelico: Art and Religion in the Renaissance
Mark Rothko: The Art of Transcendence
Frank Stella: American Abstract Artist
Jasper Johns
Brice Marden
Alison Wilding: The Embrace of Sculpture
Vincent van Gogh: Visionary Landscapes
Eric Gill: Nuptials of God
Constantin Brancusi: Sculpting the Essence of Things
Max Beckmann
Caravaggio
Gustave Moreau
Egon Schiele: Sex and Death In Purple Stockings
Delizioso Fotografico Fervore: Works In Process 1
Sacro Cuore: Works In Process 2
The Light Eternal: J.M.W. Turner
The Madonna Glorified: Karen Arthurs

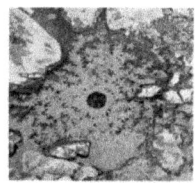

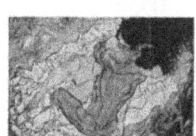

LITERATURE

J.R.R. Tolkien: The Books, The Films, The Whole Cultural Phenomenon
J.R.R. Tolkien: Pocket Guide
Tolkien's Heroic Quest
The *Earthsea* Books of Ursula Le Guin
Beauties, Beasts and Enchantment: Classic French Fairy Tales
German Popular Stories by the Brothers Grimm
Philip Pullman and *His Dark Materials*
Sexing Hardy: Thomas Hardy and Feminism
Thomas Hardy's *Tess of the d'Urbervilles*
Thomas Hardy's *Jude the Obscure*
Thomas Hardy: The Tragic Novels
Love and Tragedy: Thomas Hardy
The Poetry of Landscape in Hardy
Wessex Revisited: Thomas Hardy and John Cowper Powys
Wolfgang Iser: Essays and Interviews
Petrarch, Dante and the Troubadours
Maurice Sendak and the Art of Children's Book Illustration
Andrea Dworkin
Cixous, Irigaray, Kristeva: The *Jouissance* of French Feminism
Julia Kristeva: Art, Love, Melancholy, Philosophy, Semiotics and Psychoanalysis
Hélène Cixous I Love You: The *Jouissance* of Writing
Luce Irigaray: Lips, Kissing, and the Politics of Sexual Difference
Peter Redgrove: Here Comes the Flood
Peter Redgrove: Sex-Magic-Poetry-Cornwall
Lawrence Durrell: Between Love and Death, East and West
Love, Culture & Poetry: Lawrence Durrell
Cavafy: Anatomy of a Soul
German Romantic Poetry: Goethe, Novalis, Heine, Hölderlin
Feminism and Shakespeare
Shakespeare: Love, Poetry & Magic
The Passion of D.H. Lawrence
D.H. Lawrence: Symbolic Landscapes
D.H. Lawrence: Infinite Sensual Violence
Rimbaud: Arthur Rimbaud and the Magic of Poetry
The Ecstasies of John Cowper Powys
Sensualism and Mythology: The Wessex Novels of John Cowper Powys
Amorous Life: John Cowper Powys and the Manifestation of Affectivity (H.W. Fawkner)
Postmodern Powys: New Essays on John Cowper Powys (Joe Boulter)
Rethinking Powys: Critical Essays on John Cowper Powys
Paul Bowles & Bernardo Bertolucci
Rainer Maria Rilke
Joseph Conrad: *Heart of Darkness*
In the Dim Void: Samuel Beckett
Samuel Beckett Goes into the Silence
André Gide: Fiction and Fervour
Jackie Collins and the Blockbuster Novel
Blinded By Her Light: The Love-Poetry of Robert Graves
The Passion of Colours: Travels In Mediterranean Lands
Poetic Forms

POETRY

Ursula Le Guin: Walking In Cornwall
Peter Redgrove: Here Comes The Flood
Peter Redgrove: Sex-Magic-Poetry-Cornwall
Dante: Selections From the Vita Nuova
Petrarch, Dante and the Troubadours
William Shakespeare: Sonnets
William Shakespeare: Complete Poems
Blinded By Her Light: The Love-Poetry of Robert Graves
Emily Dickinson: Selected Poems
Emily Brontë: Poems
Thomas Hardy: Selected Poems
Percy Bysshe Shelley: Poems
John Keats: Selected Poems
John Keats: Poems of 1820
D.H. Lawrence: Selected Poems
Edmund Spenser: Poems
Edmund Spenser: Amoretti
John Donne: Poems
Henry Vaughan: Poems
Sir Thomas Wyatt: Poems
Robert Herrick: Selected Poems
Rilke: Space, Essence and Angels in the Poetry of Rainer Maria Rilke
Rainer Maria Rilke: Selected Poems
Friedrich Hölderlin: Selected Poems
Arseny Tarkovsky: Selected Poems
Arthur Rimbaud: Selected Poems
Arthur Rimbaud: A Season in Hell
Arthur Rimbaud and the Magic of Poetry
Novalis: Hymns To the Night
German Romantic Poetry
Paul Verlaine: Selected Poems
Elizaethan Sonnet Cycles
D.J. Enright: By-Blows
Jeremy Reed: Brigitte's Blue Heart
Jeremy Reed: Claudia Schiffer's Red Shoes
Gorgeous Little Orpheus
Radiance: New Poems
Crescent Moon Book of Nature Poetry
Crescent Moon Book of Love Poetry
Crescent Moon Book of Mystical Poetry
Crescent Moon Book of Elizabethan Love Poetry
Crescent Moon Book of Metaphysical Poetry
Crescent Moon Book of Romantic Poetry
Pagan America: New American Poetry

MEDIA, CINEMA, FEMINISM and CULTURAL STUDIES

J.R.R. Tolkien: The Books, The Films, The Whole Cultural Phenomenon
J.R.R. Tolkien: Pocket Guide
The *Lord of the Rings* Movies: Pocket Guide
The Cinema of Hayao Miyazaki
Hayao Miyazaki: *Princess Mononoke*: Pocket Movie Guide
Hayao Miyazaki: *Spirited Away*: Pocket Movie Guide
Tim Burton : Hallowe'en For Hollywood
Ken Russell
Ken Russell: *Tommy*: Pocket Movie Guide
The Ghost Dance: The Origins of Religion
The Peyote Cult
Cixous, Irigaray, Kristeva: The *Jouissance* of French Feminism
Julia Kristeva: Art, Love, Melancholy, Philosophy, Semiotics and Psychoanalysis
Luce Irigaray: Lips, Kissing, and the Politics of Sexual Difference
Hélène Cixous I Love You: The *Jouissance* of Writing
Andrea Dworkin
'Cosmo Woman': The World of Women's Magazines
Women in Pop Music
HomeGround: The Kate Bush Anthology
Discovering the Goddess (Geoffrey Ashe)
The Poetry of Cinema
The Sacred Cinema of Andrei Tarkovsky
Andrei Tarkovsky: Pocket Guide
Andrei Tarkovsky: *Mirror*: Pocket Movie Guide
Andrei Tarkovsky: *The Sacrifice*: Pocket Movie Guide
Walerian Borowczyk: Cinema of Erotic Dreams
Jean-Luc Godard: The Passion of Cinema
Jean-Luc Godard: *Hail Mary*: Pocket Movie Guide
Jean-Luc Godard: *Contempt*: Pocket Movie Guide
Jean-Luc Godard: *Pierrot le Fou*: Pocket Movie Guide
John Hughes and Eighties Cinema
Ferris Bueller's Day Off: Pocket Movie Guide
Jean-Luc Godard: Pocket Guide
The Cinema of Richard Linklater
Liv Tyler: Star In Ascendance
Blade Runner and the Films of Philip K. Dick
Paul Bowles and Bernardo Bertolucci
Media Hell: Radio, TV and the Press
An Open Letter to the BBC
Detonation Britain: Nuclear War in the UK
Feminism and Shakespeare
Wild Zones: Pornography, Art and Feminism
Sex in Art: Pornography and Pleasure in Painting and Sculpture
Sexing Hardy: Thomas Hardy and Feminism

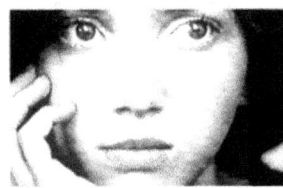

The Light Eternal is a model monograph, an exemplary job. The subject matter of the book is beautifully organised and dead on beam. (Lawrence Durrell)
It is amazing for me to see my work treated with such passion and respect. (Andrea Dworkin)

CRESCENT MOON PUBLISHING
P.O. Box 1312, Maidstone, Kent, ME14 5XU, Great Britain. www.crmoon.com

cresmopub@yahoo.co.uk   www.crescentmoon.org.uk

www.ingramcontent.com/pod-product-compliance
Lightning Source LLC
Chambersburg PA
CBHW062154080426
42734CB00010B/1687